LIVING FUTURE PULL

A Spiritual Memoir

ROSALIE DEER HEART

Cover Design by Arla Patch: artist, author, educator, creativity midwife, using art as a tool for healing.
www.arlapatch.com

Printed in the United States of America

Dedication To

June Bro who embodies a uniquely positive response to the Buddhist koan that invites each of us to imagine holding all the pain and suffering in the world in one hand and a rose in the other hand. The evolutionary challenge is to enjoy the fragrance of the rose while still being aware of the suffering in the world.

June Bro has cultivated the practice of sniffing out happiness and humor in relationship to whatever life offers up. No exceptions. For her boundless faith in God and the Goodness in everyone she meets and forever sounding a positive note, I am grateful.

Deep Bows and Appreciation To

Alison Strickland, who volunteered to edit this book and held my feet to the fire as together we figured out sequence and shine.

Nancy Carlson, who now resides in Spirit, for holding my history and helping me break out of my past.

Diane Powell for her boundless support, quirky humor and ability to practice tough love when necessary.

Lynda Marvin for her keen editorial eyes and for her courage to walk her own path and to look beyond herself for revelations.

Meghan Don for her dedication to walking and furthering the path of feminine spirituality.

Jo Ella Todd and Dan Urton, Leslie and Ed Rosenberg, Alison Strickland and Ted Coulson, Lynn Potoff and Lou Ann Daly, Ellen and Robert Powers, Penny and Larry Moulis and Pam and David Cooper for blessing me with living models of conscious, loving partnerships.

More Endorsements

"If I had to sum up Rosalie Deer Heart's memoir in one sentence I would say, "It is truly possible to find inspirational guidance and direction for your own life by exploring the life events of another."

Beginning with the unexpected death of her fifteen-year-old son, Mike, and a communication / visitation with him shortly thereafter, Rosalie takes us on a fascinating exploration of life, psychic phenomena, the survival of the soul, and relationships. Along the way we learn how much beauty life has to offer, how we are never too old to learn, the power of positive thinking, the importance of befriending one's self, and the myriad of ways *spirit* can interact with the material world.

If you are looking for a story that confirms life after death and the reality of God interacting with His Creation, I recommend *Living Future Pull.*"

—Kevin J. Todeschi,Executive Director & CEO,
The Edgar Cayce Work

"With the sudden death of her teenaged son in 1977, a veil designed to shroud the living from the realm of spirit was lifted and Rosalie Deer Heart was given a glimpse of a reality more radiantly real than anything she had ever experienced.

A glimpse became a focused gazing, and her gaze was accompanied by the inflow of profound knowledge – not only of life and death, but also of the evolutionary trajectory of humanity. The gates of perception have remained open ever since. Through courageously sharing details of her own life's journey as a woman and a healer, Rosalie Deer Heart reveals the underlying lessons of love we were all born to learn."

—Mirabai Starr, Author of *Caravan of No Despair: A Memoir of Loss and Transformation*

"Powerful...Courageous ...and wise in a way that challenges beliefs, expectations and lessons learned in our youth. Rosalie Deer Heart provides an honest and deeply personal accounting of a life lived outside social conventions with passion, joy and unfolding adventures that have brought her to a place of more enlightened living. This spiritual retrospective offers a mirror and invitation for readers to look inside and ask who we are called to be and how we hold ourselves back. A great catalyst for waking up and making the choice to step into brilliance and light by answering the future call of soul's purpose."

—Lou Ann Daly, PH.D author of *Humans Being: Creating Your Life From the Inside Out*

"This is a profound piece of life review and life instruction revealing the extraordinary spiritual connection at the core of a woman's life. *Living Future Pull*, is full of practical and well-earned wisdom—prepare to underline and savor!"

—Christina Baldwin, author of *Life's Companion & Storycatcher.*

"Many people now are experiencing deeper levels of intuition, higher frequencies of awareness, subtle changes in their capacity to communicate. Evolution is occurring to and through us, and it is a challenge to communicate its complexities. Rosie Dear Heart shares her own story here of a soul's journey into the depths and heights—a gift of insight from another dimension."

—Jan Phillips, author of *Creativity Unzipped*

"Rosalie Deer Heart's spiritual autobiography is information expressed in frequencies, which are mind, heart and soul touching. She invites us to take this love-expanding journey with her. If you say "yes" expect to be challenged to become more spacious, know more possibilities and raise your personal frequency. Her authenticity adds to the power of this book to inspire us to live in a higher vibration, from a multi-dimensional perspective. "

—Joan Chadbourne, EdD, author of
Healing Conversations Now

"In *Living Future Pull, a Spiritual Memoir*, Rosalie Deer Heart describes what an authentic spiritual path looks like. It is neither predictable nor easy, yet, it is genuine. A traumatic event sets in motion a life of both inner reflection, and service in the light. She is guided throughout her soul-journey by the wisdom from her higher self, the spirit world, and like-minded teachers. Deer Heart reminds us that what may sometimes seem confusing is in fact the pull toward our destiny. In clear and honest language, *Living Future Pull* becomes our support and encouragement to recognize our own unique journey forward."

—Asandra, author of *Contact Your Spirit Guides*

Chapters

Introduction to Living Future Pull

Writing a spiritual memoir was the last project I imagined for myself. I have dared to write honestly about my journey home to myself despite a cacophony of discouraging voices living in my head taunting: "Who do you think you are?" "How dare you?" "How narcissistic of you!" and "For shame."

After the publication of my books *Awaken* (2011) and *Soul Befriending* (2014), friends and readers challenged me to include more personal stories in future books. I was surprised and a bit daunted. Although I am an outrageous extrovert, I also come from five generations of Mainers from both my mother and father's sides of the family and privacy is a deeply ingrained intergenerational value

Writing and witnessing are synonyms for me. Looking back over forty years, journal keeping was, and continues to be, another example of Future Pull that connected me deeply with my personal stories, edge-walking stories, and soul stories. I believe that our stories, like our energy, impact others as well as our own consciousness. I also believe that a story is more powerful than a weapon because we can recreate ourselves through the stories we choose to share.

1

To write this book, I drew on four decades of journals filled with stories of losing myself, finding myself, questioning myself, loving myself, confronting myself, dismissing myself, re-claiming myself, and celebrating myself. For example, in July 1977, four months after the sudden death of my son, Mike, my guides channeled through me:

Believe in yourself and all is possible.

You are an instrument of light and power.

You are prepared: only commitment and faith are needed to bring your gifts to fruition.

There are those around you who are afraid of what you are living. They will discourage you, yet your direction is charted. You are becoming a clear channel, and your motives are pure.

I agree with Alison Strickland, my friend, editor, and co-author of *Harvesting Your Journals: Writing Tools to Enhance Your Growth and Creativity* (1999) who wrote:

"Journaling isn't just capturing experiences; it's reflection upon experience in search of meaning that yields wisdom." Through time, journaling became both a practical and later a spiritual practice. As long as I stayed patient with myself and honest with my feelings and perceptions, I learned that I could count on myself to maneuver through confusion and sometimes chaos to arrive at a place of understanding and healing.

Midway through writing my memoir, I enrolled in a six-week online memoir class offered by Roger Housden, author of *Ten Poems to Change your Life*. I have admired Roger for more than three decades, and I intuited that the class might assist me in organizing and deepening my own memoir. I was right. For starters, Roger reminded me that writing a memoir was a daring act because I would have to stand by my own voice and my own emotional experience without apology. My heart applauded when he reminded me, "What matters is not so much what happened but the sensitivity with which you absorbed the experience and the ways it continues to inform and color your life now."

When my ego directed my personal story, I reacted from my familiar roles and pain pushed me until future pulled. I eventually gave up pleasing others and looking outside of myself for validation and began to trust my intuition to source my emerging truths. Looking back from my current perspective, each choice I made reflected either egocentric will which is connected to power, control and personal stories, or soul growth which is connected to Future Pull. Over time, I moved from simple awareness to cosmic awareness.

Both breaking rank and responding to Future Pull interrupted my predictable life. Both required action. The frequencies of Future Pull invited me to move out of my comfort and control zone and live way beyond the person I knew myself to be. I grew in awareness amidst creative tension. Both rebellion and discipline were essential for me to grow into my authentic self.

Edge walking between my personal story and my soul story involved separating myself from old attachments and limited beliefs and being patient with myself as I learned to tolerate uncertainty. In the process, I gradually discovered that I no longer belonged to myself in the ways I used to. In the transformation process I learned to be more accepting, loving and compassionate with myself.

In the following pages, you will meet me as I weave, inter-weave, and re-weave my human self with my Divine self. You will also meet my guides and teachers, who had their hands full as they supported me to break rank with my learned limitations and channeled irresistible information that I eventually claimed as my internal GPS—God Presencing System.

Although breaking rank with my limiting intergenerational beliefs that did not serve my soul's journey was one of the recurring themes and lessons, the unexpected wild card was the magnetic attraction of Future Pull. I was stunned when I looked back over the past four decades of my life and discovered that the energetic frequency of Future Pull had always been present. No matter if the event was heart breaking or heart opening, I had the choice to align with the potential of Future Pull.

In my experience, which is more than enough for me, a feed forward or Future Pull event is a condition in the present with meaning that unfolds in the future. When I was nineteen, which is one half century ago, I had a vivid dream that in retrospect counts as Future Pull. In the dream, I witnessed myself sitting outside in a white wicker rocking chair on a large wrap around porch surrounded by six people. Some were younger than I and some were older. The people felt like my soul family. In ordinary reality, the dream made no sense, especially since I believed that I would marry and have children and live the American dream. At seventy-two, I am single by choice and value community. I might indeed be moving in the future direction of my dream of long ago.

After many hours of reflecting, tracking and remembering times when I said "Yes" to Future Pull without consciously being aware of the implications of my actions, I recognized how Future Pull acts like a soul switch similar to a familiar light switch. Unless we switch on the light, the potential light remains inert and invisible. Each time I said Yes to Future Pull I activated the soul switch. The frequency of Future Pull stretched me into the unknown future and I later claimed aspects of myself that I did not know were there. In order to be present for Future Pull, I risked believing that the unknown future was a place of revelations—not fear.

When I looked back in previous journals for examples of Future Pull, I discovered this gem that my guides channeled in May 1983:

> *Note the opportunities and challenges that accompany living a multidimensional perspective. As you grow more fully within the light, you fuse with all that is, and you will remember how to consistently access love-wisdom. The echoes of eternity resonate within your soul.*

I am no stranger to living in more than one dimension. I was born intuitive. Energy is my first language. Settling for being ordinary no longer claimed me. Although others referred to some of my experiences as "far out" or even "extraordinary," in retrospect I realize that each event challenged me to embrace my multidimensional wholeness. As I wove the thread of my eternal divine self with my evolving authentic human self, I experienced times when I enjoyed being a playmate with angels, Mother Mary and God. Part of my joy as a Cosmic Catalyst is to remind and teach others to dare to say Yes! to a co-creative relationship with the Divine Creative Forces that I know as God while living embodied, passionate lives on earth.

Equally true, I enjoy being a mother, grandmother, and evolutionary buddy to many people. Balancing dimensions and ways of knowing feels, at times, like juggling orbs in the air and grounding and honoring the information that each orb offers expanded my perspective, imagination, and what it means to live in a unified field of consciousness.

Although I prided myself on being an above average problem solver and later taught at the Creative Problem Solving Institute in Buffalo New York one week every summer for more than two decades, I opened to other ways of accessing meaning. I learned how to listen to my body and then to honor my body's wisdom. Over decades I learned how to befriend my compassionate, intuitive nature, which to me is the silent voice of Spirit. Ten years ago, I wrote the following paragraph in my journal:

I appreciate from experience that intuition is the language of the heart that provides multidimensional answers to my most pressing questions. I also respect that planetary evolution is grounded in service to the greater good and dedicated to the wellbeing of all.

My priorities changed in radical ways. I practiced discernment and set both physical and energetic boundaries—all in preparation to surrender to my own vulnerability, reclaim my innocence and extend love and healing to others, myself, and the world. Love became my spiritual signature and my joyful service in the world.

In my experience, the cosmic frequencies are accelerating and amplifying. The results of my present day choices feel instantaneous, while only a few years ago, the consequences required more time to manifest. We, too, are re-calibrating.

Time itself feels elastic as if it too is accelerating. Change is happening much more quickly. I sense I am moving into a deeper place of accessing my own God Self. I believe that it is time to deepen our alignment with our inner holiness and our outer wholeness. My experience is that as I claim my entitlement to my inner Divinity and weave my Divine self with my evolving authentic human self, I have the potential to become a channel of blessings and joy-filled service.

In my thirty-seven years of doing soul readings, I have noticed during the past three years that many others sense the Future Pull of conscious evolution. My human response to the accelerating energies is a daily intention to live my life from the perspective of my soul story and transform my personal stories to align with the often hidden energies of Future Pull.

Since we are all multidimensional beings, our genetic blueprints contain the potential to tap into all of the knowledge throughout time, including the future. Native Americans consciously call upon their future ancestors, who live as far out as seven generations, before making an important decision that will affect their tribal family. I often challenge myself to merge with my Future Self when facing an important decision. I ask myself, "Who do I wish to become?" and then discern whether or not my decision resonates with my unfolding future self.

What if our journey on earth is as simple as believing and trusting that each of us is the meeting point between earth and heaven? What if my life were as simple as believing that God is having a Rosalie experience here on earth through me?

My prayer is that we all recognize our inner Divinity and live our lives as if God were enjoying a touch of the earth's experience through us. Three months ago, I picked up my journal and wrote,

The present and the future invite each of us to become more than we can imagine. Our future ancestors as well as our planet's evolution deserve to inherit a consciousness that is grounded, informed and graced by our all knowing hearts as well as our multidimensional minds. As we each surrender to the power of love and expand our willingness to love each other, our Mother Earth, and ourselves we amplify our multi-dimensional natures and add our energies to the healing of each other, ourselves, our communities, our nations as well as the healing of our planet. I am ready to invite the future to have her way with me. Please join me.

My prayer is that my stories touch your heart and inspire you. Remember the future may pull you in dreams, synchronistic events, visits from inspirited ones, conversations with an evolutionary buddy, memories from a past or future lifetime, visits or communications from a guide, or "blink truths" that people often call sudden insights.

I agree with Dr. Jean Houston, author of *A Mythic Life*, who wrote that one-way to holiness is by being punched full of holes. In order to discover what is trying to be born from your wound, she advised people to stop telling their small story and begin the larger story with the wounding. That is the primary reason I chose to begin my spiritual memoir in the middle with the sudden death of my teenaged son, Mike.

CHAPTER 1

The Middle

*M*y first Soul Call came on March 23, 1977, although I did not recognize the heart-shattering event as a soul call until many years later. I don't know many people who would count the sudden death of their child a soul call. Yet the sudden death of my almost fifteen-year-old son, Mike was definitely a soul call for both of us.

My spiritual memoir begins with his death. If he had lived, he would have celebrated his fifteenth birthday in just six weeks. He had his first girlfriend and qualified for the swimming team in the same month. Two weeks before he was electrocuted in the schoolyard next door, he surprised everyone by kissing his two-year-old sister, Kelli Lynne goodnight.

The week before he died, he placed four of his school photos on the mantle over the fireplace and said, "So you will see me everywhere" and the photos remained on the mantle for months after his death. I wondered for years after if he knew he was destined to die suddenly or was just fooling around like he often did. The unanswered questions remained when one week after his death a game called Life that I had ordered for him as a birthday present arrived six weeks before his birthday. I had imagined that we would enjoy this game as a family activity and I burst out crying because Mike was dead—not alive and neither life nor death was a game to me.

Looking back from a forty-year perspective, I see that my long-established beliefs had begun to be challenged three months earlier. Twelve weeks before Mike's sudden death, I underwent an unwanted emergency hysterectomy caused by an IUD that had perforated my uterus. The doctor suspected that I might have cancer too. For the first time in my thirty-three years, I faced the possible reality that I might die and never see my children grow up. My unplanned and unwanted hysterectomy made me feel separate from all my friends and I felt punished for something I did not understand.

After the surgery, my raging hormones thrust me into the middle of menopause and the daily combination of mood swings and hot flashes reminded me that I was out of control. As hard as I tried to convince the feminist part of me that the hot flashes existed only in my mind, I had to change the sheets several times a night. To say that I felt like my body had betrayed me was an understatement.

In less than three months, my first-born child would be dead.

Before my thirty-third year, trusting life was easy. Trusting God was not an issue either. I believed in a benevolent God. After Mike's death, I did not know what I believed about anything. I wanted to believe in love and the power of love to heal, but I was immersed in grief. I wanted to believe that my two-year-old daughter, Kelli Lynne would survive and grow up and be happy, but I no longer trusted life.

My son's death forever changed how I viewed both life and death. Grief became a familiar. The pain of emptiness and feeling like I was a ghost walker seized me. I felt alone no matter how many people were around me. None of my friends or family had survived the death of one of their children. Words felt hollow. Hugs reached me but not my heart. Food tasted like cardboard. People watched me. When I entered a room, they stopped talking. I no longer cared.

Equally true, nothing prepared me for the subsequent conversations and visits with my dead son that began eight days after he died. Of course, I captured the encounter in my journal:

About midnight I noticed my body pulsating with energy. My heartbeat accelerated and I felt scared and alert. Bright lights filled the room. I closed my eyes tightly, then opened them a little to see if the lights had disappeared. They hadn't. Cautiously peeking through half-open eyes, I became mesmerized by a bright orange spiral light circling around a pure white center that had a minute black dot in the middle of it. As I watched closely, the brilliant orange border gradually turned to yellow and the vivid center remained unchanged.

Jolted, I sat up in bed. I didn't understand how or why, but I recognized the energy contained in the colors. My heart responded to this energy, and I knew it was similar to my own heart's light. Understanding exploded as I realized that this light was somehow related to Mike. Without warning, I began to float, and for an instant wondered if I was dying, but I relaxed and knew for the first time ever that I did not fear death.

While floating, I experienced myself as a concentrated point of energy, traveling easily through space and aware of Mike as pure essence and of myself as an aspect of that essence.

As if in affirmation, Mike's vibrations responded to my own with energy—not words. There was a communion that seemed to say, "That's right, Mom. There is no difference, no divisions, no separations."

We were communicating! Somehow, I could receive and interpret his message although it was not spoken; similarly, he was able to hear the questions in my mind although I hadn't uttered them out loud.

He continued, "Together we have activated a link. I have information for you and others that will sustain you and bring new light to you."

In that moment, I knew with absolute clarity that one of us had to die in order to connect in this way. Acknowledging this deep emotional truth further separated me from my family who did not believe that life continued after death. My visits with Mike also separated me from friends who lacked a similar experience and were not able to relate to mine. Stepping more fully into my evolving story felt like my only choice, even if it meant I would be alone.

I knew I was not hallucinating either the energetic sound of my son's voice or the messages he gave me, even though I was in shock. How could I explain hearing his voice in my mind when I was a psychotherapist who referred clients who heard voices in their heads to a psychiatrist? Nothing in my inner or outer world made sense after Mike's death.

I coined the word "Inspirited," to replace "Dead" because in my experience, Mike continued to have energy, motion, and intention. How was it possible to have those characteristics and no breath? I felt like I was still the mother of two children and each had a hold on my heart.

In retrospect, I grew up in a culture and in a family that did not acknowledge an afterlife. None of my professional colleagues talked about reincarnation or spiritual guides. Until Mike's death, I had never talked to or listened to a dead person and the psychotherapist within me would have labeled such an experience an "auditory hallucination." I felt isolated and bereft because of my own experiences on the inner planes that felt more real to me than gravity and my own pulse.

Less than six weeks after Mike's death, I awoke with vivid memories of a dream (or was it a visit?) in which Mike told me to place his ashes in a creel concealed under a pile of clothes in a large cardboard cylinder in the garage. I awoke from the dream with his words, "The creel is important, Mom, because I was a fisherman."

The dream seemed so vivid that I tiptoed to the garage in the early light and spotted the cylindrical cardboard container that I had seen in the dream. Trancelike, I pried off the lid and found stacks of outgrown clothes. I wildly pulled out clothes until my hands grasped a solid object at the bottom of the bar- rel—an odd-shaped closed straw basket with a slit on top and a ruler attached to one side. I recognized the creel from the dream image and remembered that my grandfather, Bomp, had given Mike the creel for his fifth birthday.

I slowly fingered the rough edges, stunned that I had dreamed a dream based in reality. My mind whizzed with questions: Is Mike really in touch with me? Is he giving me signs, reassuring me or guiding me? I shrugged my shoulders and acknowledged to myself that death has a different reality for me as long as I have this connection.

The timing of the dream was uncanny. We had planned to scatter his ashes at Two Lights State Park in Cape Elizabeth that day.

Exactly eight months after Mike's death, I dreamed of him again. Or was it a visitation? I recorded the event in my journal:

In last night's dream, Mike was confined to an institution for the mentally disabled. He could not move or speak. I hated seeing him reduced to a body with neither a mind nor vitality and I felt guilty about being repulsed. In the dream, I forced myself to visit with him. I spoke to him, stared at him, and searched for a sign that he heard me. He remained immobile and I was horrified and saddened. In the midst of my agony, I heard Mike's voice saying, "You see, Mom, there are worse things in life than death."

I sighed, put another blanket on the bed and said out loud,

"Yes, I agree, there are worse things in life than death. But damn it, Mike, why?"

"Don't you understand yet, Mom? I am a light."

I scratched my hand to make sure that I was awake.

His voice interrupted me saying, "The question is, 'Do you believe in me? In yourself? Do you dare to trust and see through?'"

"What does that mean?" I challenged.

"Rest now, Mom and trust in your senses."

I sighed and said in a resigned voice, "What choice do I have?"

He replied, "Revolving, involving, resolving, evolving, all is in process."

"What kind of an answer is that? I want something I can hold on to," I sputtered through my tears.

Silence.

My son's death broke my heart open, ignited my intuition and opened my mind to the psychic world of continuing life after death. I now believe that his death was a soul agreement that we made before he was born—an agreement to consciously bridge dimensions that called upon one of us to die and one of us to live. Years later my evolutionary buddy Lou Ann Daly challenged me when she asked lovingly, "Rosie, do you think that your soul agreement with Mike stipulated that he was the one who would die?"

The mother in me responded first, and I said that I did not believe that it mattered who left and who stayed. When I met Lou Ann's eyes, I opened my heart to her question. As a mother, I would have chosen to be the one to die—what mother wouldn't? Or maybe our soul agreement was that he agreed to excarnate and experience an afterlife and I agreed to receive his messages and write about our inter-dimensional connection.

On a human level, I believe that I was not given a choice; yet on a cosmic level, who knows? Certainly, the emergency hysterectomy felt like a wild card and death felt close by. Yet I survived. I also honor that without him I would not be the person I am today. Without him, I would not be doing soul readings and tracking people in the afterlife. Before his death, I never imagined it was possible to communicate between dimensions. Furthermore, I had no idea that dimensions existed and hence no concept of dimensional doorways, or portals.

By beginning my memoir in the middle of my story, I transformed my perspective as seeing both Mike and myself as victims. Eventually, I began to relate to myself as a "seeker" and to Mike as "Inspirited" rather than "my dead teenaged son." It took a long time for me to realize that Mike's death opened up my intuitive channels as well as my devotion to journaling that resulted in *Healing Grief—A Mother's Story*, which I still think of as *Mike's Book* and the beginning of my writing career.

Nine months after he died, I recorded this in my journal:

Silver and gold streams of light filled the room. As I watched, I could see each particle of light both separately and as part of a stream. My eyes felt like the shutter of a sophisticated camera. The streams of silver and gold coalesced, blanketing my heart. As they did, the light turned white. My body was light. I was not out of my body, but rather in the light.

Suddenly I sensed a familiar energy. I looked up, expecting to see a ghost. Instead, I was captivated by a swirl of light with a revolving center. I recognized this familiar energy as Mike. Then I sensed Mike's voice— not in my ears, but rather in each cell of my body.

"That's right," he channeled "I am sending you the essence of love, which is light. I can do that now."

As I watched more intently, I noticed tiny rays of white light emanating from my heart and joining the energy spiral that was Mike. I wasn't trying to do any-

thing; the convergence simply happened. I transmitted my thought: "I don't understand this."

"Just relax. Be with the light. You are experiencing that you, too, can send light."

"But my streams of light are nothing compared with yours," I complained.

"That's because you have not let go, you must release fully the emotion you have invested in me. Only then can we begin the transfusion."

"How do I let go?" I questioned.

"By blessing my passage. You released my body in the hospital, but what is needed now is a deeper release — for by blessing my evolution, you bless your choice to remain as an instrument of healing. And within healing, we mutually evolve. You see, our souls' evolution is connected, and to reinvest in the light, you must bless my choice of evolution."

"I can't bless your death," I told him.

"Death is your word," he reminded me. "I am living energy. I have motion and intention. If I had left for college or married, you would have given me your blessing. Both of us would have experienced a new beginning, further learnings, a different relationship."

"But that time was far away," I complained. "I can't make that jump."

"Time is all relative. Past, present, future—all are 'now' in my dimension," Mike told me. "Your blessings are a vote of confidence in our mutual evolution. You are experiencing the resonant vibrations that connect us. The radiant energy that you are impressed with can be received and channeled on a daily basis, but only after you have released me from your heart."

"In other words, it is my function to disconnect—again" I said.

"Precisely," he responded. "There are levels of releasing, depths of letting go. You have now glimpsed an aspect of your own radiance, but you must be willing to release me. I cannot do that for you, Mom. That is your learning and your work. Know that in letting go, you will experience light."

After Mike's sudden death, I tried harder to be good and available to family and please others as if in some crazy way I could make up for his death, which I did not cause. Someone told me that I suffered from survivor's guilt as if the label would ease or explain my pain. All the while I wanted to scream, mostly to myself, "His dying was not my fault." Nevertheless, I held myself hostage for his death for years by restraining my creative self-expression and over-giving to others. Eventually over-giving wore me out. Gradually I became aware of the trance I had woven around myself and my life and slowly "trance-ended, retired from sacrificing myself and began to honor my soul's path and forgive myself for judging myself in absurd ways.

CHAPTER 2

The Beginning

*B*eginning at the beginning takes me back in time seventy-three years to where I existed as a soul and before I had inherited a physical body. I have a distinct soul memory that existed before conception when I agreed to introduce a high love frequency into my birth family. From the soul dimension, I experienced love as light. From the perspective of spirit, I had no idea how ambitious and challenging my soul agreement to shine my light full beam would be on the earth dimension. Loving was like breath in the spiritual dimension. Oneness was all. Looking back, I realize that my parents did not have a clue what to do with my spirit and I was their first-born child.

Like most people, upon being born I adopted the denser vibrations of the earth and then gradually reflected the predominant beliefs of my family that life was hard and challenging. They had survived the Great Depression and carried a scarcity fear like many of their generation. Plus, we were serious, hardworking Mainers!

Since I was conditioned to believe that life was a struggle, I attracted pain and suffering. More than one astrologer has told me that my fifth house is packed and the decision is always between suffering and service. As the descendent of five generations of native Mainers on both my mother and father's side of the family, the values to be strong and work hard were branded on my teething ring! Both my grandparents and parents prided themselves on surviving long, severe winters and their ability to keep going no matter what. Play, pleasure and vacations were for others. We were responsible, hardworking native Mainers who toed the mark.

One of the family stories about my birth is how my mother refused to nurse me, even though her parents had to use food stamps to purchase milk, because, as the story goes, her breasts belonged to my father. Add to that unwelcoming behavior her allegiance to Dr. Spock's harsh feeding schedule that forbade on demand feeding.

Both my mother and my grandmother told me stories about how I screamed so loud and long from hunger that they turned the record player on loud until I eventually gave up and slept. Nobody came to hold me no matter how hard I wailed. No wonder that I have a hard time nurturing myself and a harder time receiving nurturance from others, even though my soul knows that receiving is an essential part of every relationship.

My father was in the Merchant Marines during World War II and then devoted the next thirty years of his life to going to sea. He worked his way through the ranks to be captain of a super tanker, the American Eagle that delivered white fuel from the Middle East. It wasn't that he loved the ocean or life aboard ship; he just wanted to provide for us because he had grown up poor.

For the first twenty-eight years of my life I saw him about six weeks a year when he was home on vacation. Each time he returned, I was supposed to drop my own life and be available to do family things with a man I did not know.

My mother changed from being an independent in charge woman to answering to the name "Baby Doll." I imagine they argued in the privacy of their bedroom, but I never witnessed an argument.

In those days, people stayed married even if they were not happy and if a mother with children lived alone, it was because her husband had died. As I started school, I was the only child in my class without both parents living at home. I felt envious of friends who had a regular dad who was home every night and on weekends.

For many years, the annual welcome home ritual for my father centered on pennies and piggy banks. My father saved pennies while he was away at sea for ten or eleven months a year. Always the first morning that he was home, he unlocked the bedroom door in the pre-dawn light. Moments before my brother and I heard him turn the lock, we heard the clinking sound of thousands of pennies being dumped on the shiny, hard wood floor. That was our signal to grab our piggy banks off the mahogany bureau where they sat untouched for three hundred and sixty-three days a year and scurry into the semi-dark bedroom.

Even though I was only six, I knew my younger brother and I were expected to act excited. He was. I wanted to cuddle in bed with my mother like we sometimes did in the early morning when my father was absent.

My father began the countdown for the penny race. Five—Four—Three—Two—One. We dropped to the cold, wooden floor. I was not interested in stuffing the mostly shiny coins into the narrow slot of my two-foot tall Santa Claus penny bank. My brother grappled for the pennies and shouted, "I'm winning. I have more pennies than you have."

I looked over at the bed and my mother and father whispered and laughed with one another. When they looked at us, I felt like an animal at the zoo. My brother started tickling me and I screamed. He jumped on my belly and tickled me with one hand and grabbed my stack of pennies with his other hand.

"Stop it," I shouted, and hit him.

The man in my mother's bed bellowed, "Looks like you need some help, son," and toppled to the wooden floor and joined him in tickling me.

"Stop it, both of you," I screamed, "I mean it." I looked over at my mother for help. Her eyes were closed.

"Quiet or you will wake your mother," ordered my father.

"Quit tickling me or I will pee my pants," I squeaked.

They kept tickling me. I peed my pajama bottoms and they laughed and teased me. In a flicker of a moment, I made a decision to numb my body so I would never be humiliated ever again.

Everything changed when my father returned home, even the way my mother laughed. When he was home her voice sounded softer and friendlier. We were in bed with lights out at seven o'clock without our normal bedtime story. Our dog, Thunder, no longer wagged his tail or begged for dog biscuits and he stayed outside.

I was confused. I was warned to never talk to strangers. Yet when my father came home, I was supposed to tell him funny stories and to sit on his lap and kiss him good night. Nobody asked me how I was feeling. Who was this man who smelled of garlic and made drinks called Manhattans every night before supper?

When I started school and my father was home for his annual four-week vacation, I was under orders to come directly home from school and be a family. No play dates or hanging from trees for one month. Inviting friends over was off limits. Making up for lost family time was lost on me. I protested because I wanted to be with my friends and my grandparents.

I got in trouble when I asked, "Why do we have to be together all of the time in this house that is just right for three people and too small for four?" I missed my life and said mean things and got spanked on the butt with a stiff hairbrush. I clearly remember making a decision to never cry no matter how hard I was spanked. Then my mother accused me of mocking her and spanked harder. I held my breath, stiffened my body and did not cry— not even when I was alone in my room.

While I was growing up, my feelings were mostly ignored, ridiculed, or judged. I have spent a lifetime learning to honor my own feelings and giving voice to my own emotions without second-guessing myself or trying to please others. Emotional safety was not present. Yet bypassing my feelings did not feel like a healthy option even though I was labeled Sarah Bernhart.

As a child I learned to close down and become less than I was to please others. Gaining love became my survival strategy. To remain safe in the family, I perfected the art of being just enough— never too much.

Religion did not play a big part in my childhood or adolescence. I was expected to attend Sunday school at the local Methodist Church. As a reward, I had my choice of an ice cream cone as soon as the class was over. If I also attended the hour church service, I qualified for a double decker ice cream cone, which my grandmother scooped! As an adolescent, I attended the Baptist Church in a nearby town because after the weekly program we all piled into a car and went to the local pizza shack.

Most of my friends attended the Catholic Church and for years I secretly wished I had been born Catholic. One of my best friends was very religious and a mutual friend referred to her as "pious." Later I looked the word up in the dictionary and I was upset because I convinced myself I would never learn how to be pious in a Protestant church.

During my adolescence, which was emotionally turbulent by unanimous agreement of all the adults in my family, I begged to convert to Catholicism. My parents and grandparents were appalled. I wanted to become a nun and practice being pious. As I looked back, the idea of living a sheltered life among other "girls" appealed to me because sexuality was such a compelling puzzle with many missing pieces.

Given my spotty history with religion, imagine my surprise, forty years later, when I obeyed an inner impulse to travel across the waters off Scotland to embark on a one-week retreat at the secluded island of Iona, a small island off western Scotland in the southern Inner Hebrides. Many people who lived at Findhorn, the spiritual community in Moray, Scotland, spoke of their "epiphany experiences" that happened there.

During my first walk around Iona a few dilapidated buildings attracted me. My heart beat faster as I approached the ruins. My legs began to shake and I rested on a large nearby stone. Then tears eclipsed my sight. Familiar with the emotional impact of past lifetime memories, I asked to remember specific details of the lifetime that the ancient edifices had shaken loose. Nothing. My body shook and my tears became sobs and then moans. I pleaded for insight. No information. My only awareness was a fleeting sense of betrayal, intense emotional and physical pain and an overpowering sense of injustice.

I returned to the retreat center with red eyes, chills, and raw emotions. I felt like I had unwittingly punctured a deep wound that had been scabbed over for centuries. Since the other twelve retreat participants had agreed on a voluntary seven-day vow of silence, I could not ask anyone about the history of the island; however, I found a book about Iona in the retreat center's library. I learned that the remnants of the buildings were originally a Benedictine convent for the order of nuns, built in 1203. Reading further, I learned that the present Benedictine abbey was the most complete remnant of a medieval nunnery in Scotland.

I was determined to break through my resistance and discover the roots of my pain. Once more I walked the trail to the convent. This time I walked to the ruined structures and placed my hands on the rocks. Then I opened my mouth and spontaneously licked one of the stones, hoping for information. Once more tears blocked my sight. Brushing the tears from my eyes, I trudged around the old building hoping that the earth and the structures would open my memory bank. My body shivered and I returned to my sitting rock.

Not knowing what else to do, I half closed my eyes and prayed to be shown whatever remained hidden. Instantly, my eyes were drawn to a high part of one of the ruined buildings and I knew I had lived in that corner once upon a time. I prayed harder and as if a movie were playing in front of my eyes, I saw a young nun kneeling in prayer. I studied her and knew from deep within my present womb-less body that she was pregnant. The movie was fast-forwarded and I watched in fascination and trepidation as a monk denounced her for stealing the sacred relics and ordered her to be "done away with" and her body dumped in the harbor. He further decreed that other nuns never speak her name on penalty of being cast out of the order. Instinctively, I understood that the monk who sentenced the nun to death was the father of her unborn child and her beloved. Although I did not want to watch the sentence carried out, I knew I must re-live the experience of drowning and feeling my innocence and the injustice done to my unborn child and me if I intended to release the emotional memories. So I did.

No wonder as a teenager I desired to be cloistered to escape my physical passions. No wonder love is complicated and painful for me this lifetime. No wonder that I experience a huge tension between spirituality and sexuality. Perhaps now that I had released this traumatic past life memory, I could heal the inner split between spirituality and sexuality and enjoy a deep, loving, long relationship.

Returning to my chronology, I was a freshman in high school, when I fell in love with Mike's father. He was two years older than I and we got "pinned" during my junior year in high school. He was handsome, intelligent, ambitious, and aspired to be a doctor. I was unhappy living at home and played the biology card and got pregnant during the first semester of my senior year. I was not allowed to continue school once the principal found out.

The morning that I gave birth to Mike, my best friend of twelve years tearfully announced that she and my husband had had sex the night before while I was in the hospital. The double betrayal and the onslaught of post-partum hormones made for a chaotic introduction to motherhood. Disillusioned, I filed for divorce within six months.

As a first born child, my parents expected me to go to college. I followed their dream. During the sixties, the two professions open to women were nursing and teaching. My dream was to become a photojournalist, but that was not offered at the commuter college in Portland. Since I fainted at the sight of blood and I enjoyed children, teaching seemed like an easy choice. My mother cared for Mike while I commuted to college.

College was serious business. I grew up in a family that valued neither creativity nor music. Although I was an imaginative and intuitive child, I, like my family, discounted both as frivolous. No room for creativity or courage. I knew how to memorize facts and theories and my intuition, which was a wild card, served me well because I knew in advance what questions or essays topics would appear in exams. Although I studied, I credited my intuition for alerting me to the questions and essays on exams and I sped through college in three years and graduated with high honors.

My parents validated me by how hard I worked, how much I produced, and how much money I earned. Secretly, I valued creative self-expression and fortune telling. Yet my self-esteem was tied to working hard and being successful. I pushed myself to excel in my career as a junior high school teacher, later as a psychotherapist and then as a consultant. To this day, I still struggle to relax and take it easy.

For most of my life I have majored in doing, achieving, creating, mediating, teaching, channeling, and winning recognition. Earlier in my life, I expressed my personality by being good (mostly), being smart, being dutiful, and being whoever the adults wanted me to be, especially being pleasing. I also wanted to be popular. Yet looking back, I now question whether that was important to me, to my mother, or both of us. Although my mother is dead, sometimes it is still hard to know my own needs, feelings, and preferences.

Being the daughter of a narcissist is hard work with no time off for good behavior.

I met my next husband during my first semester in college while I was a single mother and overwhelmed with the demands of both college and motherhood. Nine years older than I, he was steady and loyal. My family loved him and, in truth, he became more like their son than I was their daughter. We married as soon as I graduated from college and moved to Montreal, Canada where he'd found work. With him I was free to learn and grow and study and have friends, but he was not interested in growing either emotionally or spiritually. Over the years, I grew bored and Mike's death foreshadowed the death of our fourteen-year marriage.

After I met my mentor Bob Eberle, an accomplished educator, when I first attended the Creative Problem Solving Institute in Buffalo, New York in 1972, I co-authored two books with him. In *Affective Education Guidebook: Classroom Activities in the Realm of Feelings* (1975), we stated, "the ultimate goal of a classroom community is to establish interpersonal bonds to create a higher level of human nature so that the sharing of psychic energy becomes possible."

I was the first teacher in my school to co-author a book, let alone one about creative and caring education. Being an author made me feel special and I gained recognition as an innovator. Again, I felt isolated from my colleagues who were envious of my accomplishments and connections. Four years later we collaborated and wrote *Affective Direction: Planning and Teaching for Thinking and Feeling*. Mike died during the writing of this book and after that I felt like I had lived through a lobotomy and no longer felt like a contributing partner. Bob Eberle remained both determined and patient to the end.

Reviews called the book "scholarly and applicable to classrooms." We had designed developmental maps that included strategies for thinking and feeling to incorporate aesthetic sensitivity, interpersonal relations, moral-ethical development, and self-knowledge into the curriculum. This book gained us much attention and we conducted in-service teacher-training workshops around the country. I enjoyed the recognition, yet I realized that I preferred my classroom to large professional workshops.

CHAPTER 3

Breaking Rank

I broke rank with my parent's dream for me when I quit teaching after the birth of my daughter, Kelli Lynne, and trained to be a psychotherapist. I had no interest in pursuing traditional psychotherapy. The cookie cutter approach did not appeal to my soul.

Self-actualization was my goal and assisting people to connect with their soul was my path. Somehow, I knew, although I did not have the words, that integrating our human nature with our divine nature was part of my soul path. I pursued holistic studies that included psycho-synthesis, guided imagery and music therapy, body centered psychotherapy, mediation training, and women's adult development. I also studied and then taught with Matthew Fox whose book, *Original Blessing*, remains on my bookshelf. Although I felt like a renegade, I built my private practice where I specialized in psycho-spiritual integration. Ten years later I served as a holistic therapist on the Maine Governor's Task Force for establishing licensing credentials.

My family did not support my new career choice because they did not approve "of charging people to listen to their misery." Nobody in my biological family ever worked with a therapist. Problems were private and dealt with in house or denied.

Three years after Mike's death, I divorced and again broke rank with my parents and my grandparents who believed one marriage was forever. No exceptions. I was not willing to allow my soul to stagnate in a marriage, even if my decision meant distancing myself from my family.

I have a freeze frame memory of when I told my parents that I was getting a divorce. We were at camp and as I walked up the gray wooden stairs to my bedroom, my mother hollered, "Where did you ever come up with the idea that happiness and marriage were connected? If you are not happy, welcome to the real world."

In that moment, I realized how different our worlds were and I knew that once again I would receive no support for a choice that felt soul directed. I also acknowledged that we were of different generations. My generation looked at relationships as developmental and we understood that people came together to learn from one another and when the learning internship was over, different options were available. The freedom to re-choose a partner or a life direction did not exist in my grandparents or parents generations. Even now I continue to question whether it is possible to grow in love and authenticity over decades and decades with a partner or if settling becomes the norm.

I met my third husband at a residential Gestalt psychology workshop two years after Mike's death. A psychotherapist, artist, and journal keeper, he and I shared a passion for personal growth, the spiritual journey and growing together as a couple. He became a nurturing stepfather to Kelli Lynne—an unexpected gift to our relationship.

When I answered another soul call and studied channeling and mediumship with Patricia Hayes in North Carolina, I unintentionally created emotional and psychic distance between my husband and me. The psychic world opened and became more real to me than my normal life. During the intensive training, I was asked if I would give permission for Mike to be our focus during a group séance, which was part of our training. Mike showed up! My classmates channeled information from him and I was allowed only three responses: "Yes," "No," and "I don't know." The objective was for my classmates to give evidential information that proved that they were in contact with my son. He told me that he desired me to gather my journal entries and experiences of him into a book and publish it. Also, he told me that the turquoise ring that he had given me for a birthday present three weeks before he died would be returned to me within three weeks in a surprising manner. He was right! Kelli Lynne found it tucked inside my mother's jewelry box and recognized it as mine.

My new husband played his role perfectly as an extension of my family because he was not supportive of my fascination with the paranormal world. He was a Taurus and believed only what he could see, feel, and know with his five senses. His motto was "I'll believe it when I see it," and mine was, "I'll believe first, and see it eventually." We both enjoyed growing psychotherapy practices in Maine, but according to his cherished beliefs I had gone over the edge when I incorporated soul readings into my ongoing therapy practice. I believed that if I was not living on the edge, I was taking up too much room on this planet.

When I left for a two-week spiritual journey to Egypt on our fifth anniversary, my husband felt abandoned and did not want to hear a word about my revelations when I returned. I felt like I had to choose between my seven-year relationship with him and the growth of my soul. The choice was painful because of all I had given up to be with him. Years later he told me he could not live up to the idealized image that he had presented to me when we first met. I bought the illusion of who he presented himself to be and my heart ached when he was unable to acknowledge me for who I was becoming.

Once again, I broke rank with my personal story and dared to imagine who I could become beyond my personal story. Once again, I returned to my journals for the thread:

I am stepping into my own reality and my own life and if my family wishes to be part of my world, they are welcome. However, I will no longer dim my light or be invisible or struggle to figure out how much of me is acceptable. It is over.

In retrospect, I acknowledge that I did a perfect job choosing both my parents and later my husband to act as my brakes. Like my parents before him, he encouraged me to be normal and act as if I were someone I was not. Although I pretended to be who they wanted me to be in order to be loved, eventually my soul rebelled and I broke rank with my past, conditioned self each time I chose to live more deeply into my emerging soul story.

I enjoyed being a psychotherapist, and my clinical supervisor, Joe Melnick, challenged me by asking, "Rosie, when do you know it is time to throw out the flowers?"

I was surprised by his question and even more curious when he confronted me with the same question upon several occasions. I wondered how he knew about my secret habit of clipping flowers back, removing dead leaves, treating the almost gone by bouquet to fresh water daily, removing individual petals in hopes of preserving the bouquet for at least one more day. Letting go is difficult for me.

Even if I had not chosen to be a therapist, I believe I would still track relationships, beliefs, and energy to ascertain whether passion, pain, fear, or boredom was the decision maker. For me writing is another way of tracking. I record beginnings, middles and endings of cycles in my life. Over the years, I have disciplined myself to track waning cycles and notice when the energy begins to dwindle, or I become bored or irritable. I pay attention to the inner and outer signals that warn me of completion. Blink truths are often reminders that something in my life has reached its expiration date. Dreams, too, often serve as clear harbingers of change when I remember them.

My purpose in tracking is to let go of any deadwood in my life. For example, I noticed that I no longer looked forward to swimming three days a week. Rather than give myself a hard time for eliminating swimming from my exercise schedule, I acknowledged swimming had entered the completion stage. When I signed up for a Pilates class, I was aware that I was beginning a new cycle. On a more practical level, I collect all the clothing and shoes that I have not worn during the year. Off they go to Goodwill and I smile at the empty hangers.

Around the beginning of each New Year, I do a completion inventory. In preparation for writing, I remind myself to check in with my heart and then I write my responses to the following questions:

Where am I flourishing?
Where is love growing?
Where does inspiration and creativity abide?

Does this relationship, project, and belief add to my energy or restrict my energy?

Recently, I acknowledged that a ten-year-old friendship felt more duty bound than connected to my evolving journey and lacked joy potential. When I was honest with myself, I acknowledged that the energy had been waning for months. Several times I wrote in my journal about being impatient and I avoided returning my friend's calls. Our conversations began to bore me and our time together lacked connection. I acknowledged that we had enriched each other's lives; however, I needed to let go of her friendship like the wilting bouquet.

Breaking rank with my sense of duty happened naturally as though life herself determined that I was ready to let go of my open-door policy. My journal excerpts captured the event:

More clearing the decks! On our way home from church, my friend complained that she did not feel appreciated by me. I admitted to her that I was tired of listening to her torture herself with obsessive thoughts and fears. Being compassionate to someone who is intent on re-creating drama felt like enabling and crazy making. I had offered understanding, guidance, and healing for years and she typically responded with, "Yes, but..."

For years, she consumed herself by trying to outsmart "the critters" as she called the dark energies that pursued her. She experienced herself as a victim who was being relentlessly pursued by evil energies that were determined to steal her light, take over her body and prevent her from being a creative artist.

I told her that I felt sad that the only way she expressed her creativity was to obsess about how to outsmart "the nasty critters" that lived in her imagination. I wondered out loud what might happen if she used the four or five hours a day that she devoted to clearing her energy field for her art.

She said she did not know if she was avoiding grief or what. Without thinking, I replied, "It is your fear that runs you. Let it go and laugh heartily. Fear is a magnet for the negativity that you attract."

From my perspective, she gave her power over to the darkness when she forgot her soul agreements and soul purpose. She compromised her energy, focus, creativity and health. Her personal story was one of struggle without end.

Then she said "Never work with anyone who regards you as a teacher because they will expect you to take care of them." I realized that she herself regarded me as her teacher and therefore expected me to take care of her. "When did that happen?" I wondered to myself.

I tracked my energy as I listened. I noted to myself that I felt like I was working harder than she was and I was muddled until I realized that I was interacting from the edges of my personal story. Instead of defending myself about not appreciating her, I witnessed my part of the process and ducked being part of her personal story by defending, complaining or shaming.

Later I realized by avoiding the impulse to jump into her drama, I had planted at least one of my legs in my edge-walking story.

I also track my spiritual guides and teachers. When I sense a guide feels distant or uncommunicative, I ask if each has completed his or her service to me. If one or more are ready to move on, I bless and release them and invite in new guides and teachers. One of the aspects of my soul story is that I recognize people by their frequency. I read energy all the time. Energy has always been my first language. When I honor my energetic knowing's, I am the best smut detector in the universe. I also carry a high, energetic frequency and I have learned over time that I am responsible for maintaining my frequency. That is one of the reasons I do my best to avoid gossiping, watching violent movies, befriending needy people or putting myself in an integrity breach where I am not honest, withhold information, or keep secrets. Being kind does not mean being co-dependent. My commitment is to be real.

Eventually, I banished the cute and entertaining Gracie Allen archetype that I embodied to win love. Letting go of the part of me that was entertaining and shallow, often at my own expense, did not mean that I sacrificed my sense of humor. I aligned with my soul story by making a commitment to be an active agent of evolutionary consciousness. That's when I printed "Cosmic Catalyst" on my business card. Crab walking around my soul purpose was no longer acceptable.

For months, I recited the following quotation from Terry Tempest Williams when I got out of bed each morning:

"I am going beyond my own conditioning—breaking set with what was breaking me."

How many lifetimes have I recycled my life lessons? I returned to an old journal dated February 1980 to track myself and was startled to find this entry:

Deliver me from always being strong.
Deliver me from looking to others for insights and validation.
Deliver me from settling for mediocrity.

After putting my pen down, I realized that I am my own deliverer.

Most of my life I have prided myself on being more philosophical than heart centered. Being in control was directly related to what I knew and understood. Added to that analytical and rather rigid way of knowing, I expected myself to know effortlessly. I took responsibility for bringing in high expectations this lifetime. I chose my parents well and they expected me to excel; plus, I was the first-born child and grandchild on both sides of my family. I adopted the motto "Excel and exceed" and I did my best to live up to that perfectionistic expectation.

In a mysterious way that I did not yet have words for, I know that my journey was a return to the feminine ways of being and knowing. Not only does the feminine relate to stories but it is also the energy that weaves and interweaves and shifts consciousness. I began to pray that I would open to a greater understanding of how I have allowed my inner patriarch to override my feminine ways of knowing. Within no time, I became aware of a triad of beliefs that has ruled my life: Work hard. Work often. Work before relaxation.

I was trained early that over-giving was a way to show love and be loved and that self-sacrifice was service. Over a glass of wine, my soul friend Leslie Rosenberg reminded me, "Rosie, people want to consume you—eat you up because you are a magnet of light." I allowed her words to impact me. When I am honest with myself, I know that I am light in formation. I also affirm that shining my light bright brings me and others joy. Equally true is that setting realistic boundaries with my time and energy is an ongoing life lesson. How do I honor my soul purpose and beam light to others without losing myself? Setting limits and being honest rather than co-dependent is another way I broke rank. For an over-giver, the line between enabling and empowering is murky.

The goal of moving from our personal story to taking up residency with our soul stories is not to escape our personal stories, but to make our stories sacred. I question myself about why it took me thirty-four years to recognize the impact of Future Pull in my life, especially since my guides channeled this information in July 1982:

"A magnetic resonance accompanies your decision to be in alignment with your soul story. Future Pull is a magnetic resonance."

I returned many times to Gregg Levoy's book *Callings: Finding and Following an Authentic Life* and his wisdom regarding soul calls: "Saying Yes to the call places you on a path that half of yourself thinks doesn't make a lot of sense, but the other half knows your life won't make sense without."

Looking back, each time I said "yes" to a specific soul call, I let go of my limited definition of who I thought I was and became present for my more spacious soul story. The question that helped me to align with my soul story became: Who do I desire to become instead of what should I do?

Moving into my unique soul story required me to ground myself in awareness and intention. When I was not present, my familiar personal story often hooked me. From a soul perspective, the emerging question was: How big do I need to make myself in order to step into the spaciousness of Future Pull? Often, I reminded myself that Be Spacious was the summary of all spiritual teachings and being spacious was not egocentric. In fact, Be Spacious is connected to being theocentric. Again, when I returned to old journals to track myself, I found this one liner in a journal written in 1982:

Straying from the light creates pain and isolation. You incarnated to activate your soul to receive and express joy in human ways.

When I made the decision to divorce my therapist husband, I no longer wanted to carry his name. Friends urged me to return to my maiden name, but that name felt as though it belonged to someone else. The idea of naming myself felt both exciting and daunting because I challenged myself to choose a name that reflected my spiritual path. For weeks I searched through name books unsuccessfully, and then I turned to numerology and struggled to find the right combination of vowels and consonants that embodied the frequency that I desired. After three weeks of force-fitting letters, I almost gave up.

As a last resort, I invited my dream guides to assist me. I decided to retreat to the spare bedroom for as long as it took for a dream to come. In preparation, I filled a four gallon LL Bean thermos with water, placed candles in the spare bedroom, posted a Do Not Disturb sign on the bedroom door, smudged the room with sage, turned on meditation music, and settled into dream time. It was 9:31 P.M.

At 1:29 A.M., I recognized that I was in the midst of a lucid dream. A large circle of men and women gathered around a bonfire. I stood alone a few yards from the circle. I watched as one person at a time threw something small into the fire. Then they all leaned forward to watch the object burn. When there was only a shape on the parched ground, someone ran about ten feet to an old man who had a long stick in his hand. The elderly, hunched over man drew something in the ground that I could not make out. He repeated this action at least seven more times. Finally, I caught a young woman's eye and asked her why I was excluded from the circle.

"You called us here to do what you do not know how to do," she said simply and without emotion.

"Yes, but it is my dream and I don't like being on the outside," I responded passionately.

"When it is done, we will call you," she said calmly as she turned her back on me and resumed her place in the circle.

Then everyone in the circle walked over to join the old man with the crooked stick. After several minutes, someone motioned me to join the large circle. The elderly hunched over man pointed to the scribbles on the ground and motioned me to watch.

Then the group began to chant, rattle, and drum. As I watched, the squiggles transformed, one after the other into letters. I was mesmerized. I have no idea how long the process took. Time did not matter. When I saw the name "Deer Heart" spelled out, I cried.

Next, six men approached me and I panicked because I had no idea about their intentions. Together, they lifted me high into the air and held my body facing toward the sky.

Then they turned my body over so I faced the earth. Slowly they carried me around the group and the vibrations that resonated with Deer Heart were drummed, rattled and sung into my bones. I felt like I was being baptized with my spiritual name.

A few weeks later I told my dream to a group of friends who gathered for my going away party, prior to moving to New Mexico. I asked them to bring rattles and drums because I wanted to re-enact the dream ritual with my friends. Once again, I vowed to carry the name Deer Heart until my death and into my afterlife if that were possible.

The morning of the divorce hearing my lawyer explained to me that my request for a name change was complicated unless I convinced the judge that I had used Deer Heart previously. Otherwise, we would have to petition another court.

"Do past life times count?" I asked with a smile.

"Rosalie, in the case of changing your name, the judge will ask you if you have used the name before and I advise you to say, "Yes. Your honor."

Then he continued, "He might also ask if you have shared your name with your professional colleagues."

"Yes, they all participated in my naming ritual," I said enthusiastically.

He interrupted me and said, "Rosalie, your response is, "Yes, your honor."

I took a deep breath and agreed to follow instructions.

The divorce was granted within five minutes. Then I watched from my seat as the judge conferred with the two lawyers and I felt impatient and angry that three men had the power to decide on my right to have my spiritual name. I started to stand up and protest, but my friend yanked me down. Being left out reminded me of my naming dream.

Then the judge invited me to approach the bench. I felt confident that I knew the drill. And I did, until he stood up from his seat behind the raised podium, looked directly at me and said, "This is an unusual name. Why this specific name?"

Since I had not rehearsed for this question, I took a breath, put my hand on my heart, and said, "Your honor, I want my spiritual name—my soul name—so I will never go off my spiritual path again. I plan to carry this soul name until I die.

He took a breath and said, "Never let it be said that I stood between any woman and her soul." Then he announced, "Change of name granted," and pounded his gavel.

I bowed. He bowed back and before I could say a word my lawyer ushered me from the courtroom.

Later in the day, after a celebratory lunch, I sent the judge a bouquet of flowers as a thank you. A few days later I received a note from him thanking me for the flowers and saying that in his twenty-two years on the bench, nobody had sent him flowers. I continued to send him flowers every year on the anniversary of my naming for thirteen years until he died.

The soul call to move to New Mexico, where I knew no-body, felt like a wild card. I was forty-seven and my daughter was seventeen. First, I had several dreams of The Land of En-chantment. Then someone from New Mexico called me and then realized that she had dialed the wrong number. When a friend gave me a book about New Mexico, I felt like I was being stalked.

My daughter was about to enter her senior year in high school. I enjoyed a flourishing psychotherapy practice and belonged to several women's communities. My family lived in Maine. I did not even know how to spell Albuquerque!

As I listened to my guides and let go of my fear, the message became clear.

"You will find your next home within a ninety-five-mile distance of Albuquerque."

Both friends and family thought I had gone off the deep end. Comfortable with my life, the timing felt absurd. Still the soul call felt right, even though I had no idea how I was being asked to grow. Furthermore, I had no clue what the lessons might be and lacked experience to know that blessings are also part of a soul call—eventually.

Two of my friends from Colorado met me at the Albuquerque Airport and for five days we methodically drove in circles from Albuquerque until we reached Arroyo Seco, a small, Hispanic village on the way to the Ski Valley, just north of Taos. I no longer remember which one of us called for meditation time. We piled out of the car and sat on the grass, not knowing that the pasture was on Taos Pueblo land. That's where I spotted my first buffalo.

While meditating, I saw an eagle on the inner planes. When I opened my eyes, I spotted an eagle for real flying overhead. Instantly, I knew the eagle was a sign. I ordered John and Rendle to jump into the car and we drove about four miles up a bumpy, dirt road, following the eagle that we all acknowledged as a way-shower.

When we got halfway up the mountain, the eagle's circles became smaller and smaller. We turned a corner and pulled up outside a tall wooden gate, where the eagle circled directly overhead. Nobody was surprised that the sign on the gate said "For Rent."

I scribbled down the telephone number and we backed up and started back down the road. A woman waved at us from her doorway and we stopped and asked her about the house behind the wooden gate. She invited me to call the owner from her house. Sight unseen, I rented the hippie house that had been built in stages over twenty years.

The best part was the outdoor hot tub and an inside solarium filled with small trees and exotic plants. The worst part was the absence of a furnace—only two fireplaces that did not heat the house because at an elevation of 7600 feet, winter brought lots of frost and snow.

After I signed the lease, I returned home, put my home up for rent, hired movers, paid someone to drive my car across country, and Kelli Lynne and I flew to Albuquerque. I found a small, private school, Chemisa Mesa, that specialized in environmental education, personal growth and academics for Kelli Lynne. There she became one of four seniors.

I was not familiar with the demands of living in a small community where three cultures struggled to live peacefully. Here I was an Anglo living in the midst of an entrenched Hispanic community surrounded by Native Americans who lived at the nearby Taos Pueblo. Because I was single, I was suspected of being either lesbian or a witch. Neighbors took bets that we would not survive the winter. We did and we won a jackpot of over $200!

Nature opened my heart and grounded me in my body. The un-partitioned sky, the winding trails in the woods and the seven waterfalls atop El Salto Mountain captivated me and opened me up to beauty and wonder. I bought a tee shirt with a quotation from Emily Dickinson emblazoned on the front: "I dwell in possibilities."

For the first time since becoming an adult, I did not have a full-time job. While Kelli Lynne was at school, I hiked and explored and surprised myself when I sang out loud, "I am Thanks Giving" and meant it. In the evening, I sat in the outdoor hot tub and visited with the shooting stars, welcomed the wind and played with my ocean drum. I felt like the little girl in the story *Heidi* who went to live with her grandfather and Nature became her companion. In the evening, I gathered together journal entries and wove together *Healing Grief—A Mother's Story*, which I still refer to as *Mike's Book*

I began to channel the Shaman of the Mountain, an ancient Native American medicine man and joined Taos Healing Network. For the first time, I admitted to myself that I had healing abilities. My consciousness expanded. I doubt that these heart expansions would have occurred if I had continued living my life in Maine.

During my second month in my adopted state, I attended a large conference on science and healing in Santa Fe. I spotted a woman from across the room who felt familiar to me. She looked up and we giggled. At break time, we found each other and hugged. Then she invited me into friendship asking, "What is your story, sister?"

Without planning what to say in advance, I shared the story of my recent move to New Mexico. I ended the saga by confessing that I still did not know the purpose of my move—only its rightness. Then I took a deep breath and whispered, "I think my soul has plans for growing me up."

We giggled and hugged again. Then I prompted, "Your turn, sister."

Without hesitation, she told me how she had recently quit her stressful job as head nurse in a local intensive care unit because she no longer felt fulfilled and she too yearned for freedom. She too had no clue about her next steps although she knew in her heart that she had made the right choice.

I nodded and hugged her, appreciating how both of us had responded to our unique soul calls without knowing much more than our souls would suffer if we had not. Instinctively, we both trusted that the next steps would emerge. Together we acknowledged that we were not in charge of when or where. The not being in charge part was a huge paradox since we prided ourselves on making things happen. No longer. Being receptive to the unknown mystery and admitting that we did not know and trusting that, in time, we would grow into knowing felt right to both of us. Although neither of us had lived into our answers yet, we were both more comfortable trusting that truth would emerge. Holding the field of not knowing and wanting to know felt healthier than feeling like a victim of our limiting personal story. Geneie Everett, now Dr. Genie Everett, became my first evolutionary buddy in my adopted state.

In my experience, soul calls often felt like break though moments and sometimes epiphanies. For a time, I existed in liminal space where my former ways of being no longer fit and a new, more expanded way of being in the world had not yet taken hold. Like a snake that has shed its skin to make room for expansion, I felt vulnerable (especially since my soul skin was invisible.) My familiar former roles no longer felt fulfilling.

I wished someone had pointed out to me that beliefs have consequences and that I build my own fictional world by believing what I believe. I remember reading the following quotation when I was in my fifties and regretting that I had not understood the implications earlier in my life:

"I thought you would never get here," she said.

"I know and that's what took me so long," he said.

How many times have I experienced that dissolving the ego is the work of the soul? I know that my ego majors in the past and the future in order to control. I remind myself often that ego is that aspect of myself that is a core resistance to growing into my authentic self. Plus, I know from my own experience that ego lacks a spiritual perspective.

I practiced listening to the stories I told for two weeks and I discovered that whatever I chose to believe became the reality that I created. I also was attentive to listening to others and recorded some of their beliefs in my journal:

"Life is never simple," my daughter Kelli Lynne said to me one evening. True to her belief, hers has not been simple.

Without thinking, I replied, "I am sorry that your life is not simple. Mine is and part of the reason is that I believe that life flows."

I am convinced that beliefs have consequences. I read somewhere that it takes seventeen seconds for a thought to manifest in the etheric. We hold beliefs in our body. Scientists and psychologists agree that whether you trust life or not, it is a somatic experience. Both my unconscious and conscious mind determines whether I feel safe or unsafe, lovable or unlovable, and empowered or victimized.

I am amazed by the power of unconscious beliefs. Unless I challenge myself to be honest with my feelings, I victimize myself by creating an integrity breach that lowers my energy.

Beliefs are pre-conscious. For example, I once heard a psychologist tell a story of a teenager he worked with who was arrested for robbing food from a grocery store. The young man did not need food and said he stored it in his bedroom closet—just in case. After working with the teenager for a couple of months, the psychologist invited his mother in and asked her about the details of her pregnancy with Gavin. She talked about the time her husband had locked her in the bedroom for five days without food hoping that she would have a miscarriage. I agree it is a quantum leap to connect

Garvin's impulse to rob food stores to his mother's story. Yet the mother's experience provides another window of the connectivity of consciousness.

While I pondered the power of personal beliefs, my buddy Joan called and began our conversation by saying, "I did not realize that when I moved into Chuck's house, I left behind my rugs, wall hangings and pictures. No wonder I refer to our home as Chuck's house. I was surprised because Joan has an eye for beauty and her homes in Maine have been pleasing to all of my senses.

She continued, "After living together for three years, I admitted to myself that I hated the living room because it feels dark, small, and ugly to me. Yet I am embarrassed to say that I complained a lot and made a decision not to buy new furniture until we moved into another house. It never occurred to me to buy a slipcover for the couch or to change the look by bringing my favorite belongings from Maine. The only room in this whole house that feels like mine is my office. The bizarre thing about this three-year saga is I didn't know that I had the option of bringing more of my treasures and myself to his home. He never would object. In fact, when I told him about how much I have felt like a stranger in the house, he was surprised. It was all me limiting my own self-expressing!"

I recognized myself in her story and shared that whenever I settle or create an integrity breach where I do not speak my truth, I end up resenting someone else and lower my own frequency.

The next day a friend complained about how upset he became while watching a football game on television. In a loud voice, he said, "The players roughed each other up and there were lots of fights on the field, and four men got concussions. It was horrible."

I watched his body contract as he continued to explain how upset he was. When I asked, "Why didn't you turn the game off if you were so upset?" He shrugged his shoulders in response. As long as we do not question our preconceptions, we rob ourselves of clarity and understanding.

In my own experience, some months after Mike's death he no longer related to me as "his" mother and told me continuing to relate to him as "my son" hindered his journey rather than supporting his choice of evolution. Could it be as simple as realizing that clinging to our beliefs and roles limits us and when we pass from our life on earth into our afterlife our limited ways of being dissolve?

CHAPTER 4

Multi-Dimensional Consciousness

When I was forty-nine, Mother Mary added her light to mine when I was grieving the fifteenth anniversary of Mike's death and realized that he had been dead longer than he had lived.

I returned to my earlier journal to refresh my memories of that time and my first Mother Mary encounter:

Between the ages of thirty-three and thirty-six, I learned how to be a veteran of loss. Grief demanded everything of me—my days, my nights, my dreams, at times even my breath. I survived all the firsts—birthdays, the beginnings and endings of the school year, Thanksgivings, and all the Christmases since Mike's death.

Each year since Mike's death in 1977, I dreaded the month of March and began preparing myself for its eventuality sometime in February. March marked my birthday and Mike's death day. Fifteen years after his death I considered myself a veteran of grief; however, I sensed that this year's anniversary of his death was different. I had no idea why. All I knew was that I felt assaulted with intensity.

As I walked the familiar path through the deep pinewoods in Arroyo Seco, I mentally counted how many years Mike had been dead. Fifteen. The number thundered through my heart as I realized that my son had been dead longer than he had lived with me. I felt bereft. Always before, I prepared myself. Not this time. My heart felt hijacked.

To honor this significant anniversary, I drove with two of my friends to a small circular church in Crestone, Colorado to offer prayers, and then we agreed to head to the mineral springs for a soak. The small church was empty as we entered and I took a seat in the front pew. My heart hurt. My eyes felt dry. I wanted to pray, but I had no idea what to pray for. At 10 o'clock in the morning, the bright March sun filtered through the stained-glass windows painting colorful designs on the floor and the walls.

The only sound in the church was the wringing of my hands. The feeling of, "I don't know how to do this" shot through my body. It reminded me how I felt when the emergency room doctor said, "There was nothing we could do. He was dead on arrival. If he had survived, he would have been a vegetable." Once again, I felt helpless and beyond being able to comprehend words and life and death.

I did not know how to begin my prayers. I missed Mike and I grieved his death and the future that we did not share. The reality that I eventually embraced—that Mike and I had a soul agreement to communicate between dimensions—did not ease the pain in my heart. I missed him and who I was as his mother. My

*friend handed me a Kleenex and then got up quietly
and left me alone.*

*My mind filled with memories and regrets. My love
was not enough to keep him here. My sobs ushered in
a choking prayer and I closed my eyes. Even with my
eyes shut, I could see the bright light flooding the front
of the church. When I opened my eyes half way, I saw
that the energy that engulfed me was not Mike's. As I
slowed my breathing and focused on the energy growing in front of me, I began to distinguish a face that
looked as though it were made of shimmering light. It
pulsated and vibrated rapidly. The eyes mesmerized
me. I felt like I was locked into an eye gaze and nothing
else mattered. From a place beyond my understanding,
I intuited that the face and emerging figure belonged
to Mother Mary.*

*She held my gaze and transmitted pure love and
compassion. As her energy surrounded me, my heart
overflowed with love—not pain. As I merged with her
eyes, she energetically invited me to participate in an
exquisitely choreographed dance. With no idea or even
a need to understand how it happened, I was inside
of Mary's eyes observing myself sitting on the pew.
Like erasing chalk from a chalkboard, all distinction
between Mary and me dissolved. I no longer knew if
I was the one sending love and compassion to myself
or if Mary was the channel or if we were both being
Resources for the Source. It didn't matter. Nothing mattered except the pure immensity of the healing love.*

*The next time I tracked my awareness, I was in my
own energy, sitting alone in the front pew, and breathing in and filling up with loving compassion. My body*

felt light—not burdened with grief. Gradually, Mary disappeared and I felt flushed and hot. Tears flowed down my face as joy and healing filled my heart.

When I looked in front of me, the light had disappeared. I glanced behind me and the church was empty. I wondered if I remembered how to walk or talk. As I carefully stood and slowly walked out the chapel door, I saw a small sign that I had not noticed when we entered—Mary's Church.

For weeks, I had no way to explain how Mary overlighted me. Each time I returned to the inner experience of remembered radiance, I re-entered the eternal energies of love and compassion. I have never felt like my former self since my experience with Mary. She introduced me to myself as a multidimensional woman.

I wish everyone had a visit from Mother Mary to restore the vibrancy of unbounded love. When I discovered I had the energy to reclaim love, I felt free.

My guides added their voice:

Your spiritual perspective has a higher energy and it gives your soul much pleasure to infuse your human story with spiritual awareness. When you live in alignment with your soul story, you channel and radiate light, love, purpose, and passion. Your journey toward God becomes a love story.

Looking back, I appreciated that Mary's unexpected visit marked my first evidential experience of believing that it was possible to experience myself as a meeting place between heaven and earth. My consciousness expanded to include the multidimensional nature of consciousness. Never again would I be seduced into believing that my consciousness ended at my skin. I re-awakened—like the first time that I received messages from my dead son. Plus, each time I remembered the experiences, I re-entered the realm of "remembered radiance." I knew instinctively that being a channel of blessings was part of my soul story and I volunteered my readiness to be a channel by repeating daily, "Use me! Use me! Use me"

The universe responded to my invitation to become a channel of blessings at Findhorn, the international spiritual community in Scotland well known for its gardens. In 1993 in a small darkened meditation room dug out of the earth, I sat on round, colorful pillows meditating and felt like I was surrounded in an earth womb. Suddenly I felt light move around inside my head and looked around the dimly lit room in search of the source of this light. The champagne bubble sensation in my head was unfamiliar. I did not feel lightheaded, but like light was moving within my head. Words didn't serve me. The strange light in my head continued to grew more intense each day. I wondered about the possibility of a stroke and then questioned if I were growing a new pulse.

When I confided in a friend, she suggested I make an appointment to meet with Eileen Caddy, the co-founder of Findhorn. Although I had read Eileen's book, *Opening Doors Within*, we had not met. When she graciously welcomed me into her home, I felt nervous and did not know where to begin. As I tracked the energy in my head, it expanded and I wondered how my head could hold so much light.

After Eileen served raspberry-mint tea from fruit harvested in Findhorn's gardens, she reached over and held my hands. Although she was silent, I sensed she was reading my energy. I sighed and relaxed a bit. She stayed silent as she listened to my disjointed description of my experience and then asked me if this was my first time entertaining an angel.

Hesitantly, I described my unexpected visitation with Mary in New Mexico and she squeezed my hands and smiled.

"But that was different," I said. "I saw Mary. She had hair and a face and radiant eyes and a body. This energy that lives in my head arrived without visuals—only sensations."

Eileen sighed and said calmly, "That's perfectly okay, dear. Trust that the angel knows how best to gain your attention in preparation for you to channel."

I must have looked startled or frightened because she continued,

"Yes, dear, the angel channels for the good of the community and we celebrate the thirtieth anniversary of Findhorn in a couple of days. I am very excited that she will give us a message through you at the annual celebration in the Community Hall."

"But I have never channeled an angel before," I stammered. "How many people do you expect will be at the community party?"

"Well, the whole community and also many friends from the nearby town of Forres will be here. I don't know exactly how many, but perhaps upwards of five hundred people."

I have never fainted before, but I thought this might be the perfect occasion.

"You will be fine, dear. In fact, I predict that you will enjoy the channeling experience. The angel always uplifts everyone and besides she is charming and funny, too."

She sensed my panic and assured me that she would sit beside me and hold my hand if I wished. Then she poured me another cup of tea and described some of her experiences with the Angel of Findhorn as naturally as if she were talking about washing dishes. Slowly, I relaxed. I trusted her experience with the Angel of Findhorn and respected her for encouraging people in the international community to access their own intuition rather than relying on her to channel.

The night of the party, she introduced me to the group of about four hundred people at the Community Hall and then pulled up a chair next to mine and adjusted the microphone. I reached out to hold her hand and realized I squeezed too tightly. Eileen gently returned my squeeze and smiled.

I began breathing so fast that I hyperventilated and my vision blurred. Then I questioned my commitment to be a resource for the Source. I had never experienced performance anxiety before and I hope I never do again. I took a few breaths and dropped into a meditative state. Then I felt raspiness in my throat and a tickling sensation in my heart. I opened my mouth and words flowed. According to the angel, the community was smack in its early adolescence and had growing pains. The channeling centered on The Four R's: Responsibility, Roles, Rules, and Rituals.

I had no idea how long I channeled. I was aware of Eileen's hand on mine. My eyes were closed. When the words stopped, I took a few breaths and began to feel like I was the only occupant of my body again. The group applauded and then everyone stood up. I felt overwhelmed, and had no words. Eileen leaned over and hugged me and we both cried.

I did not consciously call these extraordinary events to myself. Each time I became over-lighted, I felt expanded and enjoyed a lightness of being for weeks after. Each time that I consciously cooperated, what I knew or believed in my human consciousness expanded. At times, I wondered if my consciousness was imbued with Divine madness or Divine clarity until I realized I was creating another duality and let it go. Somewhere, somehow, I understood that revelation waited in the midst of paradox and I was not in charge. In time I began to trust that the unknown future was full of revelations.

About a month after channeling the Angel of Findhorn, I ran across an article by Brother David Steindl-Rast in which he defined angels as the Eternal breaking through time. I agree. My journals are filled with questions about how to continue to befriend angels:

> *How do I wrap my heart and mind around communicating with an angel?*
>
> *How do I explain to others that angels are allies and have no understanding of our human tendency for failure to thrive?*
>
> *How might my angelic connection benefit others?*

Angels became my familiars. The Angel of Findhorn created a pathway or a magnet for other celestial guests. For sure, the divine spark that is me expanded into more light. I reflect in wonder at my journey. Being blessed by angels, guides, and the Holy Ones added to my light and my soul purpose, which is one of service.

Opening myself up to receive and channel angels required surrendering—not easy for this strong Maine woman who enjoyed being in control. As a cosmic catalyst, I spoke my truth and told my multidimensional story in an attempt to spark connections and remembrances within others because that is part of my soul purpose.

Another unexpected soul call seized me when I turned sixty. I moved from central coast California to Scarborough, Maine to be a full time resident grandmother to my two young grandchildren. My daughter had accepted a residency in the anesthesiology program at Maine Medical Center in Portland. We agreed that my grandchildren, Malia, age four and Noah, age eighteen months, were too little for day care and money was scarce. Little did I know that my one-year agreement to nurture and grow up my grandchildren would evolve into a full-time commitment that spanned nine years.

Being of joyful service (not self-sacrifice) is one of my soul threads. The soul call to raise my grandchildren became a new form of service. If I were allowed to take only a few memories into my afterlife, my time of nurturing my adult daughter and my grandchildren ranks top on my list.

Malia was only eight when she described me to a counselor as her "multi-parent"—part grandmother and part mom and dad. Getting a second chance to be a full-time parent to my daughter and a loving source of support for my growing grandchildren seemed like a healing to me. This felt profound since my son's sudden death interrupted my role of mothering my daughter who was only two and a half at the time.

Nurturing my daughter and my grandchildren without working fulltime as I had before became a way of re-weaving my role as a parent. Not only was I present to take my grandchildren to school, extra-curricular activities, doctor's appointments, sleepovers, and outings, I was also present for my daughter while she completed her four-year residency program. When she began her career as a licensed anesthesiologist, I moved with her to Bangor, Maine and we continued to grow each other up.

In 2008, when I was sixty-four and still a fulltime resident grandmother, Big Angel entered my consciousness. I sensed the angel's energetic presence encircling me for a few months before I received a message. Since the initiation by the Angel of Findhorn, I recognized the subtle shifts of energy that signaled the presence of an angelic being.

However, the circumstances surrounding my initial encounter with Big Angel were humorous. I was in the middle of giving a workshop at Leapin' Lizard's, a metaphysical bookstore in Portland, Maine, when I took a bathroom break. While I peed, a light filled energy filled the bathroom and announced itself as Big Angel. Although I am a nudist, this invasion of my privacy seemed extreme. Yet I have learned through experience that guides tend to be impersonal and I let go of modesty.

As I welcomed Big Angel, "he" announced that he wished to teach the group how to align with their future selves. Momentarily, I was caught off guard. Then my curiosity cast a Yes vote. Big Angel asked permission to merge with my human energies. I agreed because I valued both efficiency and innovation.

None of the workshop participants guessed that they were in the presence of an angel because Big Angel had merged into my heart. I looked normal and he was invisible. Although I spoke the words that allowed the participants to merge with their future self, I was in awe of the simple yet profound process. It was way beyond what I had prepared to teach and I felt like I was pregnant with the Divine.

Big Angel enjoyed channeling for groups. I was shy and questioned whether I was showing off or being of service. Participants assured me that the presence of Big Angel opened their hearts and minds to other possible realities. That positive feedback was good enough for me.

Here is an excerpt from a group channeling:

Big Angel: I am an inter-dimensional, which means that I serve many dimensions. My assignment is to remind you of the Truth and Beauty that lives within each of you. Many are the ways to attract us: silence, intention, beauty, fragrance, curiosity about past lifetime or future time beyond this moment, reading the words of the prophets and mystics, creative acts, love, writing without thought, joy, kindness, living in your heart, and prayers. Allowing yourself to believe that everything is possible is another way of connecting with the angelic realm. I was attracted to The Lady (me) because she made a commitment to live Big Truth. I, Big Angel, honor each of you for whom I know you to be. My mission is to help you remember all of who you are.

In my experience, there is no way of knowing in advance what will be asked of me and what will be offered when an angel or a guide pops in. My ongoing relationship with Big Angel was intense and required courage and determination. Gradually, I learned how to be comfortable initiating contact. Dialoguing in writing became one of my favorite ways of interacting:

Me: Greetings, Big Angel.

Big Angel: Greetings. I appreciate your willingness to entertain me on this day. Being with your breath and your high heart and being receptive to guidance opens the portals and allows guidance to flow. Presencing yourself is a daily practice.

Me: I appreciate collaborating with you. Please know that I am very willing to give you as much space—even all of it—as we invite people to remember and deepen.

Big Angel: Thank you. That is a big part of our mutual mission. It is a mystery to us in the angelic realms why humans resist love, light, and healing. Showing up in your humorous and intense way opens the hearts and minds of others. They respond to your presence, which is your essence. Think of our interchange as a frequency upgrade. Another word, of course, is entrainment. Being a channel of grace becomes you.

Me: What? Being a channel of grace! I think I just missed a significant part of this conversation. When did I agree to be a channel of grace?

Big Angel: A little more than one year ago when Melchizadek initiated you and your soul friend John at Mountain Light Sanctuary in North Carolina. You, in turn, agreed to remind others of their divine potential. You invite by your light. Then you invite others, by your presence, to align more deeply with their own divine plan, or cosmic report card, as you call it. You model, lead, witness, and affirm by holding the frequencies of the future. Once you experience and express the frequency of the future, there is no returning to the familiar ways. Use your own life experience as a guideline. Remember that spiritual growth is experienced not analyzed.

In my experience, angels sometimes visit for a short time and we are unaware of their presence until we admit to ourselves that a transformation has occurred and we have no other plausible explanation.

I recognized a part of me that wants nothing to do with revelation because it orphans me from my old personal story. It was the unknown future that awakened me. When I dared to be open to a larger story, angels sometimes arrived. Then I experienced myself as being at a choice point between my expanding soul story and my more limited human story.

I wrote about the angel who blessed me with healing in my book *Awaken.* Yet I felt moved from within my heart to include it again in this book because, unlike Big Angel, this celestial being visited with me for only a few minutes and yet her impact was profound.

The story begins when I dislocated the kneecap in my right leg when I tripped over a curb because I was staring at an eagle flying overhead. I pushed myself to cook, clean, and care for Malia and Noah rather than resting and icing my swollen leg. Since I did not heed the initial wake up call to do less, two weeks later I tore two ligaments in the same leg. Being brought to my knees twice scared me and I surrendered to more time on the couch.

Still, caring for my two rambunctious grandchildren during my recovery time was physically exhausting and emotionally difficult. When my daughter had a weekend off, I decided to treat myself to a thirty-hour getaway. Driving was painful and I gratefully checked into a motel about twenty miles from home. I was delighted to find the handicapped accessible bathroom with a tub I could soak in. The woman who checked me in told me to ask the chambermaid for extra pillows. When the woman delivered the pillows, she asked me what had happened to my leg. I gave her the Reader's Digest version of my injury and she offered me a Reiki energy treatment. She told me her name was Rashina and I noted that she was about the same age as my daughter.

Since I am familiar with Reiki healing energy, I relaxed and opened my eyes three hours later. My leg felt lighter and pain free. I walked around the room to be sure that I wasn't fooling myself and then noticed that the swelling had gone down, too.

I had no memory of the healing session. I wanted to thank Rashina and put some money in an envelope and went to the front desk to search for her. The desk clerk looked at me strangely and said nobody named Rashina worked there. I thought maybe I had mispronounced her name and described her as about thirty-five years old, dark skin and long black hair.

The woman at the front desk shook her head and said, "The only chambermaid that works here is a middle-aged Scottish woman with short, white hair."

During the night, I felt gentle vibrations on my right knee. It felt like a gentle massage. Then my knee pulsated with heat. I distinctly heard a voice in the dark room declare, "You are eighty percent healed." I put the light on and looked around the room. I was alone.

On Monday I visited my chiropractor and declared myself 80% healed. He looked surprised and told me to sit on his table while he checked my leg for stability and mobility. Then he asked me what had happened because three days ago he would have put me at only twenty percent healed.

Before I answered, I asked him, "Do you believe in angels?" Before he answered, I continued, "Have you ever been visited by an angel?"

He stepped back from me and said, "Why, yes, I do believe in the presence of angels, but I can't honestly say I have been visited by any."

I nodded my head and smiled and then said, "Well if you had been visited by one, I trust that you would remember." Then I told him my healing angel story. Rarely expressive, he simply nodded his acknowledgment.

The healing angel continued to touch people beyond me. When I told Fred Gagnon, the minister at First Congregational Church in Scarborough, Maine, my angel story, he invited me to share the details during a special healing service. He was clearly edge walking by offering an ancient hands-on healing service and he invited me to join him. Although I felt a bit nervous standing up in front of the congregation, I also believe that we have an opportunity to change consciousness when we share our stories. Just before I walked to the pulpit, I remembered a vivid dream from forty years before. In the dream, I was standing in a church and a large Bible was open in front of me. I looked down at the Bible and closed it and said confidently, "When you speak from the depths of your heart, you are your own Bible."

Before I had mounted the five steps to the pulpit, I felt lit up from the dream recall. I told my angel story as my two grandchildren beamed love and smiles at me from the second row. Later I joined Fred in the reception line after the service and I felt blessed again when five people whispered their encounters with angels to me. Each one began by saying; "I have never dared to tell this to anyone. Your story reminded me of my own angel visit." As I left the church, I wondered how many other people silenced their angel stories. Then I smiled as I gathered the angel stories of the five people into my heart.

While I appreciate that many people relate to angels as Beings above and beyond us, that is not my experience. Angels track human potential. They behold us with a sense of wonder. I smile as I return to my journals to re-visit angel wisdom:

Most humans have anxiety around pleasure. Imagine pleasure as love of self. Allow yourself more pleasure in life. Pleasure connects to soul as long as your chosen pleasure does not dim your light. Each soul contains many levels and layers that extend and expand beyond the earth. You must be fully embodied in the physical in order to be receptive and safe bridging the spiritual realms with the physical in order incorporate your essence.

I felt like I had enrolled in an accelerated soul growth course and I had no control. My life looked normal to others. I was a resident grandmother who nurtured and played with Malia and Noah, cooked and cleaned, and listened to my daughter's stories of her hospital experiences. Neighbors thought I was grounded and devoted to raising my grandchildren. Nobody had a clue that I was engaging with angels before I spoke at the Congregational Church. Yet looking back, my soul growth was progressive and the timing was connected to my eternal nature, not my human nature. Even if I had challenged myself to answer the question, "What could be more entrancing than angels?" I could not have imagined the world that opened to me when my third eye exploded open.

The last channeling from Big Angel arrived one day before my third eye opened:

As your soul consciousness is activated through practice, it infuses your human consciousness with a lighter frequency. This transformational process brings spirit and matter into one and it requires enormous trust. This experience can happen in meditation or with a kiss.

Looking back, I have a strong intuition that Big Angel's final gift to me was a hint of what lay ahead. However, I was clueless. Although I do not think of myself as dramatic, my story of the emotional catharsis and the subsequent opening of my third eye qualified for high drama. Once again, I return to my journal to re-visit the event:

I was alone in the house today and I put on the Canadian Tenors CD and turned up the volume. As I listened to their rich voices, my heart opened and I began sobbing—loud, deep cries from the bottom of my belly. I was surprised since I had no memories connected to my tears. Then I made a choice to ride my emotional rapids and cried louder and deeper. Memories of being alone and cut off from my mother's love ripped through my body. No words. The memories came from when I was very young—maybe even before I had language, or maybe even from a past lifetime. My body shook until I had no more energy or tears. My Younger Self, who lives within me, demanded my full attention. I felt bereft and alone. When I asked My Younger Self what she needed from me, she replied, "Attention and popcorn." I agreed.

An hour passed as I nurtured my inner girl. Then I questioned whether to cancel going to the chanting session at Sadhana Center in South Portland and I decided to go in spite of my swollen face and red eyes. I felt vulnerable and lighter.

When Ashok put the music on, I relaxed. I knew I was edge walking with my emotions and feared I might cry. I never cried in public and seldom cried in private. As I reminded myself to breathe, I noticed that my forehead hurt and I remembered how menstrual cramps felt from memories of decades earlier. I giggled out loud at the thought of feeling menstrual cramps in my forehead. Gradually, I understood that my third eye was opening. I had no visuals or sounds to validate my reality—only my inner experience. I had read about this experience in books, but never expected it would happen to me.

Once again, I felt like the inside of my forehead and head were bathed in light. My physical eyes felt different—like I had telescopic vision. Then I sensed a new energetic presence that felt masculine. Simultaneously, I was aware that I no longer felt the presence of Big Angel. Before I felt the fullness of my grief, I saw a visual imprint of my new guide. His energy felt stronger and more demanding. He, like me, tended to be impatient. In my mind, I referred to him as "the Dude." Gradually, I noticed that my concentration during meditation increased and I tended to be more disciplined about writing and organizing my seventh book, Awaken.

Two months went by before I spotted a photo that looked exactly like him: bearded, thin face, deep set eyes and an intense stare. Muktananda had become my new guide. A researcher at heart, I discovered that he was acclaimed as a meditation master and known as the guru's guru during the seventies.

This soul call, like all the others, felt sacred and mysterious and I practiced discernment by keeping the experience close to my heart. I did not want friends to project their fears or their excitement onto me. I was tired of the skeptical looks I received from people when I described my inner world. I no longer needed to be affirmed by others. Besides, I did not know how to explain numinous experiences in words. My inner life felt grounded with energy, vibrations, and frequencies—not words.

Eventually, I decided to come clean and share my experience with a few of my evolutionary buddies. Each time I returned to my journals to re-visit the experience, I felt Goddess bumps all over my body:

I told the story of the opening of my third eye three different times in two days and yet I continued to avoid leaning into the implications of that unexpected event. My friend Maryam pinned me down when she said, "You are coming into your guru-hood." I knew she was right. For starters, I am amazed what I know when I sit with someone or do a soul reading.

Ashok was curious why I had waited several weeks to tell him, especially since it happened at his Meditation Center when he was present. I explained that I did not want anyone to think that I was filled with self-importance. He listened carefully and said that there were two contrary thoughts about sharing this kind of experience in India. One opinion is that if you "brag" about your experience, it will dissolve or disappear.

The contrary view is that people need to hear the stories because they inspire.

When I thought about not wanting to draw attention to myself, I laughed. How can I expect to have impact on others if I remain silent? Once again, I broke rank with my family system, which censored bragging.

Then he asked me if I was aware of any changes since my third eye popped open.

I replied, "Life feels more precious. Love motivates me to love more expansively. Life feels easier since I have let go of many attachments. I recognize projections—both shadow and light—and I refuse to play. I expect miracles to happen daily. My healing abilities have escalated. My laughter is deeper and more genuine. Grace is becoming a presence for me. Channeling and doing automatic writing, which are different than journaling, have also deepened."

Later I felt deep relief talking to Hiromi who "got it" and was not envious or suspicious about my journey. Since she lived in an ashram for a few years, I value both her experience and her wisdom. I described how tears are my daily companions and it seemed like my heart expanded, too. Then I described how I cried when I spotted a bird carrying straw to build a nest, or when I saw lovers embrace, or how an innovative display of chocolates at the grocery store elicited tears. Other times, it was the energy and power that flowed through me that filled me with awe and delight. She listened intently and shared that her guru laughed a lot. Then she smiled and said, "Joy was his constant companion."

When I said, "I was not prepared for the opening of my third eye," she said with authority, "One never is." When she told me her own epiphany story, she beamed.

At one point in our conversation, I said, "I know this sounds bizarre, but..." as I told her about the disappearance of Big Angel after my third eye opened and how Muktananda assumed the role of my major guide. She said, "It does not sound one iota bizarre, Rosie."

Even when I described how I stomped about and had a full-blown temper tantrum because I did not have an opportunity to say "Goodbye" and "Thank you" to Big Angel and my familiar guides, she simply smiled.

With tears in my eyes, I continued saying that I had no way of knowing if Big Angel would return or if this was another example of a guide promotion where I have no advance warning and no opportunity to say "Thank you" and "Goodbye."

Then I remembered the first time that a familiar guide was "furthered." I was angry because I did not understand why I was not informed in advance. My ego capitalized on the event. I tracked my anguish to the sudden death of my son, Mike. That too happened without warning and I was left without explanations—only questions and deep grief.

As we said goodbye, she asked me if she could kiss my forehead. I was surprised and nodded. She did and responded, "Gosh, your forehead is on fire, Rosie." Then she said, "You are a guide now, Rosie. You are blessed."

CHAPTER 5

The Frequencies of Love

One morning I awoke at 3 A.M. with the ending of a dream that asked me, "What about love matters to you?"

Out loud, I answered, "Everything," and woke myself up.

As a follow-through response to my dream I made a commitment to adopt the affirmation, "I am loving awareness" for the week. As I participated in the conscious evolution of love for that week, I was aware that there were no qualifying exams. I centered myself in love and reflected in my journal the many ways that love graced my life before I slept each night. Then I wrote the following Love List in my journal as a reminder.

> *Love of nature, which extends to the lusciousness of my salad garden*
> *Love that erupts while watching children frolic under a sprinkler*
> *Love of friends and celebrating Ted's seventieth birthday*
> *Love of my daughter that is fringed with pride*
> *Love of my two grandchildren, Malia and Noah, who return home tomorrow after being with their dad in Florida for six weeks*

Love of each bright and waning day of summer
Love of sculpting
Love when I walk in the woods in the rain
Love when I dance to the music of Wah.

Somewhere I read that if one person loves you, no matter how many mistakes you have made, that bond can change your life in positive ways. My grandmother, my mother's mother, was that special person for me. Not only did she love me unconditionally, she modeled how to be a nurturing grandmother. This journal entry tells all:

Beginning when I was in the third grade, I worked with my grandmother three days a week after school. She had arthritis in her hands and knees and had a hard time bending down to get penny candy from the large, closed in cabinet. I was her helper and most of my young customers thought my name was "Honey" because that was her name for me.

I remember how her face lit up when I bounced into Mr. Emmon's Drug Store at the end of my school day.

"Hi, Honey," she said, no matter if she were waiting on a customer or alone, and then she hugged me. I always felt like I was the person she most wanted to see walk through the screen door. When we were alone, she asked me how my school day was and she listened. Then she took my hand and led me over to the silvery ice cream cabinet that contained at least twenty different gallons of ice cream. Her favorites were rum raisin and maple walnut. I preferred cherry vanilla and teaberry. When she nodded her head that was my signal to get the ice cream scoop. She praised me when I dipped into

the large cardboard container and turned out a perfect scoop of maple walnut ice cream for her. Then I closed the cabinet and moved down three lids until I spotted the cherry vanilla container. Two scoops—never more, although I knew she would have said nothing if I added a third scoop.

Nanny taught me how to make change, frappes, sundaes and banana splits, greet customers, and do a semi-annual inventory. She taught me other things too—how to spot a genuine piece of cut glass, what the brown wrapped Kotex was used for, the meaning of a condolence card, and that the customer was always right—no exceptions. She paid me fifty cents an hour to be her knees. I saved most of my money and she walked me to the Saco and Biddeford Savings Bank every Saturday morning to deposit money into my Christmas account.

A few years before she died she confided in me that she always wished she could have been an interior designer, but she settled for arranging the blue bottles of Noxzema into a pyramid pile and decorating the top shelves of the drugstore with expensive cut glass dishes.

When I was nine years old, I started to brush her long, gray hair as she sat on her red pillowed oak chair in front of her three-way bedroom mirror. We were silent and smiled at one another in the mirror as I arranged the ivory fanned shaped hair comb just the way she liked it. When I finished re-arranging her hair, she reached for her cut glass atomizer, squeezed the small, white crocheted ball at the end and sprayed Evening in Paris perfume into the air that separated us. I remember thinking, "This is even better than dessert."

Nanny was part fairy godmother and part angel to me. Without any effort, I remember the distinct taste, color, texture and smell of the biscuits she made every Saturday night to accompany a pot of red kidney beans and red skinned hot dogs. I watched her whip up and pour the ingredients for her biscuits into the same large brown mixing bowl for five decades. Never did she reach for a measuring spoon or cup. No matter how many times I asked her how she knew how much of each ingredient to put in, she shrugged her thin shoulders and said, "I was just born knowing, I guess." Then she wiped her floury hands on her clean apron.

Always, she insisted that I peel the stinky red onions as she watched. Then she poured on just the right amount of vinegar and sugar.

When I was in junior high school, I developed a craving for her lemon meringue pies. If I close my eyes now, I see a freeze frame picture of her standing in her small, wall papered kitchen in her half-tied apron, whipping the egg whites until they stiffened. When I begged her to teach me how to make the treasured pie, I could not make the meringue. I remember how she wrapped her arms around me and said quietly, "No matter, Honey, don't feel sad. Almost everyone can whip egg whites and heavy cream into stiff peaks—except witches and witches are special people who have more to bring to the world than stiff peaks." From that day on, I stopped trying to whip cream or egg whites and focused on mastering spells.

When I finished graduate school, she urged me to get my doctorate. She told me she wanted to brag about me to all of her friends. Although I loved her and wanted to make her happy, my heart was not into acquiring another degree. She was disappointed. When I published my first book, Healing Grief—A Mother's Story, I dedicated it to her writing, "To Shirley Jellerson, who has loved me since the beginning of time." When I handed her an autographed copy, I said, "Nanny, this is my version of a doctorate." She hugged me and said, "Honey, you did the right thing."

When my daughter turned sixteen and entered into her rebellious time, I complained to my grandmother. She listened and then she hugged me close and said, "Honey, I know you worry about her, but in my experience, she does not hold a candle to the antics you put us through when you were her age. Just love her. She will grow into herself just like you did. It takes time."

Then she sighed and I said, "Like you have loved me my whole life, right?"

She looked at me for a long time without saying a word. Then she sighed and said, "Yes, Honey, I hope so." Then she invited me to sit down with her and play a game of gin rummy with an old lady.

I thought I was finished writing in my journal when my guides weighed in on love:

Your frequency is a reflection of your love.

Self-love is the process of appreciating yourself without objections. The more love you radiate, the more you align with your soul and its evolving story.

Withholding or turning away from love is grounded in scarcity and cements you to your personal story.

Resisting love adds to your pain body.

Sometimes I wish that I believed in love in the innocent ways that my grandkids do. I think I will ever hold in my heart a conversation about love between Malia and Noah:

"How are families made?" asked Noah

"By love," his 9-year-old sister, Malia replied before I thought of an answer. And even if the mother and father grow out of love with each other, they each still love us and we are still a family even if we don't all live together anymore and even if they marry someone else and we get another adult to love us and be our family."

It is more complicated for me because I have lived longer and I notice more.

Two days later, I took refuge in a comfortable, quiet neighborhood restaurant the day after a busy and inspiring all day workshop with hundreds of other dedicated writers at Maine Festival of The Book in Portland, Maine I stretched out my legs as I sipped my cup of dark house blend coffee. I was happy to be alone after a day of workshops, book signings, and conversations. As my body surrendered to the softness of the cushioned chair, I appreciated the uncluttered walls and the leisurely feel of the energy surrounding me. I savored another delicious sip of coffee and reviewed my week hoping to lasso a theme for my blog.

Suddenly, my eyes darted to a couple sitting next to a large window. The energy coming from the young man and woman felt intense and compelling. The music from Vivaldi's Four Seasons played in the background and I tapped my fingers and feet to the escalating rhythms. The music drowned out their conversation and I felt as though I were watching or perhaps even participating in a silent movie. No longer revisiting Maine Festival of the Book in my mind or figuring out what to write about in my weekly blog, I stared at the couple.

The young woman leaned forward, slammed her coffee cup on the table, wrapped her arms around her chest and shook her head vigorously from side to side. Her lips moved but I could not make out her words. The man sitting across from her pointed his right index finger close to her face, and then he pulled his hand back and lunged for her arm. Motion and emotion collided as I watched the energy erupt between them.

Then the woman abruptly motioned to the exit sign, grabbed her coffee cup and winter coat, and stumbled from the table. The man ran after her, only a few seconds behind.

I looked around me. People sipped coffee, conversed, read the Sunday paper, or concentrated on their computers. I was surprised that I seemed to be the only one aware of the angry encounter that, despite a change of scene, continued in the parking lot. Looking out of the large picture window, I realized I was holding my breath. I was afraid someone was about to be hurt in this angry collision. Still no sound as the action outside continued.

Watching the interaction between the two warriors, reminded me of times I had reacted in anger, usually directed to a partner whom I thought had betrayed me or some value I held sacred. I remembered how I too, expressed my outrage because I needed my feelings to be acknowledged or to be right. Usually my anger created walls, more distance than intimacy and often a counter attack rather than reconciliation and tenderness.

Returning my attention to the escalating drama outside the cafe, I watched the woman throw up her hands, hurl the coffee cup against the pavement, and make an "it's over" gesture in the air. Then she spat at him. Without looking back, she opened her car door, slammed it shut, and careened out of the parking lot. I doubt if she saw him sticking his middle finger up at her before he ran to his car and raced out of the lot after her.

Their story did not end here. I finished my breakfast, satisfied that I now had a beginning idea for my blog and headed for church. As I drove, I thought about the couple, aware that it was both Palm Sunday as well as April Fools' Day. That somehow seemed relevant. Before I figured out the connection, I noticed flashing blue lights on top of a police car on the opposite side of the road. I recognized the two cars even before I spotted the two warriors. A police officer stood between them writing on a pad. I didn't know if he was issuing a ticket, preparing to arrest one or both of them, or writing out the preliminaries for a restraining order.

As I drove slowly past, I imagined the angry couple's relationship permanently damaged. Even though I had heard not one word spoken from either person, energy can scream. Yet other times it can overflow with love, compassion, and forgiveness.

We do react like April fools when we forget that love is for giving, or when we override the Palm Sunday message to love and serve one another in favor of being right. Both frozen anger and out of control anger diminish our ability to love each other and ourselves. I know the truth of that statement in every cell of my being. As I looked though my rear-view mirror and realized the silent movie had ended, I re-committed myself to live love in a simple, and more peaceful way.

The only love that is missing in my life is an intimate, committed partnership. For forty-two years of my life, I have either desired to be in a committed relationship or ached to exit one. Each time I was the one who ended the relationship and I blamed myself for failure because together we were not able to meet my ideal of conscious loving. Perhaps the answer was simple: I chose the wrong men.

As I grow older and more honest with myself, I acknowledge that I could not be authentic with anyone else until I belonged to myself. My evolutionary buddy Diane Powell surprised me one day by saying "I am good at relationships." I paused, not knowing how to respond. Although I have enjoyed many committed relationships, I am not comfortable saying I was good at them. I am more authentic in my friendships with women than my relationships with men and I am ready to transform that limiting belief and my subsequent expectations and behavior. For example, I expect more from my women friends than my men friends. I am most authentic in my relationship with God.

John O'Donahue, in his book, *Eternal Echoes,* posed an essential question: To whom do I belong? My first response was to my soul, which is eternal. Some of my longing to be in a conscious, loving relationship is connected to belonging. At the same time, I also know that I am unwilling to abandon myself to belong. Freedom and belonging feel like polarities to me and I wonder if there is a way to heal the split in my consciousness.

I believe that in an intimate relationship both people are the guardians of each other's hearts. Also, I acknowledge that one of the reasons that I came here was to co-create and experience a soul centered, committed partnership. And I am unwilling to settle for anyone who crabwalks.

I was born with a soul memory of conscious loving. Then I forgot how to consciously co-create that state. Maybe that is why the following two lines from a poem by Rumi spoke to me:

"This is how I would die into love I have for you.
As pieces of cloud dissolve in sunlight,"

I assumed everyone else responded to Rumi's way of loving, too and embraced intimate relationships as powerful places of transformation. I believed that healing and the expansion of consciousness evolved within partnership. I believed that two people could flourish both as individuals and as a couple.

However, I question if I was being too idealistic because I have seen too few examples of love that thrived over time. I continue to entertain many questions about partnership: What drives us, beside hormones, to mate? If both sexes were androgynous and had the necessary genitalia to pro-create, what might intimacy look like? At what cost do men leave their herd, their buddies and their talk of competition and rough housing? How do they learn to source gentleness, connection, and vulnerability?

What do we compromise and how do we grow?

I read somewhere that when a woman begins a relationship at least one of her friendships with other women becomes less intimate. At seventy-three, passion no longer has the power that it had decades ago. Companionship and kindness have replaced passion or at least that is what I imagine. Being comfortable in the silences appeals to me now. When I announced to my soul friend Genie that I wanted to believe that a conscious partnership was still part of my destiny, she smiled. Then she asked me what kind of man I wished to attract.

I replied, "Kindness is top of my list, followed closely by an ability to enjoy, emotional, mental, and spiritual maturity, a passion to collaborate and travel, and a love for of people.

She listened appreciatively and commented, "No tall, dark, and handsome?"

We both giggled as we acknowledged that we had both shattered that illusion.

A wise person once told me to be aware of what I didn't like in my partner and then to check to make sure it was not some character defect that I had not forgiven my parents for. I wished I had applied this wisdom earlier in my relationships.

Recently a friend asked me if I believed that there was freedom in marriage and I answered "No." For me, it is a balance between belonging and freedom and I look around and do not see many successful marriage acrobats.

From my experience, withholding or turning away from love is grounded in a scarcity belief that cements me to my limited personal story and my energetic pain body. I have gathered personal evidence that moving toward love adds to my bliss body.

My guides weigh in on love:

> *The heart knows no polarity.*
> *The heart knows no separation.*
> *The heart knows only love.*
> *Practice love until you become love.*
> *Then watch your resources expand.*

The last eighteen years of my life have been a time of valuing, choosing, and loving myself. No longer am I tempted to give myself away to gain love. I never imagined growing older alone. All the women in my family married and remained married until they died. Almost all of my friends are in relationships. For the past weeks, I have been aware that the entire world seems paired. Even my friend Jonna, who is enjoying her sixties and never expected to be in a relationship, is partnered.

I listen intently to friends who are involved in long relationships and I am fascinated by their stories of how they made their partnerships work. I know that compromise is a key and yet I do not know where the balance is between compromise and authentic growth.

The next day at lunch Debra Stanley told me about meeting her partner of eight years on Match.com. Her prime intention was to enjoy a committed relationship with a man who was willing to be her prayer partner. Within twelve hours after she posted her "prayer partner" intention, three self-nominated prayer candidates emailed her. When I went home from lunch, I added prayer partner to my list of attributes that I seek in partnership.

I feel like Anais Nin when she wrote about her struggle to figure out the place of love in her life and what happened after the chase. Her head was filled with romantic ideas gathered from books that she had read and her mother and father were separated although neither parent talked about that. She tried to find the middle ground between idealism and cynicism through writing in her journals. I, on the other hand, have the experience of multiple marriages, and I question whether love lasts or people just settle for what they have.

Someone told me about a Sounds True tape by a neurosurgeon who believes that the primary purpose of relationships is for partners to co-parent one another. He claims that it is both natural and unavoidable. I too believe that we unconsciously attract our mother/father or both in a partner so it makes sense that we work through the unconscious projections and re-parent each other and ourselves.

A couple of years ago, when I re-located from Maine to Virginia Beach for the winter and spring, a local dating group that promised personal service contacted me. Since I was re-entering my life again after being a devoted resident grandmother for nine years, I listened to the sales pitch and answered a few personal questions. All went smoothly until the interviewer asked me when I had dated last.

I replied honestly, "Seventeen years ago."

She was silent and I thought she had disqualified me. Then she asked, "Why have you not dated in so long?"

Again, I answered honestly, "I have not found anyone who interests me more than myself."

She was silent again and I figured that she was probably searching in her guidebook for an appropriate comeback. No matter, because I had decided I was content living by myself. In an attempt to gain an historical perspective, I returned to my journals

FLASHBACK to a May 2004 journal entry:

In two weeks, I walk into the last year of my fifth decade. Today I consulted with Gero, the trance-channel woman in Bali who screamed at me during a trance healing session, "Never marry again. Never. You give all your energy to your man and you came here to heal many." Although I felt the truth of her words, I was lonely for partnership. Now I appreciate that partnership does not have to be marriage. A hearty hug at the end of a day, cuddling in front of a fire, insightful conversation, loving glances and silences, exploring together, giggling, networking with others resonates with partnership for me and I have proven to myself

*that I can live without a man during the last seventeen
years.*

What a coincidence. I had my first sexual experience
when I was seventeen years old. Later I surprised myself
when I ran across this one liner in a 2010 journal,

*I am done adoring men. My intention is to adore
the Divine!*

A friend, who is my age, mentioned that she is in the eighth
year of a committed relationship. She treats the relationship
as her spiritual practice. When she feels like running away,
she stays. When she feels like shutting down, she speaks.
When she feels like screaming, she is silent. When she feels
like being silent, she speaks.

My guides once channeled a similar strategy:

*"When you feel like leaving—stay, when you feel
like blaming—forgive, and when you feel like giving
up—love."*

Last night while we played gin rummy, Malia, my fourteen-year-old granddaughter with whom I have a soul agreement to always be honest, asked me why I got divorced.

I replied, "Because I wasn't happy."

"Did your husbands not give you attention?" she asked.

"Not the kind I needed," I replied candidly. "I expected
we would grow together and that did not happen. I continued to work on myself and grew and ultimately outgrew the
men I loved."

Later I reflected more deeply on my relationship history and Malia's question about why I divorced. I expected to grow and transform in intimate relationship because I intuited that our mutual soul's growth was at stake. Each time I risked partnership, I felt diminished in the end rather than expanded.

One of the things I did not tell my granddaughter is that I am convinced that each of my committed intimate relationships was karmic. Unfinished business from past lifetimes remained in my soul memory and although I did not remember the specific details of the life times, the dynamics of the struggles felt hauntingly familiar. I never figured out whose karma was being acted out, although I definitely experienced what happens when karma activates karma and how that leads to personal misunderstanding, pulling away, and shutting down. Edgar Cayce believed that most karma was self-karma and as I age, I agree with him. Therefore, I take 100% responsibility for my life and the decisions that I made. Blaming others is no longer an option.

Husband Number Four presented himself as a healer and promised a journey around the world to network with other healers. Unlike my other partners, he was an extrovert. He also valued processing and promised sexual and spiritual intimacy. However, within a few months of traveling to Europe, I discovered he was insecure and wanted to impress others and the world with "We." He had no tolerance when I wanted to do things on my own. His self-esteem was tied to whether he could make me have an orgasm and sex became where we acted out our mutual control issues. My soul felt eclipsed.

I continue to question what is real and what is illusion in relationship, especially sometimes when I see "looking good" couples and then learn that even the marriages that look good are in trouble. I have heard different versions of the same story from six women in the past month and I wondered to myself why I had attracted stories that reinforced my questions about the possibility of growing into our authentic self in partnership. For Christmas, each of the six women wanted to fall in love with their husbands again. All the men had had affairs and each woman had chosen to remain married while secretly grieving and missing the magic.

Each confided that they feared that their husbands were clueless about how to initiate the reconciliation process. I sensed they wanted to be courted, appreciated, and wooed all over again. Each of the husbands professed his love, yet the women no longer felt the intimate connection. The lack of emotional intimacy felt like another betrayal. The approaching Christmas season amplified their emotional distance because family time and togetherness no longer felt real. The words that one of the women said to me feel etched in my heart, "I have tried to be a good wife, mother and partner since his affair. I cook good meals, I work out and I look good, I dress nicely and we sleep in the same bed. And I feel empty, alone and old."

My heart ached with each story.

Recently I told a friend, "You set yourself up when you expect your husband who lacks emotional awareness to be empathetic!"

Then she described her husband by saying, "Rage is the only emotion he allows himself. I never felt <u>MET</u> by him."

When she told him her feelings, he responded, "But I provided for you. I left my wife and young family for you. I chose you over my own children. How can you say that I have never MET you?"

"Emotionally, emotionally. You never FELT for me. You were not empathetic when I needed you to be."

He questioned, "What's empathy?"

She replied, "When I was in the hospital suffering from a crushed pelvis, you told me you resented me for creating stress in your life."

"I'm sorry about that," he said with no affect.

"Those are only words, words, words, what are you feeling?"

"Angry."

I asked myself how could they find resolution when a twenty-year pattern fueled their personal stories. He was an engineer who prided himself on processing emotions mentally, while she processed emotions subjectively and felt every emotion in her body.

When I asked her, "Who is the love of your life?" tears of grief and recognition of a deep and hidden truth surfaced. Her new partnership is the first relationship in her life where she had experienced joy upon waking in the morning. That gave me hope.

Today a close male friend dared me to let my heart be blown wide open by the beauty of another. I accepted his challenge—not once but five times— and fell deeply in love with each person that I beheld.

The only kind of an intimate relationship I will consider is an evolutionary relationship. Here are my criteria:

One in which both partners agree to serve the highest good and hold each other accountable.
One where celebration takes up more space than pain and suffering.

One where who leads and who follows is a constantly changing dance.

One where both partners are free to invest in their passionate, creative pursuits.

One where the sensual and the nonsensical merge.

One where the Divine is present and acknowledged.

One where both people make a commitment to do their individual shadow work.

One where both people value being of joy filled service.

Although I consider myself a masterful manifester, I have not applied the principles of manifestation to attract a partner. I know that I do not manifest what I need—instead I manifest who I am. That's why I do my best to be free of fear, denial and projection when I set an intention to manifest. The list above remains in a desk drawer. If a man who fits my ideals walked into my life, I would be open to exploring a relationship. A friend confronted me yesterday saying, "Rosie, nobody is going to come knocking at your door and invite you to be in relationship." I agreed. Yet I teach that if a choice is not a 100% Yes, it is a No. For the time being, I am content being committed to myself and my own soul journey as well as open to the possibility of meeting my destiny partner.

I am aware of timing; in fact, I consider myself a time watcher. That's one reason I was not surprised when David Cooper's forthcoming book, *The Journey of The Mariner,* arrived in my email box. However, it struck me as ironic that he asked me to write an introduction for a book centered around applying the principles of sailing to partnership since I have no experience sailing and I do not consider myself an authority on partnerships. As I perused his manuscript, I wrote the following questions in my journal:

> *How have my life experiences shaped my desire to be in partnership?*
>
> *What resources and/or karma did I bring from past life experiences?*
>
> *How do I know my partner has my wellbeing at heart?*
>
> *How do I know my partner's wellbeing is a priority for me?*
>
> *What is the partnership legacy that I wish to leave for my grandchildren?*

I felt excited and a bit scared when Mary Ann Russell, a psychic friend, said that a soul relationship was very close and I was at last ready to be loved for who I am. "This man who is coming to you wants to take nothing from you, Rosie. He wants to support your gifts and who you are." She advised me to cut the remaining fear cords as well as the cords of protection that I have surrounded myself with.

"You will not be betrayed or abandoned this time," she said compassionately.

My guides break through with their wisdom:

> *Love expresses through an open heart.*
> *The loving heart knows no polarity.*
> *The loving heart knows no separation.*
> *The loving heart knows only love.*
> *Practice love until you become love.*
> *Then watch your relationships transform.*

Always before, when there was no mutual beneficial outcome, I chose to leave relationships and move forward. In the releasing process, I strived to be clear, kind and firm. Then I grieved because grieving is a process of making peace. I know from experience that if I grieve fully, I won't get sucked in again. And I do my best in ending to avoid creating further karma.

I do believe that the more love I give and receive, the more I align with my soul story. I also am aware that one of the ways I have learned how to love myself is to identify how I withheld love from myself. Then I re-wrote the victim script of my personal story and challenged myself by reflecting about how love invited me to grow. My guides chimed in and added their perspective:

> *From an inter-dimensional perspective, there are no victims. Look for the Goodness in every event, relationship and even catastrophe.*

In an attempt to break through my body armoring and free myself to love fully, I contacted a woman whom several of my friends recommended. Janice Mitchell worked with angels during her healing sessions. My body was comfortable around angels and I decided to give her body work/massage sessions a try. I entered the healing session saying I knew I was holding myself back in relationships and I wanted to let go of whatever I was holding on to. "I want to cherish and be cherished," I said.

Janice said, "The issue is in the tissue and it can be released without drama and trauma." She was right. I softened. I was safe in my vulnerability.

My mother's words, "We are the only ones who truly love you," never felt right or real to me, yet I acted as if I believed them. Janice reminded me that in my mother's time, family was important and now it is community of kindred souls. Looking back, I was caught in a double bind. I could not trust others to love me and I could not trust my family to love me. As a result, I armored myself, stayed safe and looked like I was happy. A memory of taking an inventory about personal independence popped up and I remembered how proud I was that I scored the highest mark in the class. Years later I realized that I had covered up my vulnerability with independence.

A few days after the session, I wrote:

> *No wonder that giving has always been so much easier for me than receiving. When I am the one to receive, I risk being vulnerable. Trusting was the issue.*
>
> *I choose what I bless with my energy each day before I get out of bed. I choose whom I invite into my world and my confidence. I choose love. I choose to be open to beauty and mystery and grace. I choose to align with my soul and befriend others who have made a similar commitment. I choose to give back and be of joyful service. I choose to be open to the ongoing mystery.*

The following week, I challenged myself to become more comfortable with my vulnerability—another paradox since for decades I have prided myself on being strong and self-sufficient. Somewhere deep inside myself I sensed a vague soul memory that vulnerability is a resource. I do know from experience that when I open my heart to the Divine, I am vulnerable and protected. Becoming vulnerable with intimacy is my next big stretch.

As another clear signal to the universe that I was open to the possibility of partnership, I set aside a weekend to complete a recapitulation ritual that I read about a long time ago in one of Carlos Castaneda's books. It involved remembering each partner that I have shared my body and love with and recalling each memory and then saying goodbye—one memory at a time. I counted time by the six long tapered candles that I threw in the trash at the end of the ritual. I have no concrete evidence that the process worked except I felt lighter and my heart felt freer. That counts.

Later I gave thanks for each of my intimate relationships and what each lover taught me about love. Since I know I will continue to be a student of love until I take my last breath, I vow to continue to hold the ideal of conscious loving.

In preparation for partnership, I say upon entering the house, "Hi Sweetheart, I am home!" I appreciate that it will happen if and when the time is right. Then as a way of grounding my commitment to be ready for an intimate relationship, I wrote in my journal:

> I commit myself to be present in the world in a profound and spacious way and to joyfully contribute my energy to the evolution of love and peace in relationships, families, communities, nations, and the world.

The following week, during an evening gathering at my home, one of my women friends began to speak passionately about her experience of being raised by a narcissistic mother. As she spoke several of us acknowledged that our stories resembled hers. One by one we each spoke of feeling insignificant and undeserving of our own place in the world as we grew up. In unison, we spoke about being raised to add to our mother's light without knowing that our own light mattered. I shared that when I graduated from college in three years with high honors, my mother boasted, "Why of course you excelled, after all you are my daughter." I remembered being stunned and then angry because even my accomplishments were not mine.

Together we talked about feeling like we were understudies, always waiting in the wings for our turn to shine. For each of us, to be more of anything in comparison with our mothers meant either punishment or silence. One by one we spoke about how we each still struggled against our own inner oppression of the feminine. No coincidence that each of us chose to work in the helping professions in order to heal ourselves.

I talked about the few times when I dared to read true stories of my life to my mother and she shook her head and asked, "Did this really happen? It is unbelievable and you are such a dreamer." Being resilient I remember later reading my mother some of my stories that later found their way into *Awaken* (2012). She listened intently and then challenged, "Did that really happen to you?"

Before I responded, she said, "Are you sure that really happened?"

Looking back, I am not certain which stories I shared, most likely my adventures in Egypt at the pyramids or my story about remembering that I was a male dancer in Bali, Indonesia.

When I assured her that my stories were true and I had not exaggerated, she looked sad. Then she said, "Compared to you, I have led a very boring life."

I did not know what to say. I tried to lead a conventional life to please my parents and I felt unfulfilled. Traveling, teaching, and learning excited me. Looking back, they felt like passions and I felt like they chose me—not the other way around. The unknown future called me and eventually I developed the inner strength and answered the call.

I don't know if my mother settled for an ordinary life. I do know that I tried to be satisfied being ordinary and leading a similar life to my grandparents and parents. My soul rebelled. Conforming and rebelling and belonging and being free took up many pages in my journals.

The next day I spotted an article on narcissism that said that narcissism originated in revenge and retaliation and that genuine interpersonal relationships with narcissists were impossible since they lacked empathy. I credited myself from moving out of my restricted personal story and into my expanded soul story by owning my own voice and vision through writing, teaching and creating. In addition, I made a bold decision to shine my light only where I am received.

CHAPTER 6

The Irresistible
Frequency of Soul Calls

I sensed another shift in my consciousness when I made the decision to work with a spiritual advisor. The choice was another example of breaking rank with decades of being a strong, self-sufficient Maine woman. I intuited that a spiritual advisor was different than a therapist and I was right. My soul's growth and journey became center stage and my ego was ready for battle. The life lesson about integrating light returned for another round and this time I was determined to be responsible for grounding the light in my body and consciousness.

During our first telephone meeting, I told Meghan that my intention was to learn how to sustain balance in all areas of my life, especially since I was experiencing an abundance of light. Then I told her that I had experienced being flooded with light a few times before. During these times, I did not know anyone who understood the nature and demands of soul calls and in retrospect I realized that isolation did not serve me.

I also voiced my fear that my devotion to my emerging soul story might lead to more isolation and abandonment. On the other hand, I acknowledged that when I took responsibility for validating my inner life and let go of asking for approval from friends, I felt more soul centered and less in need of outer validation. What a paradox!

Toward the end of the session, I said, "I don't know how to make the transition from being productive to being present. When I added the word "perfectly," we both laughed.

As I look around me, distraction feels like an epidemic in the world. I am convinced that being receptive and holding the unknown future until it unfolds is connected to feminine ways of knowing and being. Learning how to be comfortable with not doing and not knowing is an insult to my inner patriarchy and cherished family traditions. I appreciate how tightly I have woven impatience and uncertainty as well as how I push myself to finish a project prematurely rather than face uncertainty which often feels to me like inertia.

When I honor my inner life, I know that there is depth to not knowing and waiting for Source to reveal itself. I've read enough books to appreciate that one sign of a contemplative life is learning to be comfortable with uncertainty. Recently all I know is what I am feeling in the moment and I refuse to rush myself toward closure, which ultimately feels too narrow and shallow.

In April of 2012, my soul called me back to Taos, New Mexico, one of my soul's homes, after a twenty-year absence. I left my daughter and grandchildren to participate in my second vision quest. I was determined to learn more about what the future was asking from me. Intuitively, I sensed that my service of being a full time resident grandmother was changing.

Upon my arrival, I slept the night at the Adobe Motel in Taos and left early the next morning to pick up my horse and meet my guides at a farm near Sacred Blue Mountain The trip up the mountain was long and steep in places and riding a horse was not considered practical for a woman of my age.

It's challenging to exist four days and three nights outside on the side of a mountain. Snow covered the ground and my horse seemed skeptical of my adventure and walked slowly. I had fasted for three days before my extended sit and made prayer ties in the traditional way. I brought a down sleeping bag, a blanket, gloves, water and tobacco to offer the land.

I have told the full story of my second "cry for vision" and how the mother bear became my familiar in *Soul Befriending*. Even after four years, I still have a freeze frame of gazing in fright at the mother bear and her three cubs that stopped about six feet in front of me at sunset. I reacted by remembering every single Davie Crockett movie I had ever seen until I recalled how he stared the bear down because he knew he could not outrun it. I remained sitting on the earth while my body shook in fear. Then I imagined my friends saying something like, "Well, Rosie was always a risk taker and at least she died doing something that she believed in."

The bears were close enough for me to see their breath in the almost freezing temperature. As I stared at the mother bear, I made a decision from a wisdom place deep in my body that if I were about to die, I did not want my last breath to be fear filled and I chose to discipline myself to remember times of love and beauty. It worked. The bears ambled into the forest and I wondered if the purpose of the vision quest was for me to face my own dying time.

The next day the same bear and her cubs returned at sunset. I heard the sound of their shuffle before I spotted them. Like the evening before, they stopped about six feet away from me in exactly the same spot. Nothing had changed except me. Instead of feeling terrified, I felt awe and appreciation. As I gazed at the mother bear, I was fascinated with her body and the texture of her fur and the way her brown eyes and nose matched. As I continued to breathe in her beauty, I was aware that I loved this four-legged creature. Fear was not present. Like the night before, they ambled away before I could shout, "thank-you and goodbye."

The next morning as I prepared to break camp, the bear family returned and I thanked them without moving from my blanket. I was happy that three of the men from Taos Pueblo witnessed my encounters with the bear because I was almost certain that nobody would believe my experience. In between the three visits from the bears, I had two dreams that showed me that I was being prepared to move beyond being a teacher into a leadership role.

When I returned home, I remembered that I had sculpted a small bear out of white alabaster before my trip. It was complete except for sanding and polishing. I was astounded that I had amnesia about that while on my vision quest. I wondered, once again, if the energies of Future Pull grounded my vision quest and then deliberately surrendered cause and effect thinking because that way of understanding belonged to an outdated view of how I had been taught the universe operated.

The real challenge of a vision quest comes after the actual four day vigil ends. The implementation stage requires actions. One of my takeaways from my cry for vision was my commitment to reclaim my role of teacher and then to step into the role of leader. I was comfortable expressing my soul through teaching, but not with the leader part.

When I told my friend Maryam about my fear of stepping into my role as leader, she laughed and said, "Rosie, why does that scare you? You have been on the leadership staff of the Creative Problem Solving Institute for twenty years. You were honored with a coveted Leadership Award. Everyone welcomes you as a leader." I laughed because I had blocked that part of my life out, too, yet I also acknowledged that this call to leadership felt different.

Another takeaway from my vision quest was a commitment to reinvest in my creativity. Three months after my vision quest, I took action and wrote a $1200 check for a one-month residential artist retreat at Starflower Farm in Monroe, Maine. This soul call thread began when I walked into the Blue Heron in Bangor and spotted a twelve-inch white and brown ceramic angel on the wall. When I asked the owner for the potter's name and address, she told me that she lived about eighteen miles away from me. I waited two weeks to call her because I really wanted a sculpture teacher, not a potter.

True to previous soul calls, the only thing I knew for sure was that I yearned to immerse myself in my creative process and Nature. Malia and Noah were with their father for the summer and I was free. However, a month seemed financially extravagant and scary, especially since I had not worked for five years. To satisfy the curiosity of my friends and family, I said that I planned to experiment with combining clay and stone. In reality, I had no clue what my soul called me to become. In many ways, this deep dive into my creative process felt like another vision quest without the warrior's sweat, fasting, and keeping vigil for four days and three nights.

Breaking rank is sometimes connected with claiming or re-claiming a soul quality. Creativity was that for me. Unlike my children and grandchildren, I was not validated for creative expression—just the opposite. I was a daydreamer and often got "called to task" for gazing out of the window or scribbling in my room. "Wasting" was the word most often used to invalidate my imagination and my sense of magic. Looking back, I see that creativity stalked me. As a middle school teacher, I often invited my students to wonder and fantasize and entertain other possibilities.

I was anxious when I finally telephoned Squidge Davis to make an appointment to interview her as a potential mentor; yet in retrospect my heart knew the stakes were high. Future Pull was at work again. When I walked into Squidge's studio, I was surrounded by life sized clay angels, wolves, and bears. She had even designed a large kiln to bake her life-sized figures. My soul knew that I had found my creative abode within minutes of my arrival. Before I left, I had committed myself to being her student for a month. She explained that clay was more forgiving than stone and suggested I work with clay in the morning and stone in the afternoon.

Driving home from Squidge's studio, I re-affirmed my bold decision to devote a month to my own creative process. Not only did I invest money, time, and energy—I also invested in my future. The unknown beckoned and although I was anxious, I was mostly excited. On my drive home I entertained myself by acknowledging how sculpting and healing are like an engagement ring and a wedding ring.

I was first called to sculpting two decades ago when my friend Sara submitted her fragile body to chemotherapy. I was determined to give her something she could hold in her hands during her treatments. When the idea of making something from stones popped into my mind, I was startled.

I remember the exact moment when I picked up my first piece of white alabaster stone and how I stared at the two-pound rock and started to hyperventilate! When I recovered my breath, I felt flooded by every negative statement that I had swallowed since childhood about my inability to create art. Then I sensed a strong current of energy that seemed to emanate from the stone. I responded to the loud negative voices inside my head and the inviting energy from the stone by shrieking, "I will make something healing for Sarah to hold." Then I sensed the stone saying, "Yes." My healing relationship with stone had begun.

Five days later I gave Sarah a small polished figure of a woman in the child's yoga position. She smiled, unable to speak because of the ventilator in her mouth. Then she caressed the figure and turned her over and over. She sighed, nodded her head and then we both cried.

Three decades later I continue to be a student of stone and healing. Even now before I pick up a diamond-studded file, I hold the stone. Then I lift the stone close to my ear in case this is the one I will hear sing. Next I turn the stone over and over studying the texture, the angles, and the way light enters. If the stone is not too big, I put it under my pillow and dream with it.

Before I make my first cut in the stone, I am deeply aware that my first gesture will forever change the stone's structure. I hold my breath when I file the first time because I appreciate that transformation waits somewhere in the wings. Then I breathe, listen and watch for a response from the stone. Once again, I look at the stone from all angles waiting for it to call me into a collaborative relationship.

Often I file too gently at first because I am cautious and I don't want to make a mistake. Then the stone calls me to file deeper. Surrender is part of my creative process. I let go of the first few abstract forms that appear in favor of being curious. Then I stand back and gaze again at the stone and remind myself that each time I let go of a familiar perspective, I create space for other possibilities.

Stone teaches me about persistence and vulnerability. When I get frustrated, I walk away. Then the familiar refrains return—I am not good enough, smart enough, creative enough, or committed enough. Once again I feel my vulnerability. Eventually, I befriend myself and return to the stone with more patience and a degree of self-compassion.

Before leaving for my artist's retreat, I reached out to friends and asked for prayers. They responded. I made a collage of their prayers and each time I read the words of encouragement, wisdom, and love, I smiled. Then I recorded their blessings in my journal so I could re-inspire myself anytime I drifted away from my creative intention and myself. My favorite invitations included:

"May all that you think drop away, may all that you have achieved in the past drop away, may all that you think you can do drop away, may all that you think you can't do drop away. May God's sculpting tools have free reign to re-sculpt and recreate you, as you are busy sculpting and creating another." Meghan

"My prayer for your July adventure is only this:

That you find joy and delight of discovery in each moment...

That you merge with and enjoy "Nature" in all its forms,

That you approach your work with clay as though you were a child...the only purpose to have "delight" in the experience, with no expectations about the results.

That you deepen your Love and Appreciation for yourself, in all of your magnificence." John

"May your retreat open a new door of awareness, creative inspiration and further deepen your connection to your divine essence. Ya Fattah!" Maryam

Squidge began our day with silence and then moved into inquiry. The first morning she asked me, "Who are you?" After a long, thoughtful pause, I replied, "I am a woman living in between raising my two grandchildren and rejoining the world." Then I took a short breath and added, "I am a woman of courage and also a woman who has crab walked around my creative expression for too long." I inhaled and finished by saying, "I am committed to speaking my truth and clearing my life of illusions, grudges, and any other strategies that separated me from my creative, healing process."

Later Squidge suggested that I buy a big journal because I carried big energy and the medium size journal that I brought with me was not nearly big enough. I was startled because nobody in my whole life ever invited me to be bigger or to live bigger—with the exception of my guides.

As I wrote in my journal, I remembered to soften my breath and sink more deeply into my body. Then the echoes of a familiar song erupted from my heart: "I am an old woman, I am a new woman, I am the same woman, deeper than before." I cannot count the times I have chanted the words to that song—but never alone. Always I sat next to other women in circles and felt our combined voices move straight to my heart. That night the chant felt like my heart's song.

The second morning began with an eight o'clock formal class about the life of clay. Squidge reminded me that clay was our first art. Then she gave me a block of clay to play with. Next, she taught me how to make coils as we passed the clay blocks back and forth.

Then she invited me to put my hands on hers and together we made coils in preparation for a pinch pot. She led, and then I added a layer. It seemed easy and fun. My assignment was to retire to my studio and make a pot. I was enthusiastic when I went downstairs to my studio; however, when I placed the coil around the circle either the sides caved in or I felt holes. I did not know if I was pressing too hard or too soft when the coil separated from the base. I felt discouraged—not curious. It seemed so easy upstairs and I had looked forward to playing.

I destroyed the first misshaped pot and then continued to make more coils and experimented with a smaller version, but when the same thing happened I got frustrated. I was not sure what was going wrong, but I knew I had to have a strong foundation before I could build up. I crushed the second embryo of a pot and acknowledged that the clay was too hard to work. When I pressed down harder, the clay weakened—not strengthened. Even when I kept at it, the clay continued to resist. It felt like leather and no matter how hard I rolled it, the cracks remained.

When I admitted to myself that I was leading with my will by trying to force a form, I took a giant step back from the table. Clearly, the clay was not cooperating. In frustration, I retreated to my sculpting corner and worked on the pink alabaster stone heart and tried to re-balance my energy. A few hours later, I returned to clay for one more try. Fresh clay did not yield fresh results. Feeling hopeless, I called upstairs to Squidge and she was not around. No coincidence, because I knew this was the time to build my own relationship with clay.

Realizing I was not enjoying the process, I left the studio and let NJ, the calico kitten that I had brought with me out to play. I needed space. Then I returned a few telephone calls. Without a clear plan, I retreated to the forest and approached Grandfather Tree. I reached out my arms and hugged the ancient tree and then fell to my knees and rested on the ground and pounded out my frustration. Later in the day Squidge invited me to help her weed the garden and we talked about my experience.

She asked, "Would your friends describe you as dynamic?"

"Yes," I said.

She smiled and after a long pause said, "The way to approach clay is quietly, in surrender, with an attitude of deep humility."

Then she said she saw my strength when I worked with stone and reminded me to lead with softness when I worked with clay. She surmised that I was pushing down too hard.

"Clay will never throw you a curve, Rosie. It is predictable if you understand it." Then she paused and was silent as she looked toward the horizon. I sensed she was not finished and was relieved when she said, "You will never win with clay. You must do the yielding. Thinking and will are not qualities that will impress the clay."

When I sculpt, I know from experience that any time I impose my will, the stone cracks or breaks and instantly lets me know that I am out of harmony. She suggested that when I switched from clay to stone or vice versa, I do some body movements first. Intuitively I knew that she was right. Getting on board with my body was the first step.

Later in the week I was surprised when she commented that I have a tendency to focus on what is wrong when I look at a piece of my own work. Her observation threw me because I take pride in being an optimist. However, she was right. I know from my own experience that judgment eclipses creativity. She also reiterated that she believed that my intuition often overrode my instincts. I had no clue what she meant. Could it be that my instincts, which Squidge explained were connected to my body awareness, were my shadow?

Before I reflected further about that thread, she cautioned me sternly, "Become more aware of your instincts or your intuition will overrun your body's wisdom."

I must have looked vacant because I had no idea how to become aware of my instincts. Then she reached out and touched my hand and said softly, yet firmly, "Those of us who were not nurtured in safe, loving ways as children do not trust our instincts."

A phone call from a friend of more than sixty years interrupted my retreat at the end of the first week. Darlene's voice was subdued as she told me that her doctors predicted she had a couple months to live. Cancer had ravaged her body despite chemotherapy and radiation treatments. She was scared because her parents were dead and she had no brothers, sisters, or children.

Although we had become estranged during the last four years, she demanded that I interrupt my artist retreat and stay with her until she was no more. I have a well-earned reputation for being a loyal and responsible woman. Like many women, I also have a history of over-giving and sacrificing myself. Compassion fatigue has claimed me more times than I care to count this lifetime. Yet she knew I had been a death doula to my grandfather, my Uncle Bud, and my father during their dying times and she banked on me supporting her. The choice between devoting myself to my art or midwifing Darlene in her dying time was complicated, especially since she had abandoned me for Mexico. I felt like I was being tugged between creativity and caring for a friend and I was confused about what choice aligned with my soul path

Grounded in my heart as well as my body and surrounded by ancient trees and a clear, starry sky, I asked if I had a spiritual responsibility to be with her. The response was immediate and guided me to remain on retreat for the next twenty-two days and then join her. I prayed for her to live into a merciful and peaceful death. Then I struggled with being selfish.

I called her early the next morning and I promised her that I would join her in three weeks. I also reminded her that I knew how to send her energy. Then I reassured myself that I would be more present for her after three more weeks of solitude and creativity. When I returned to my clay and stone, I practiced being creatively generous to myself.

My intuition said she would live for another six or seven weeks. Yet trusting my intuition with timing felt huge. What if I were wrong? Letting go of what I ought to do in favor of following through on my longing to express my creativity felt like serious edge walking between my personal story and my soul story. Remaining on my retreat while my friend prepared to die felt selfish and it also felt oddly right.

In an attempt to make sense of how my long-time friend Darlene straddled her own death, I returned to my journal and re-read journal entries that I had written six weeks before her phone call when I had spent the weekend with her:

I am settled into Darlene's basement quietly remembering myself as the foggy day unfolds. Last night we drank wine, and I listened as she spoke disparagingly of our aging bodies and the many life dramas that we had both endured. She was angry and bitter and

complained about how ugly and hard getting old was. She is only two years older than I and she spoke as if she were one hundred. Her immune system is compromised and doctors said it would take her a year to recover from the chemotherapy. The recurring leg pain was her ever-present reminder that cancer almost killed her. As we talked, she drifted off. Her body, which was once the source of her power over men and life, has become her shadow.

She was always the beautiful one. When her looks began to diminish, she used oxygen treatments to smooth out the wrinkles. Then she elected to undergo other surgery to enhance her looks. I, on the other hand never related to myself as a beauty and growing older did not feel like an insult.

Our conversation felt exhausting, especially when she complained about how hard growing old was and mourned her unfulfilling love life. Drama drains me even when it is not mine! Yet I wanted to be present for her now especially since she has no family and few friends.

The next morning I awoke from a crippling dream of being younger and unable to move in any direction. In the dream, I lacked vision, momentum, and a belief in the future. My body felt decrepit and I wondered how much of my dream was connected to the energy of this house or the reality that Darlene is living with, and how much my own shadow. Is it possible that I was the recipient of Darlene's dream?

The following day, she shared that her life continued to be intimately connected to horses. If not for her service to horses, she would choose death. She talked about mentoring a forty-three-year-old woman who was involved with horses and she told me how she rode one yesterday and was exhilarated for a while until exhaustion took over. She was determined to write a book about horses before she died. She hoped the book would be her legacy.

I did not expect that three threads of my journey—my body, my intuition, and an unfinished sculpture entitled The Pregnant Nun—would interweave during my artist retreat experience. Although I recognized that the unfinished Pregnant Nun stone was a teacher for me, I did not know how to untangle my history and I re-read my original journal entries in order to spot some tangible clues about how to proceed:

I spot the twenty-pound white alabaster stone before I sleep and upon waking. For two years, I have crab walked around the stone—picking it up, holding it, filing tentatively, and then putting it aside.

The name, Pregnant Nun, emerged from the stone months before I had a clue about her form. Instinctively, I understood that I had the opportunity to further heal the traumatic past lifetime in Iona by sculpting myself free. I had already experienced the emotional impact of that past lifetime, yet from somewhere deep inside my heart or womb, I resisted making a commitment to bring her form out of the stone.

Initially, I talked myself out of filing deeper by convincing myself I did not know anything about anatomy. Then I decided I needed a teacher. I searched the web and asked friends for recommendations for a sculpture teacher who lived nearby and had no luck. Then I re-

turned to writing and published Awaken (2012), which occupied my time and my mind for almost twenty-three months. The attraction toward freeing the Pregnant Nun from the stone was relentless. My unconscious pursued me in dream after dream until I returned to work on the Pregnant Nun. My soul would not permit me to abandon this project or myself.

Intuitively, I knew the stone held an important key to my healing. I reassured myself that I was ready to file deeply. Slowly, I became less tentative. In retrospect, I appreciate how my fear overrode my willingness to file deeper.

I brought the incomplete torso with me to my artist retreat. She sat on a separate table nearby as I worked with clay in the morning and returned to file and chip her free in the afternoon. Toward the end of my month's retreat, I summoned my courage and asked Squidge to critique the white alabaster woman. I watched as she picked her up carefully, turned the form around in her hands, rubbed the protruding breasts and swollen belly, closed her eyes and said softly, "Hmmm, no arms. That is why you are stuck."

"How could I have missed that?" I said out loud. Then I whined, "There is no way I can make arms. There is not enough stone."

As soon as I said that out loud, my heart understood the paradox. This stone woman had no arms to reach out to anyone. She could not even embrace herself. Immediately, I lit a candle, put on a CD entitled "Goddess," said a prayer out loud and waited. When I approached the woman without hands, I was determined to use my strong arms and my whole body, if necessary, to set her free.

With my intention firm, I felt a surge of energy go through my body. Instead of grieving about her missing arms and hands, I concentrated on her roundness—her milk-laden breasts and protruding belly. Mentally I counted the hours that I had studied the contours of my own breasts and I remembered joking with my friend Ed Rosenberg that I had become as obsessed with breasts as most men appear to be. He winked and laughed at me and replied, "I don't think so, Rosie."

As I continued to chisel and file, I sensed that self-forgiveness was the missing puzzle piece of my unhealed story. I filed deeper until I convinced myself that my forcefulness might shatter the stone. Yet the stone felt soft under my hands. On a cellular level, I understood that by freeing her, I was also liberating myself from a strong karmic overlay that held me hostage to a sexuality-spirituality split in my consciousness and I persisted. The spell of karma almost kept me hostage until I yelled, "I forgive you, Rosalie Ann for loving and choosing love of a man over your love for God. I forgive you for getting pregnant and trusting in love and your future family. I forgive you for being human."

My heart opened and I wept. The tears felt ancient and present. My journey to reclaim my wholeness felt closer than ever before. Even though I did not find a way to give her arms, I felt embraced by the Pregnant Nun.

The next day Squidge ordered me to wear a blindfold while working with clay so that I would experience that my body was the home of sensations, instincts, feelings, and creativity. For two and one half weeks, I wore a wide red blindfold for several hours of the day. I became more aware of texture, sensation, and the feeling of the clay and let go of figuring out how to make a shape in my head. I was stunned that the pots I pinched and coiled blindfolded appeared more symmetrical and attractive than the ones I created with my eyes open!

Squidge began our daily clay lesson with a body scan and then a short meditation. Early on, my inner three-year-old presented herself. She was fascinated by rhythms of all kinds, the sounds of feet going upstairs, the patter of raindrops, and the piercing sound that the wooden banister emitted when hit. She skipped in rhythm, said rhymes in rhythm, and learned early that her rhythm was not acceptable in her family. She felt vulnerable and made an early decision to enjoy her rhythm in private.

Later I wrote a journal entry about the return of my little girl self:

After a long, sweaty hike in the woods, Squidge reminds me that I bring my inner little girl along in addition to my grown-up adult when I create. Growing up, I was expected to learn fast, be perfect, and be smart. Excel and exceed became my lifeline. When I did excel, my mother declared, "Well of course, you were brilliant. After all, you are MY daughter." I seldom felt like I was the one who accomplished.

As an adult I carried out the family expectation of perfection and I get frustrated when I do not know how to do something perfectly the first time. I am surprised that when I slow down enough to linger in my vulnerability, I seldom have to ask Squidge for guidance or support.

Befriending my lonely and misunderstood three-year-old self after so many years felt unfamiliar. I asked her what she needed to feel safe, comfortable and loved. Music was her only request. I felt her inside me and was grateful to have her with me. How insulted she must have been during seven years of traditional dancing classes! "I am sorry that I did not know how to make you happy and safe," I said.

Then I was flooded with memories of my mother reinforcing that I was un-coordinated. That is why she insisted I take those dancing lessons three days a week for seven years. I learned how to be obedient and follow the robotic steps of a middle aged, rouged teacher named Mrs. Reuben. I do not remember a time when she invited us to listen to the rhythm and beat of the music and move to our own inner rhythms. On the days free from dancing school, I was forced to practice. Rhythm and self-expression felt separate from movement. I felt the rhythm of my emotions only in rebellion. and I was punished for rebelling. The message that I internalized was that I could not trust my body.

Decades later, when I lived in Cayucos, California, I enrolled in Gabrielle Roth's Five Rhythms course. I felt awkward and embarrassed with my locked pelvis and tight hips. Movement felt alien. For a few weeks, my ego ruled as I convinced myself that I needed to attend a special class in remedial movement. Yet I returned. I showed up and slowly felt more comfortable in my body. I even bought some tapes and moved to the music at home. Healing happened gradually.

"Of course!" I said to myself, remembering that I have carried those early memories for decades. Yet when I teach intuition classes I remind people to be aware of their unique body signals and to track which ones register truth and which body sensations alert them to a non-truth. I tell people they do not need to buy a pendulum because their body is a trustworthy pendulum. Relating to my body as a place of truth connects me with unhealed wounds.

Each time I engage in any type of creative self-expression, I challenge myself to go beyond what I believe I am capable of creating. Occasionally, I merge with the infinite possibilities that are forever present. Often, I dream at night and awaken with insights, inspiration and excitement. Then my consciousness transforms and expands. My journal reminds me to return to my own experience—even if I feel alone and confused.

My days are full of art and diversity. I am happier than I ever remember. Pieces of the puzzle that is me continue to fall into place without drama or judgment. Dreams of integrating self-acceptance and creativity, whether in words, art, or body awareness, remind me that growth happens on the inner dimension before we manifest it in our human form.

Pleasure is becoming familiar and I have a growing sense that pleasure is a forerunner to joy. The part of me that thrives on knowing in advance would appreciate a map of this journey of awakening consciousness while my soul trusts the unknown future to evolve in perfect timing and order.

Surrendering to pleasure is a theme that has stalked me since I began my retreat. Today I lay down on my bed with our kitten NJ, our kitten that joined me on my retreat. Within minutes, I was asleep. When I awoke a couple of hours later, I felt groggy and pulled between getting up and returning to sleep. When I listened to my body, the message was clear: more sleep—even though that meant losing time in my studio. I knew from experience that integration often happens in sleep time; nevertheless, I went back and forth three more times

115

before making a deliberate choice to close my eyes and let go of other agendas. That's when my guides arrived with a personal tutorial about time. I vaguely recalled that Big Angel had channeled information about pleasure before he departed and I returned to my journals and smiled as I read his words: Pleasure is a form of self-love unless it becomes an addiction.

My creative process insists that I set my mind aside along with my tendency to overachieve and then override my limiting belief that I know nothing about how to create. Each time I choose to create, I challenge myself to go beyond what I believe I am capable of. Eventually, if I stick with my project long enough discipline and flow merge.

Being creative awakens my yearning for wholeness. Texture and form replace words. Meaning and healing mingle when I file stone and pinch clay. As I trust my instincts, I surrender to What Is. Then I spontaneously merge with Earth and Spirit. In that moment, I feel as if Art is my outbreath. Earlier today I emailed friends describing my retreat experience:

As an artist, I intentionally invite the elements of earth, water, air and fire to have their way with me.

As an artist, I ground myself in my body, my instincts, and my intuition as I await inspiration.

As an artist, I remind myself to intentionally use my hands as extensions of my heart.

As an artist I enter the mystery each time I interact with stone or clay.

As an artist, I overflow with appreciation for the earth each time I am creatively generous with myself

Later that day as Squidge and I weeded and harvested her vegetable garden, she inquired, "What is your work?"

I surprised myself with my quick response, "My work is love, to love myself, others, the earth, the process of living, and then expand my love and its expression."

When I ground myself in my unique soul story, love is my Source and Resource. Miracles arise from love. I was created in love to love. Could it be this simple? That my soul purpose is to learn to love me being me and sharing my experiences with others?

During the second week of my artist's retreat I became entranced with making rattles. I understood instinctively that creating clay rattles was somehow linked to my soul story. Yet my ego challenged and questioned whether my passion for making rattles might be my way of avoiding learning how to throw pots on the wheel. After I effortlessly crafted a few dozen rattles, each with its own shape, color, and sound, I found myself once again doubting myself. Again, I questioned whether I was wasting my time and energy making something that didn't matter and had no value. That night I dreamed of rattles and I heard the sounds of rattles in my sleep. The next morning I drew pictures of rattles and channeled this poem:

> *Rattles as grounding instruments,*
> *Rattles as sound smudges,*
> *Rattles as timeless as eternity,*
> *Rattles as inducers of altered consciousness,*
> *Rattles as ritual containers,*
> *Rattles as healing instruments.*

117

In the morning, I asked Squidge if she thought I was "going nowhere" with my rattle making. She smiled and said clearly, "Rosie, rattles are one of the most ancient archetypal images. If they are calling you, listen. If you are attracted to creating rattles, why question your motivation?"

For two weeks, I surrendered my resistance and delighted in making rattles. I still do not know how rattles are connected to my Future Self. Perhaps they are remnants of a past lifetime or maybe linked to a future lifetime. For sure, the act of collaborating with the clay and creating both sound and beauty filled me with pleasure. For the moment, I do not need to understand more than this.

I must create time and space for beauty daily. It's a basic need for me. I agree with the late John O'Donahue who wrote, "In the experience of beauty we awaken and surrender in the same act." I challenge myself to participate with beauty daily because I know beauty only visits; it does not take up permanent residence. I feel as if I am seeding my expanding consciousness with beauty. My commitment to beauty, which spans four decades, nurtures my soul. I absolutely agree with the observation by Richard Holmes, "Beauty is the explosion of energy perfectly contained." Sculpting is my favorite medium for creating beauty. Writing is another. Other times I choose to be a beholder of beauty. I participate in beauty by beholding the starry night sky, licking a snowflake, spotting a spider's intricate web, smelling an apple tree in bloom, or responding to the laughter in the eyes of my two grandchildren.

CHAPTER 7

My Service as a Death Doula

*T*he day my artist retreat ended, I returned to Old Orchard Beach to be with Darlene during her dying time. A lifetime of memories bounced around me as I drove. We attended twelve years of school together and lived on the same street. Her parents and my parents were best friends. I was at the New Theater at the end of Main Street when she got her first kiss. She gave me her long white gowns to wear for Rainbow Girls. Together we earned extra money cleaning up after our parents' parties. I watched her play the accordion at countless recitals. I remember when she got married the first time.

One of my most potent memories of her dying time happened when we were curled up in her big bed. The day was hot and humid and Darlene was cold. The Hospice nurse who visited earlier in the day confirmed that she was definitely dying when she saw that Darlene's toenails were turning blue. Earlier in the week, I had painted my toenails blue. As we talked quietly, she looked down at (my) feet and then laughed saying, "Oh Rosie, the nurse had it all wrong. You are the one who is dying." I wiggled my toes. Before I responded, she said, "Or maybe we are dying together."

Later I retreated to my journal and wrote:

We both wanted her dying to be fast and merciful. It was neither.

Gradually she withdrew her energy from the daily ritual of beautifying her home.

Gradually she stopped rising from bed early to beat the sunrise.

Gradually she slept more and spoke less.

Gradually she withdrew from music.

Gradually she forgave some of the people who "had done her wrong."

Gradually she stopped eating lobster and coffee ice cream

Gradually she gave up her resolve to die at home.

As a midwife to dying, I knew how to bridge dimensions of consciousness. I knew how to ground myself with my breath in order to be present while Darlene gradually let go of her breath. I returned to breath and love, love and breath as I affirmed her preciousness.

Detaching with love became her work as well as mine. As she slept, I wrote:

Letting go of needing to know how, why, or when,
Letting go of needing to speak,
Letting go of the illusion that I could make her dying less painful.
Letting go of the future that I imagined we would share together.

As a midwife and friend, I continued to surround Darlene with love. I maintained our connection as she lived inside morphine. I breathed consciously to quiet myself and disciplined myself to stay tuned to her essence rather than the diminishing life force of her body.

Several months earlier, I remember seeing a life sized, hand hewn wooden cradle made by the Shakers. In their dying tradition, the family rocks the dying one. The meditative rhythm of the rocking brings comfort and perhaps a remembering that death comes when breath goes. For the Shakers, the cradle is a bridge between birthing and dying.

I have a vivid memory of the exact moment that Darlene made her decision to practice dying. I was standing in the hallway at the Hospice Center with three other women listening to a young woman tell a story about how she knew when her grandmother was ready to die. I was on alert in case I sensed or heard Darlene call out for me.

In the middle of the story, I felt Darlene energetically reach out for me. I hurried to her bedside. Her eyes remained closed. I bent down to touch her head and she whispered, "I have been searching for you everywhere." I squeezed her hand. She smiled. Without using words, I energetically asked if she were ready to practice dying. She nodded. Then I tracked her energy and intuited her response: "I don't know how."

She, who prided herself on being in control and manifesting her intentions easily, had little life experience with letting go or counting on anyone to be there for her. We had mirrored that way of being for one another all our lives, and who knows how many previous lifetimes.

"No worries," I said out loud. "I know the way."

A tiny tear fell from her left eye.

I whispered in her left ear, "Let's travel through space together. Maybe you will remember dying before. Maybe you won't. It doesn't matter. Together we will practice the way home."

Before we began traveling, I reassured Darlene's human self that I would not abandon her. Energetically, she agreed to practice leaving her physical body behind by merging with her light body. Before we pushed off, I sent gratitude to Ben Bentov and Robert Monroe, who had mentored me in ways of journeying out of body. Then I asked Darlene for permission to lead the way and she nodded. We were off.

To me, our light bodies were like airplanes and Darlene energetically joined me as I remembered how Richard Bach, author of *Jonathan Living Seagull*, described doing loop de loops in his airplane. Then I remembered that I loaned her that book many years ago, before she decided to take flying lessons. Was I reaching too far to imagine that re-connecting with her flying lessons was her calling card from Future Pull? I reminded her that as the co-pilot she could take over the controls whenever she wished.Then I reassured her that she could return to her physical body, too.

"We are tracking your own GPS (God Presencing System) route home and repetition is allowed," I said. "This is practice."

Yet we both knew this was a dress rehearsal for dying.

"I trust you will know when you are ready to leave the earth plane," I said energetically.

Three or four times, Darlene was within a nanosecond of surrendering her last breath. Each time she gasped and returned to her physical body. I waited until she signaled that she was ready to venture out of her body again. Each time we lifted off and traveled out of body, she seemed to be more comfortable and confident.

As I sat with her after our practice flights, I appreciated how much she allowed herself to take in the love that friends offered during the final days of her life. I remember crying when she asked, "Can you believe it, Rosalie, only now when I am dying do I appreciate that friends loved me all the time—even when I did not return their love?"

Many times, I retreated to my journal and wrote about the sadness I felt for her. Darlene's personal story was filled with abandonment and betrayal as well as passion, travel, adventures, accomplishments, healing, service and magic. I choose to believe that she willed herself to stay alive, in spite of much pain and suffering, in order to fill up with the love that she had desired and denied for her entire lifetime. I choose to believe that love gave her courage to die. I choose to believe that the love she accepted from friends accompanied her on her journey.

I honored Darlene's request to create a celebration of life ritual with my clay rattles. Before she died, she made up a guest list as well as a list of people who were not welcome to celebrate her life. I agreed to make twenty-one clay rattles and create a ritual to rattle her home because she was afraid that she might get stuck between dimensions. I flashed back to a few weeks earlier when she had asked me to teach her how to make rattles and she had talked about making embroidery like designs on her handmade rattles. I remembered how we drove to Portland in her car to buy dark and light clay. When we returned home to the hammocks and tables in her garage, I demonstrated how to make pinch pots by fusing the top and bottom together. However, she had no strength in her fingers and said, "Rosie, I'll just watch you do it and pretend that we are doing it together."

After Darlene excarnated, I was left with many questions:

How do we remain conscious of both our human and spiritual needs as we gradually take leave of our physical body?

How can we live our life from a love-centered perspective so we don't rush to catch up on love at the end?

How would our dying time be enhanced if we actively engaged in forgiveness?

How can we prepare in advance to respond positively to the question: How much pleasure did I enjoy from my life experiences?

I am deeply aware that each time I midwife another during the dying process, I am practicing for my own dying time. I yearn to embrace my dying as a time to unravel and then re-weave some of the threads of my life. I believe that if I am consciously present for my dying time that my heart will take refuge in death. I intend to leap into my dying time without fears or regrets. I promised my Dad on his deathbed that I would return to a consistent meditation practice because I wanted to be conscious to answer the call.

During a phone conversation a few weeks after Darlene's death, Meghan asked me if I had grieved Darlene's death. I felt guilty when I said I had not had time. She died the same day that my grandchildren returned home from being with their father for five weeks. School and food shopping enveloped us. Plus, I had inherited a litter of newborn kittens born on my bed the same day that Darlene died! No time for transitions that included grieving.

When I shared my plans for the rattle ritual with Meghan, she predicted that the ceremony would be spiritually beneficial to Darlene as well as all who came to celebrate her life. She also remarked that creating the rattles and giving them away to people who came to the ritual was an example of my generosity. I agreed. Then I added, " Now I knew why I had been obsessed with creating rattles."

The death theme did not stop. I learned that beloved pets can also be way showers who initiate us into the demanding and sacred work of being present for a Beloved who is dying whether the beloved has fur, fins, wings, or skin.

My friend Ellen discovered that it is never too late to grieve. She told me the story of caring for her cat, and being confronted with the reality that she never cried after her mother died when she was twelve years old. She did not go to the funeral because she knew she would fall apart. Since her mother's death, she had avoided funerals and grieving and made the choice not to have children.

Yet there was something about Sister Mary Calico and their fourteen-year relationship that motivated Ellen to being present for both dying and grieving. As her cat was dying, she reached out to friends and asked for support and prayers and spoke about her sadness, her dread, as well as her wish to be present for her cat as she died.

She grieved in advance and counseled herself to let go gently when the end time came. Not only did she make the decision to be present for her cat's dying and her subsequent grieving, she also consciously partnered with her inner twelve-year-old self and led her step by step through the rituals of dying: the crying, the bargaining, the memories, the regrets, the confusion about what to say to people—all of it! In the process, she understood that grieving was cumulative and she carried the china doll that was her favorite when she was twelve years old and placed a photo of her mother and herself into the burial box when she said her final goodbye to Sister Mary Calico. The tears she cried came from long ago as well as present time and opened her to possibilities that she had closed herself off from decades before.

As she told me the story of her epiphany, she expressed surprise and awe that her heart had opened so wide because of a cat. She thanked me for an earlier email that I had sent saying, "Time to grieve and celebrate, celebrate and grieve," and said the dance between crying and celebrating claimed her several times a day. She wondered how Sister Mary Calico's death might impact her vow never to have children and said she was content to allow evolution to have its way with her. What a gift to be present for her being present.

I am aware that whether we grieve a beloved pet, a person, a place, or the death of an illusion, death makes demands. As the one left behind, we are the memory keepers. As the one left behind, we honor the person or pet and the love we shared as well as the lessons we learned. I enjoy believing that each time we remember someone who has died, a bell rings in heaven.

Death continued to stalk me. As Noah and I delighted in a pre-dawn beach walk. I spotted a fish gasping for breath about four inches from the water. In an attempt to save it from dying, I bent down and tossed the gasping fish back into the ocean. While the fish was in mid-air, a seagull swooped down and flew away with the fish in its mouth. I held back tears. Noah looked at me intently, shrugged his shoulders and said, "Don't be sad, Grandmom. It's just the cycle of life."

One day a friend emailed me a vintage picture she had snapped seventeen years ago. There I was at fifty-five with mahogany red hair. As I studied the photo, I remembered the love and laughter of the six women surrounding me in the photograph. Memories flooded me. Darlene had taken the photo during my "Giving Away Party" the night before I married.

As I examined the faces in the picture more closely, I began to cry. The faces of three of my friends who are dead now stared back at me. Piroshka died fourteen years ago, from kidney failure. I remember the exact moment that she commanded me to switch from sending her healing energies to singing "dying songs." I resisted. She insisted. When I told her that I did not know any "dying songs," she ordered me to remember. I did. And I also remembered that we had mid-wifed each other through our dying times before. Jenai died six years ago, by her own hands. Half of my intimate circle of women friends has disappeared from this earth realm. Just seeing us all together and alive in the picture ignited my memories and magnified my grief.

As I stared at our faces, I counted the years. Their deaths spanned fourteen years. During that time, I moved four times. As I continued to stare at our faces, my grief felt fresh. Only in that moment did I appreciate the multiple impacts of their deaths. I remembered that we all made a pact to live together when we got old. During the same conversation, we talked about who might be the last one to die. We failed to consider who might be the first, and the second, and the third.

As I continued to study the vintage photograph, I was overwhelmed with the love I continued to feel for each friend. Without their presence in my life, I would not be me. I was also aware that my body and my spirit felt stronger than at any other time in my life. Although my bones creak louder now that I am seventy-three and the time that it takes me to get to the bathroom has lengthened, my grandson Noah reminds when I can't remember someone's name, still I think of myself as young at heart.

"How can this be happening?" I asked the empty room. How come death is stalking my peers when only a few years ago, I adjusted to receiving monthly social security checks?

Yet I am also a death walker who is comfortable midwifing others in their dying process. I am present for death. As I continued to gaze at the picture of my six friends, I was sad. I breathed deeply and honored the lives of Piroshka, Jenai, and Darlene. I wished we had lived together longer.

Later that day while I was going through boxes of stored clothing, books and assorted incidentals, a piece of typewritten paper fell to the ground. There were tiny holes in the back of the paper and I remembered how typewriter ribbons made those indentations when the ribbon ran out of ink. I was not prepared to read a poem from Mike that he had written forty years ago, when he was twelve years old.

Winter

Winter is shooting a snowball at a truck,
And hitting the windshield is you have luck.
Building snow forts out of wood and never doing what you should.

Some people go South,
But you'd like to punch them in the mouth,
For when they go to New Mexico,
They call you a Maine Eskimo.

Staying out till nine at night.
Snowballing your teacher and getting out of sight,
But when you go to school next morning,
Your mean, old teacher will be scorning.
You'd better look out 'cause she's a schooler.
And she knows how to use the ruler.

But did I mention skating, skiing, and sliding?
Or even the old sport...sleigh riding?
While ski-dooing has won its fame,
And ice fishing stays the same,
While sliding is going down hill
And skating is standing still,
Fluffy white carpet falls to the ground
White washing everything around.

And when you go to bed that night,
Hundreds of snowflakes are still in flight.
All through the night snow flutters down
Covering streets throughout the town.

In the morning you wake up with a start,
And there's a sudden leap in your heart.
You turn on the radio as fast as you can,
And soon are listening to WGAN.
The moments silence seem like death,
And then you hear...Cape Elizabeth.
—Michael Hall, age 12, 1974

Initially I cried and then I smiled as I honored my son's writing ability. Then I grieved again because he did not live long enough to write more. On an impulse, I made a copy of

129

the poem and mailed it to my mother because I knew she loved him as much as I did. She did not respond. I also gave a copy of the poem to my daughter and grandchildren. Nobody knew what to say, including me.

I remember as though it were yesterday a conversation with my grandmother who confided to me how painful it was to say "goodbye" to her all of friends and most of her family members. Her voice held her pain. I remember how I held her hand as she listed the funerals that she had attended over many years. Looking back, I wished that I had listened more deeply and asked her more questions. I thought I had lots of time before death became a familiar. Back then I thought death was for other people.

One of the values of keeping a journal is that I can travel back through time and re-connect with a "word snapshot" of what was important to me then. I returned to a 1991 journal when I took private retreats with the sisters at Bay View Colony, in Saco, Maine and felt like I re-entered the conversation with Sister Anita who said, "When I am dying, I want no distractions. I refuse to have sisters around watching; they can pray in the parlor. I wish to be totally absorbed in God's approach." Her way of dying, as waiting for God's approach, is the way I pray to make my final transition.

My elastic mind returns to my own dress rehearsal for dying when I was bitten by a brown recluse spider in San Cristobal, New Mexico more than twenty years ago. Earlier in the week a man from our village had died from a brown recluse bite. A local Hispanic healer, known locally as a curandera, rattled over my body for nearly thirty hours while I traveled between life and after life. I witnessed myself detach from continuing to live my life or moving on to explore my afterlife. I visited both realms and felt like an observer as I waited for a soul call in order to make a choice.

I had no sense of time passing. I was neither in pain nor bliss. Yet my awareness felt laser sharp. When I discovered myself in the midst of what I thought was a past life review, I imagined that I had died and I was at peace with my evolutionary choice. During the "life review," I was surprised and confused when I was not able to say "Well Done" in relationship to three people. Intuitively I understood that I could heal those three relationships from my afterlife or I could return to my body and make peace. It was my choice, and I wanted to have no regrets.

I did not go through a lengthy process of weighing the options. I cannot say that I "instantly" came back into my body because where I was time did not exist. Nevertheless, my return to my body felt sudden. I lay in bed, feverish, thirsty and disoriented. Upon my return to my body, the Hispanic healer kissed the spot on my upper arm where the spider had deposited its poison and told me that I now carried spider medicine which empowered me to see into the heart of eternity. I believed her although I had no clue what she meant. She and her mother had both survived a brown recluse's bite and I joined their clan.

CHAPTER 8

Surrender

*A*fter the month of being with Darlene in her dying time, I yearned for a nest of my own. I craved "womb time." The last day I did a soul reading at home, I went upstairs to find that Noah vomiting in his bedroom. When I cleaned that mess up, Malia wanted to know what a condom was and the Federal Express man knocked at the door. Too much chaos for me!

I crafted an intention to find a cave-like environment without windows, close to home and affordable. Paying rent for an office place of my own felt like an outrageous gamble. My ego warned me of danger while my soul voted for freedom and solitude. When I put up cash to rent a space of my own, it felt like both a courageous and loving act. I signed a nine-month contract and surrendered worrying.

I divided my new space into two areas—my art studio and my office space where I met with clients for soul readings or soul mentoring. I purchased a large, wooden roll top desk where I concentrated on writing *Awaken*, and a small couch and a rocking chair from a second-hand store. When clients commented on the healing energy in the room, I knew I had manifested my intentions.

Retreating there filled me with inspiration, comfort, and silence. Nobody visited unless invited and I invited almost nobody. I named my healing nest Grace Place and dedicated it to soul readings, creativity, and healing.

Each time I walked through the door, I entered a loving energy field. The first thing I did was light a candle, sniff my flowers, sit, and then meditate. Tea followed. Then I felt deliciously supported because my energetic imprint reigned here. Spirit awaited and responded. The call to solitude and quiet deepened. Virginia Woolf was right when she urged every woman to have a room of her own.

In order to reinvest in teaching and doing more soul readings, I chose to break rank with my primary role as full time resident grandmother and mother. Balancing being of service to my family and assisting others to align with their soul purpose filled me with joy. My family sensed it was time for me to begin to re-enter my own life. Malia and Noah were not as dependent on me since they were both in school full time and Kelli Lynne had settled into her first job as a doctor at Eastern Maine Hospital in Bangor.

We all agreed to cooperate while I figured out how I wished to live my own life. Kelli Lynne volunteered to do the food shopping and Malia and Noah agreed to help me cook and to keep their bedrooms neat. Kelli Lynne also agreed to take more responsibility for her children on weekends, giving me more free time. Our new agreement felt like a natural transition that benefitted all of us.

Soon after I moved into my office, my friend and Pilates teacher, Val Kitchen, invited me to do a group presentation on the video interview that I made at Yale University with interviewer Augusta Albin titled, "Don't Retire, Inspire." I expected a small group and was stunned when I walked into a large crowd of people in her studio.

After spending the majority of my days in the company of children, I did not know if I had words of more than one syllable left in my vocabulary. I was relieved and surprised to find I felt comfortable answering questions and giving examples. I even cracked jokes that were not of the bathroom variety that peppered the language of my grandchildren and their friends.

After the lively discussion, a tall, lean man came up to me and asked, "Did you used to have a different last name?"

I nodded and smiled. I had no idea of who he was and where he was going with his questions.

"A long time ago did you have an office on Route One in Scarborough, Maine?"

I nodded again and said, "Yes" with increasing curiosity.

"Do you remember me?" he asked, with a glint in his eyes.

I shook my head, "No."

"Do you still do soul readings?" he inquired.

I felt as though he had bridged time by reminding me of a person who had been missing in inaction for years.

Then he grabbed my hands and said, "My name is Dennis and I didn't expect you to remember me after twenty-eight years. You gave me a soul reading the day before you flew back to New Mexico." Then I vaguely remembered him because he was about to leave for a trip to the Grand Canyon.

He squeezed my hands and said, "Your soul reading changed my life. I still listen to the tape you made. If you ever want to hear how you sounded twenty-eight years ago, come visit. We live about half an hour away. In fact, we have a retreat center called the Gathering Place. Say, do you still do workshops and retreats?"

I told Dennis that I had not designed or facilitated workshops for the last six years in favor of being a committed grandmother. He listened intently and said he understood because he and his wife, Georgia, were also devoted to being present for their two great-grandchildren.

Then he turned to leave, but not before saying, "I think you would really like our place. Come visit. Here is our email."

Intuitively, I sensed that our meeting again was another example of synchronicity although I had no clue about the specifics. I put his email in my pocket. Then it disappeared for three months until he reached out to me four months later.

As another follow-through action step after my second vision quest, I designed a seven-month training course called Embodying Soul. My ego's voice screamed about the current scarcity economy and then I almost convinced myself that nobody would be interested in what I desired to teach. Later I wrestled with the possibility that the training might be a "spiritual bypass" which happens when I override or deny what my soul is communicating to me. I am familiar with spiritual bypassing because that is what I did when I reassured everyone that I was dealing with Mike's death when in reality my heart felt ripped apart.

Applying the principle of over-belief, I imagined everything in the universe lined up with my intention to fill my Embodying Soul training. For a moment, I was back in time clapping my little girl hands together so Tinkerbelle would live in the Peter Pan movie. The training filled up and I declared myself a magnet for miracles. After the first four-day meeting in Florida, I affirmed myself as a leader in my journal:

My knowing that everything in my life led me to design and teach Embodying Soul was spot on. I felt

135

that deep truth like a shawl around my shoulders for the first four days of the training. I marveled at the synchronicities, the deep connections that participants created, their willingness and courage to go deeper, clear layer after layer of limited thinking, laugh, and celebrate themselves and each other. I referred to principles when it was appropriate, gave lots of concrete examples, invited questions, challenged and comforted—effortlessly. I even created a new word, "flowth," for the fusion of flow and growth. Women allowed themselves to be vulnerable, heart centered, powerful, and unfinished with one another. A lovely combination of structure and reflection led us to new awareness, understanding, and appreciation. There is no doubt in my mind that we came together as a shared group soul agreement that created a group readiness to grow, let go and flow.

During my time away in Florida leading Embodying Soul, Dennis Kosciusko called and asked me to lead a workshop at the Gathering Center in April because the teacher who had guided the established group of ten people was not available. He sweetened his offer by inviting me to teach anything I desired. The timing of his call felt perfect. I decided on the spot to teach people how to identify and clear past lifetime vows that kept them out of alignment with their present soul purpose and then reclaim soul qualities, which is where an individual's power and healing are grounded.

Also during my workshop in Florida, my daughter decided she no longer wished to suffer through another Maine winter and decided to relocate to Virginia because Noah had decided to live with his father who lived there. It became clear that the time had come for me to once again live on my own, especially since she was entering a new relationship. I made the decision to reenter my own life with the promise that I too would move to Newport News, Virginia within a few months of her departure.

Initially we had planned that I would find a place of my own within walking distance of her home so Malia and Noah, when they visited, could walk or bike to my house. Although I looked and looked for something close by, the energy in Newport News did not feel right.

Noah expected we would always live together. In the midst of our daily pillow talk one morning he said, "You know Grandmom, when I decided to be born and live with you I did not look at the whole movie. I thought we would live together forever and I am very sad. But next time when I am thinking of being born, I will watch the whole movie." The deep gratitude for the nine years we lived together brought tears to my eyes.

When I realized that both the Edgar Cayce Association for Research and Enlightenment (A.R.E. Center) and Virginia Beach were only about forty-five minutes away, I recognized the soul call and was struck by how another thread in my life seemed to be interweaving my past with my present and future. When I was in graduate school at the University of Maine, I wrote my master's thesis on the Society for Psychical Research in England and came across many references to Edgar Cayce. His book, *My Life as A Seer,* and his autobiography, *There Is a River,* remained on my bookshelf for decades. Throughout the intervening years, I had planned to visit his A.R.E. Center, but never carried through with my plans. As soon as I decided on Virginia Beach, I found a house to rent across the street from the A.R.E. Center and a block from the beach and that felt perfect.

Between stepping into leadership with my new workshop and deciding to live alone some distance from my daughter and grandchildren, I anticipated my ego yelling it's loudest since I acknowledged that I was on the edge of a transformational threshold. It did and I persisted. In an effort to override the insistent voice of my ego not to rock the boat, I leafed through old journals to remember how Big Angel related to ego and found this:

> *Ego rules when you get scared, judge, or limit yourself.*
>
> *The ego is the place of suffering and pain.*
>
> *If you are under the influence of pain, suffering, or self-judgment, you are under the influence of your ego.*
>
> *Negative thinking, a specialty of ego, brings displeasure and it is a human form of addiction. Conscious use of your intuition effaces ego.*

My guides recommended *High Beam Living and Loving* for the title of Soul *Befriending*. However, I felt shy about it because I imagined that people would expect me to show up shining full beam and I did not want friends to think of me as egocentric. So I compromised and used *Soul Befriending* as the title and substituted my guide's suggestion for the subtitle. Yet from my emergent perspective, I realize that radiance is part of acknowledging that I am a spark of the Divine and I imagine that if God is living a Rosie experience through me, She is pleased.

Ever since Soul Befriending was published, I have wondered how my experience would have been different if I had not been such a tyrant with my time while writing and revising. I seldom relaxed and gave myself scant time for leisure and pleasure. Although I intentionally set an alarm clock to ring at ten minutes before each hour to remind myself to take a body break, it was never enough time to evoke leisure or to laugh at myself when I tripped over how many times I had written "authentic elf" instead of "authentic self."

Regardless of invitations from friends to step out of my self-enforced discipline, I stayed task oriented. When I was not sitting at my desk writing, I obsessed about organizing the book. I wonder how my writing might have benefitted if I had made room for all of my senses and engaged in a spontaneous picnic, or a visit to an art museum, or a midnight dance on the beach or a swim in the Atlantic Ocean?

Always before I mailed pre-ordered books at small post offices—in San Cristobal, New Mexico, where Ram Dass mailed *Be Here Now*, and in Hermon, Maine, where the post person was a friend and I was filled with delight as I sent my new books off to friends and fans.

I expected a similar farewell ritual when I brought the neatly stacked box of seventy-four pre-ordered *Soul Befriending* books into the neighborhood post office in Virginia Beach. When the postal clerk refused to stamp and label them media mail, I thought he was joking. Then he suggested that I fill out the paper work online and assured me someone would come by to pick up the books. I preferred the personal touch and I could not understand why he refused to cooperate. My compassion kicked in when he explained that he risked getting written up if he spent more than five minutes with a customer. My creative problem-solving mind kicked in, and I asked him how long he thought it would take him to weigh and stamp my bundle of books.

"At least twenty minutes," he snapped without looking at me.

When he refused a second time to stamp my book envelopes, I recognized that I was edge walking between my personal story and my soul story and I wanted to make this a soul-befriending event.

"Okay, what if I guarantee that nobody will stand in your line for twenty minutes?"

"You can't guarantee that," he said in a sneering tone.

"What if I can?" I said as if we were bidding each other up in a card game.

Then he folded his arms across his chest and ordered me to take the box of books home.

I remained standing in place as he walked away. Before he was out of sight, I asked to speak with his manager. As I waited, I took several calming breaths and did my best to step out of the escalating negative energy and the drama without giving up my right to mail the books. The manager ordered the postal clerk to stamp and affix the media mail label to each envelope. When he handed the envelopes back to me, one by one, I placed my hands on each package and sent healing energy to each recipient. When we were almost done, I said cheerfully, "Almost done. Only about ten more to go,"

"There's no such thing in my world as 'almost done.' You are either done or not."

I continued to add a healing touch to each bundle and refrained from more attempts at adding lightness to a trying situation. Then Manny, my favorite postal worker, returned from his coffee break and joined us saying, "I wonder what is going on outside this morning. Nobody has come in for at least fifteen minutes and this is usually our busiest time of the day."

I was not aware that he was watching our interaction until he laughed and said in a loud voice, "Do you know what she is doing? She is putting 'good mojo' into those envelopes when you hand them to her."

The man who was serving me shrugged and said, "She is an author. These are her books."

His colleague looked at me and quipped, "Don't tell me you wrote a book about how to win over an uncooperative postal worker."

We all laughed. Tension dissipated. The last book was metered and I reached out my hand to thank the clerk. We shook hands and I smiled as he said, "Done."

In June I traveled back to Maine. I affirm that when I am in alignment with my soul, I am lit up with God's light and God's spaciousness reflects through me. One night while at a book signing debut for *Soul Befriending* at the Maine Holistic Healing Center in Bangor, I felt comfortable being center stage. For me, showing up is very different from showing off! I understood that being center stage is precisely where I needed to be in order to move from teacher to leader. I was speechless, however, when one of the women present told me after the book signing that she had been raised to be a leader. She seemed equally surprised when I told her that I was raised to be an obedient daughter, loyal wife and sacrificing mother. Sometimes my only response is laugher at the cosmic joke that life has promoted me to be a leader, and I delight in reflecting lightness of being.

I bring lots of energy and love when I show up for a workshop, retreat, or book signing. When the event is over, I yearn to return to solitude and nature to ground my frequency—not to re-charge or fill up, but to ground my expansiveness. I know from experience that Nature is big enough to contain the amplified energies that run through me. No demands to engage, interact, nor cats to pet or anyone to please. Within the quietness of the pine forest, I breathe in and ground the loving energy surrounded by ancient granite stones as well as the fertile earth and endless sky.

Many years ago, I adopted the practice described by Barbara Marx Hubbard, author of *Conscious Evolution,* by engaging in an ongoing written dialogue with my Higher Self or guardian angel.

Me: Dearly Beloved, Thank you for gracing me with your guidance.

Dearly Beloved: You are welcome always, Dear One of the Light. From our perspective, you are entertaining many on many dimensions, as you remain grounded in your physical body.

Me: I am becoming more conscious of my energy. When I am tired, I sleep. When I no longer have words, I am silent. When I need to ground myself, I sculpt, garden, or retreat to the pine forest. My awareness deepens. Much of the time I have no thoughts.

Dearly Beloved: Being of "No Mind" does not mean empty headed! Creating space and time for your multi-dimensional self to shine through is part of who you are becoming. Fanning the frequencies of others is demanding as well as delighting. To others, it appears that you do that effortlessly. Yet holding space for others demands that you be present on multiple levels.

Me: Yes, and that is why at the end of a workshop or training, I desire to be off by myself and cradled by Nature. Presencing for others feels more demanding than Presencing for myself.

Dearly Beloved: Engaging with others, no matter how deeply you care about them, requires energy. And as you are aware, will is energy dependent. Being gentle with your human nature is fundamental unless you wish to give yourself away.

Me: No, I have retired from giving myself away.

Dearly Beloved: Much good is coming to you and you will be amazed how synchronicity recalibrates your energies. More people are coming to you who appreciate your gifts and it is important to continue to fill yourself with light.

Me: I appreciate being in connection again. I have been negligent and I promise to make our conversations part of my spiritual practice.

Dearly Beloved: As always, we are here.

Me: Thank you.

Who knows if my inner yearning to become intimate with the rhythms, cycles, sounds and smells of nature came because my soul yearned for more expression and expansiveness or because of a response to the questions that I had written earlier in my teal blue journal in May, in Virginia Beach, when I imagined how my summer in Maine might feel:

143

Is it possible for me to substitute clock time for Nature's time and live the way my ancestors lived?

Is it possible for me to slow down and count clouds and stars as my familiars?

Is it possible for me to co-exist with Nature so I feel Mother Earth as my second skin?

Is it possible to feel the earth stretching to accommodate more light, more growth through my own body?

Nature is no stranger to me and I appreciate how brilliantly nature grounds me. I believe that has always been true because looking back, the low points in my life were also times when I got disconnected from nature.

My original decision to camp out surprised me because I have a long history of avoiding sleeping outdoors. In fact, I had only camped out three times before—always at the insistence of friends, never alone. I tented out twice in Chaco Canyon in Arizona, because there were no motels nearby and once in Scotland because it was easier to acquiesce than to argue with my partner. I felt safe knowing that other campers were close by. Memories of snores and stars intermingled as well as the aroma of bacon cooking over campfires in the early morning.

Many of my Maine friends warned me of the ever-present danger of bear, moose, and coyotes, and someone even added the possibility of a rabid mountain lion to the list of nocturnal predators. I comforted myself by remembering that I had befriended bears during my vision quest in Taos, New Mexico, and deer is my totem animal in addition to being my middle name. That left the band of yowling coyotes and they too were my familiars since I had co-existed with them for seven years when I lived in Arroyo Seco and San Cristobal, New Mexico.

I kept a journal and two pens in my tent so I was prepared to record dreams or note insights that visited during the night. I was surprised that even in the darkest time of the night that there was enough light to see to write in my journal. As I breathed deeply, I surrendered even more to my connection to Nature. In return, I experienced a sweet sensuality, a softened endurance as well as a few saucy surprises. Indeed I am a spirit keeper of the earth. The following poem arrived as I relaxed in the moon's light. I still do not know if the source was a muse, a guide, an angel or my poet self.

Be of the earth and sky.
Heal your wounds.
Honor the earth and her seasons.
Remember that sacredness is wild in the earth and the heavens.
Both are home to you.
Decorate your home with gifts from the earth mother.
Listen and respond to the rhythms of your heart.
Voice your knowing.
Refresh yourself with joy and spontaneity.
Feel your luminosity.
Ground your light in delight and gratitude.
Remember how the earth and the stars are forever connected.

I knew from experience that words often diminish heart-centered, numinous encounters. I yearned to experience Nature directly, not from understanding gleaned from books. I knew that my yearning to sleep outside at night and feel an intimacy with the earth, sky, and stars was connected to moving into a cosmic sense of vastness and I intuited that sleeping on the earth was my way of merging with cosmic consciousness. During my time with Nature, I coined the word, "Cosmicity."

In many ways camping felt like a lazy woman's vision quest—minus the prayers, the warrior sweat lodges, and the fasting. The first week I felt sleep deprived because I shifted from being scared and reminding myself I needed sleep to being mesmerized by shooting stars, fireflies, and the haunting sounds of a hoot owl.

For three months, the liminal transitions from dusk to dark and dawn to day fascinated me. The border times between day ending and night beginning and night turning to dawn felt sacred to me and filled me with adoration, humility, and silence.

Hours slipped by. I had nothing to note and nothing to prove. I was content sitting on the earth admiring the uninterrupted starry sky with the fireflies as my only company. I even let go of wondering if I were emptying out or filling up—or both.

My basketful of reflections included:

The night sky is lighter than my bedroom at night.
Just before three A.M. a audible "hush" happens.
Fireflies surrender their light two hours before dawn.
By August, the airborne fireflies retreat to the ground.

Many times I wondered if the zillions of stars think that the fireflies are their relatives and then remembered that Native Americans related to stars as the campfires of their ancestors. My body remembered that we are all made of the dust and light of far off stars, and I now include "stars" when I end my prayers with thanksgiving to all my relations. Then I marveled that fireflies know how to be fully lit and I am only learning the art of high beam living and loving.

During a phone conversation, my friend Joan asked me, "How do you get Flow from the land?"

I replied, "I feel as though I belong to the rhythms of night when I camp out. "

Sleeping outside felt like returning to the mother's womb whether the womb is in the earth or in the sky. I entered into a relationship with the Divine Mother and the earth felt intimately connected with my evolving soul story. I surprised myself later by writing in my journal:

I am a soul desiring unity, which begins in nature. Then I sighed.

Is it possible to be present to know in advance the direction a rainbow will appear even before the dance of sun and rain?

Is it possible to be more like Squidge who planted trees in order to give the wind places to express itself?

Sometimes a short poem says it best. I return to my Wisdom Journal to re-read a poem by Terry Tempest Williams:

Once upon a time,
When women were birds,
There was the simple understanding
That to sing at dawn
And to sing at dusk was to heal the world through joy.
The birds still remember what we have forgotten,
That the world is meant to be celebrated.

Then I wrote in my journal:

The outdoors is my temple. I sleep naked in my tent from mid June until mid October. I experience myself in service to the earth as well as being receptive to the night sky. The earth herself acts as my Muse. Inspiration arrives in the darkness of night. I feel held and cherished. I breathe and relax. My body softens. My breath connects me with an exquisite sense of ease that surrounds me. My pen feels like it is an extension of my heart and the heart of the earth and sky.

During the light of day, I retraced Big Angel's words in an old journal from 2012 and smiled at his wisdom and missed his daily presence in my life:

In times of challenge or change, it is important to be aware of what you trust.

Your inner wounded child part of you has learned not to trust.

Look to Nature when you are in need of trust.

Appreciate how the grass comes up every spring underneath that which looks like wood.

Flowers pop up from beneath the formerly frozen ground.

Ocean tides ebb and flow.

The moon moves through predictable cycles.

You may also trust gravity because it has worked for you.

Nature is a mirror of your inner beauty.

I have learned to Stop, Look, and Listen in an attempt to befriend my ego. If I had not consciously slowed my story down and recognized the sabotaging power of my ego to limit my freedom of choice, I would have deleted camping from my list of growing pleasures.

When I returned to Virginia Beach in October, friends asked about my summer in Stetson, Maine, and I replied, "It was the best summer of my life." The next question was usually, "What made it so good?"

"Sleeping in my L.L. Bean pop-up tent and discovering pleasure in snuggling in my yellow satin polka dot sleeping bag. The best way to summarize my outdoor adventure is to say I no longer belong to the universe or myself in the same way as I used to."

None of my friends from Maine or Virginia related to my enthusiasm for sleeping alone in the middle of a forest. June Bro, my ninety-four-year-old soul friend was the exception. When I returned to my winter beach house in Virginia Beach and told her of my summer nights outside, she grabbed my hand and said, "If I lived in Maine, I would join you, dear." She went on to tell me about her one-month camping adventure in Canada when her five children were young.

I expected to easily fill up the third annual nine-month Embodying Soul training, based on the rave reviews from the original graduates. In truth, I no longer felt passion to teach it again because I wanted to travel less and be available to follow my soul path. However, a guaranteed source of income appealed to me too.

I required a minimum of eight participants and four people had registered. I tuned into my guides and was not surprised that they did not support another training. Next time I will remember to seek their counsel before I invest time and energy promoting an event. I need to hold myself to the same standards to which I hold workshop participants. When they fail to consult their guides, I require them to send a check to their least favorite charity!

I believed that if I exerted my will, I could convince four more people to sign up, but that felt ego driven. In turn, my ego bullied me for making a stupid decision that put my financial wellbeing in jeopardy with no guarantees of another income stream during the summer. Still I trusted myself and lived on the edge of my own edge. The aftertaste of my decision was relief.

I recorded the following reminder in my journal to refresh my awareness when necessary:

> According to Swami Muktananda, "The role of the impure ego is to make you believe that what is good for you is bad for you and what is bad for you is good for you."
>
> Daily, I marvel how my outer life reflects my inner world. My friend Val Kitchen played her role perfectly.
>
> "Work first and then surrender," advised Val.
>
> "That's no longer how I live my life," I said. "Surrender comes first." Then I surprised myself by saying, "Maybe surrender is my work," and Goddess bumps erupted on my arms.

No question I have worked hard my whole life, and many would say I have been productive and creative, but I have not counted surrender as a familiar. Yet I wonder if pleasure, reverence, passion, and ecstasy are connected to surrender—not work.

I have an instinctive sense that surrender, pleasure, and leisure are aspects of my wholeness that I have either judged or denied. Furthermore, when I embrace time as an ally rather than an enemy, I feel like I am healing a deep intergenerational wound. I have no idea what to do with what feels like an abundance of time. I choose to allow myself to flow with time and leisure and resist my urge to control time. With this awareness comes freedom.

I remember how I gradually substituted the word "sacredizing" for "wasting" when I moved away from my strong inherited Puritan work ethic. My intention to align with flow and let go of control gained the attention of my ego. Immediately an old, insistent inner voice confronted me once again with, "Who do you think you are?

I replied quickly, "I am a woman who is determined to live my own story and claim my wholeness."

Sometimes breaking rank extends beyond personal beliefs to challenge cultural beliefs. For example, the energy of ferocity is not valued in my Anglo-American culture, especially for women. Even when I consider the feminine face of God, I do not see ferocity as an aspect of Divinity.

For several weeks, I awoke in the morning feeling "ferocity" on my lips without any remembrance of dreams or connection to teaching that happened during the night. I pondered the idea throughout the day and still came up with nothing. I pushed the notion away because I felt uncomfortable. Clearly, I had created a split in my consciousness and ferocity wanted to come out of the shadow.

When I heard about a creativity workshop offered by my friends Hilary Pidden and Libby Moore, I signed up to explore ferocity because they promised the experience would be centered in silence and art would be the medium. I looked forward to paints and pencils replacing words and analysis.

During the opening meditation, I saw a symbol of a large bird's nest decorated with purple and pink ferocity leaves. I had no idea how I could reproduce the image that I saw in my mind's eye and almost left the workshop. Then I looked out the window at the forest and knew running away was not the right action, especially since I had obeyed the magnetic energies of Future Pull when I signed up for the experience.

I whispered to myself, "Rosie, respect that ferocity has a face. It is asking you to take up the face."

I claimed a large table for myself, grabbed colored pencils and worked non-stop for over an hour. When I stepped back to take a long look at my brown and yellow straw-like nest, I realized I had drawn it from the perspective of looking down from heaven. That seemed a bit bizarre and also perfect. The asymmetrical ferocity leaves were bright pink fringed with purple. Certainly, not the color I imagined for ferocity. I also noticed that I had left a hole at the bottom of my nest so the energy of ferocity had an outlet. As I merged energetically into the center of my ferocity nest, words tumbled out and I quickly grabbed a pen to capture them before they disappeared.

Ferocity

Fiery
Energy
Rises
Outward
Creating
Intense Truths
Yet to be lived into

After everyone had finished, we gathered in a circle to share our artwork and the stories of our creative process. After each person told her story, the group offered feedback. I realized I was uncomfortable about sharing my ferocity nest because I projected that the group judged people who spoke about the shadow side of light, especially since most of them introduced their creations as testimonies of love, compassion, and healing.

When my turn came I spoke about my initial self-judgment and fear to build a nest for ferocity in my heart. As I read my poem, I realized that nobody looked at me. I was aware of the power and the passion in my voice as I spoke about the ferocity nest. When the time came for feedback or questions, no one spoke. Their silence did not surprise me. The facilitator invited individual responses for the second time. Silence. Then she said, "It looks like there is lots of room in your nest, Rosie."

"Yes," I replied, "This is a community nest."

As I looked around the group, they all lowered their eyes. I breathed and acknowledged to myself that I was not the only one in the group initially turned off by ferocity, yet the brown, woven nest was growing on me, softening me, inviting me to be even more curious.

After the workshop, I framed my ferocity nest and the poem. I hung it on my bedroom wall and said, "Thank you," each time I passed it. The energy of ferocity surrounded me during the following week and I grew to understand that ferocity resonated with a subterranean depth often relegated to personal shadow. I discovered that in order to integrate ferocity, I had to dare to be authentic without being afraid that I would hurt people's feelings and cause them to walk

153

away. Ferocity demanded inner strength, outward clarity and honest expression.

Looking back, I appreciated that if I had claimed the voice of ferocity during my recent Manifesting Miracles workshop, I would have challenged the women who shared the outdoor camping space with me for laughing loudly instead of observing silence. I wished I had said, "Your behavior is not appropriate when the sacred invitation is to visit with the night sky and listen to the earth."

I knew that Native American and aboriginal women's spirituality is rooted in the Earth, which is an extension of their bodies. They are comfortable expressing their emotions. My guides viewed ferocity as the polarity of apathy. I agreed to pray to Mother Earth herself and asked her how she wished to reveal her ferocity to me. I was surprised when the voice of ferocity commanded me to take a ferocious look at my relationship with my body.

Looking back, there is no question that I have a dismal history of denying the needs of my body. At times, I gave my body away, overworked, and often judged my body. In addition to trauma and neglect in this lifetime, I am certain I made vows of penance, pain, and suffering that I brought into this incarnation. Later in October, as I walked Virginia Beach, I acknowledged to myself that my body has been my shadow for decades.

Big breasts, small waist and tiny feet ruled in my family and I got lots of attention for my curves in high school. I wanted to resign from being a teenager. Looking back, I realized that I have battled between my sexuality and my spirituality most of my life and some of the karma came from "bleed through" past lifetimes. Unfortunately, I reacted to my own soul history by creating even more karma this lifetime.

Later as an adult I worked hard to release the body armor that I created to protect myself as a child. My favorite body worker commented that I held my exhale breath as if preparing myself for a blow. Being touched felt dangerous. Orgasms did not come naturally. Gradually, I let go of my long habit of numbing and stiffening my body for self-protection and surrendered to receiving pleasure.

Endometriosis created another challenge in my early twenties and I dreaded my painful monthly periods. A couple of D&Cs further alienated me from my body. Then came my unwanted emergency hysterectomy and the hormonal tsunami followed by my son's sudden death. It seemed like an all out assault on my physical body. The sleepless sweaty nights and my poor appetite during my grieving time sapped my energy and made me feel like a victim of my own body.

No question that my body has existed outside of love for way too long. Self-forgiveness and self-compassion do not come easily for me. I sense that until I am able to imagine my body as a blessing and a temple for my Spirit, it will remain a shadow wisdom teacher. When I decided to invest in bodywork, I made a big step toward being kind to my body. Once again, I returned to my journal to trace the threads of befriending my body:

What a gift I gave myself yesterday by going for a deep tissue massage in an air-conditioned space with a skillful body worker who was aligned with his soul purpose. Jonathan Hotchkiss announced that my left shoulder was noticeably higher than my right one, and it had begun to rotate due to lifelong conditioning. Using a technique called somatic experiencing, he invited me to become more and more aware of my body and its messages. Tracking my own physical experience felt foreign to me. Not only did I lack a vocabulary, my long history of numbing myself against pain and pleasure had made me insensitive to my body's responses.

Jonathan asked me to notice what happened when he deepened his pressure on my back. I felt a deep tiredness that bordered on exhaustion. As I relaxed into my tiredness, I felt scared—a feeling he reframed as terror. Letting go is not easy for me, the daughter of two battling controllers. When he gently invited me to become more aware of my breathing, it surprised me that breathing more deeply relaxed the muscles in my shoulders, neck and ribcage. Armoring my body to avoid pain and fear felt more familiar than relaxing my body. When I admitted that, I felt sad.

As I left the session, I definitely walked differently. My shoulders felt lower and my breath felt less forced. I even felt more confident about being able to relax. Somewhere deep inside I felt a small hope that I might even enjoy dancing again!

The following week, I returned for more bodywork with Jonathan. Again, he worked on my shoulders and ribcage. He explained that people who think they need to be in control often stop breathing when they get scared. As he had the week before, he invited me to bring more focused awareness to my present experience. No matter how present I tried to be, I kept returning to my inner two-year-old who felt helpless and terrified and had no language. My energy felt trapped deep in my pelvis. Jonathan gently suggested I imagine how my body wanted to move. My body responded immediately and my hips retreated into the fetal position. My fear carried the message: "I am not safe." In response, my breathing once again became shallow and I stiffened my back and my buttocks. That's when I noticed that my pelvis felt frozen in place. No wonder! Next Jonathan invited me to growl and track what happened in my body. The guttural noise felt like a relief! I growled several times—each one louder than the one before. Then I put my hands on my abdomen and growled even louder. I felt my resistance relaxing. "What movement would feel good?" Jonathan prompted. "I don't know," I said.

"Ask your body," he said gently.

Without thinking, I pushed my hands and feet into the table. The movement felt oddly comforting. Then he invited me to put my hands on my chest. That felt natural, like I was taking care of my inner little girl. For a second, I had a glimpse of myself as a sensuous woman behind all my armoring and conditioning.

When the session was almost over, Jonathan asked if my soul had a message for me. The message was immediate and clear: "You are safe when you relax." I breathed a long sigh of relief that felt like it had no end. Tears flowed.

Before I left the office, he wisely pointed out that I didn't want to be totally relaxed all the time because at times there might be a need for caution. I agreed and grabbed another Kleenex. I left his office feeling hopeful that I was capable of listening to my instincts that are centered in my body.

After the session, I felt more hope for a healthy re-connection to my body. I yearned to relate to my body as a temple of

Spirit because I have experienced that inspirational messages come to me through my body and somewhere deep inside I believe that embodiment is Divinity's explicit expression.

Later in the month I wrote in my journal:

Sleeping outside in my tent beneath a pine forest and ancient granite stones nourishes my body and my soul. I am feeling more at home in nature and more at home in my body. I don't have the words to track the connection yet—only feelings and sensations.

My granddaughter, Malia, is fifteen now. She too has shut down on her feelings and judged her body in order to protect herself. I listen to her with tears in my heart when she tells me that if she could will herself to be asexual, she would. I hug her and tell her that I am sorry that she has been hurt so deeply. We cry together. She too is an empath and, like me, she feels everything. I yearn to leave both my grandchildren a legacy of pleasure with their bodies; yet I have been celibate for the last seventeen years.

Malia asks me many questions about sexuality. I answer her candidly and preface my comments with the disclaimer, "This is my experience, Malia."

She generally asks her personal questions when we are at restaurants. Recently she prefaced her questions by saying, "Grandmom, I read an article about sex and women your age and I have a question for you."

"Okay," I replied.

"Well, the article said that women your age tend to sublimate their sexual feelings with knitting. And I wonder if that is true for you."

I wondered where she had read the article, but chose to let that question go. Instead I said, "Malia, have you ever seen me knit?"

"Oh, my God, Grandmom, don't tell me you still do it. That is just disgusting."

People at nearby tables covered their mouths and muffed their giggles. Then I replied,

"Malia, I sculpt—not knit."

She laughed and said, "Oh, thank God, Grandmom."

Her experience growing up is much more complicated than mine. She questions whether she is heterosexual, homosexual, bisexual or asexual. I did not have to deal with that dilemma when I was a teenager. I remind her that she has not had a serious crush yet and assure her that the answers will come with experience.

I celebrate Mother Earth as a living consciousness each Solstice and each Equinox. My soul begins to prepare for Solstice and Equinox a few days before they arrive. As a prelude to Equinox, I feel a deep stillness as I sit in meditation. I sustain my inner stillness for a week before the calendar event and the effects usually last a week after. Throughout I feel a sense of expanded possibilities and deepened peace.

When I was a kid, my brother and I used to take eggs out of the refrigerator on Equinox Eve and carefully place them on the kitchen counter. On the morning of Equinox each egg stood upright without toppling as it did on every other day of the year. This experiment that we did for years taught me about the natural balancing energy that accompanied Equinox.

For me, Equinox is an opportunity to review the past year and to be aware of what seeds took root, which seeds died and what seeds are ready to be harvested. The Earth enjoys balance between light and dark at this seasonal marker and I, too, listen for seasonal clues that remind me how to gain and sustain physical, emotional, mental and sacred balance.

I challenge myself to look at where I feel balance in my inner life and outer expression and where I sense imbalance. One of the out of balance patterns I notice is how much energy I devote to nurturing others. Like many women, relationships bring me joy and meaning. The balance practice that I committed myself to maintain until the Winter Solstice in mid-December is to gift myself with six hours of silence for one day a week. Time for a word fast and going within to discover who will show *up.*

Since working with Jonathan I felt more confident about listening to my body. In the early morning of the summer solstice I danced nude and alone in the moonlight to celebrate the beginning of the longest day of light.

I had forgotten that Dennis had mowed the lawn the day before until I danced so vigorously that I fell to the dew covered ground exhausted. When I stood up, my body was covered with grass clippings. Curling up in my yellow satin polka dotted sleeping bag was not an option. Rubbing the grass off my body didn't work because the night dew acted like paste for the grass. Putting my clothes on made no sense. I figured that nobody would be awake so I grabbed my umbrella and nimbly walked the quarter of a mile through the woods to my abode. A warm shower felt perfect.

Solstice afternoon I joined a group of women for a community ritual. I dressed myself in a deep purple knee length dress and wore matching dangly earrings and lipstick. I watched the other women move gracefully to the music and took cues as I loosened into my natural rhythms. I felt at home in my body and my movements felt genuine. I enjoyed the yummy experience of being spontaneous, welcomed in the group and less self-conscious dancing. Then I got blindsided.

A friend said to me, "You look too sensual to be here." Abruptly I stopped dancing to the reggae music and regressed into a shame attack. I remembered to breathe and memories of my mother being jealous of me flooded in. Before I disappeared into my past completely, I realized my friend's comment had rekindled deep feelings of vulnerability. A tiny part of me knew she meant it as a compliment, but shame swallowed me. I felt the urge to turn and run away, but out of the corner of my eye I spotted a big drum. I quickly walked over, grabbed it and pounded it hard for several minutes. Losing myself in the sound and sense of pounding the drum, I once again began to dance. Ferocity had won that day.

Driving home from the Solstice ritual, I suddenly flashed back eleven years to the time when I fell into a deep depression while visiting my parents in Old Orchard Beach, Maine. Once again, the impetus was feeling betrayed by a man whom I had I loved and trusted. Plus, I'd gotten poison ivy and it reactivated the brown recluse spider venom that remained in my body from the original spider bite from years before. Not only was I depressed, I also judged and then shamed myself for my inability to be present. Before depression struck, I prided myself on over-giving and over-working.

With little energy or life force and grounded in shame, I had no clue how to receive support from friends. I judged myself as selfish and then felt guilty for taking time out to rest and regain my energy. Friends did their best to remind me that they loved me; however, I could not take love in because I had no clue how to return love. I felt emotionally bankrupt, bereft and hopeless. Subsequently, I convinced myself that my guides had abandoned me because I was incompetent.

Somehow, I managed to exert what little life force I had to refuse to medicate myself. Although I knew the process of returning to myself would take longer without drugs, I felt determined to get to the bottom of my depression.

Nancy Carlson agreed to work with me at a reduced rate to identify and release my inner demons. Knowing I did not hide truth from myself when I wrote, she demanded that I return to journaling. Initially journaling made me even more depressed because I complained and lacked compassion for myself. During one session, I cried because I was convinced that my guides had abandoned me. Nancy challenged me to consider that I was the one who abandoned my guides and not the other way around.

Since I believed that intuition was connected to self-love, I took tiny steps to nurture myself. My coming back to myself included taking short walks, hugging trees, feeding the scrawny seagulls on the frigid beach, and visiting the library. Eventually, I meditated for short periods of time and began to contact friends even though I had few words to reassure them that I was coming back to myself.

My daughter's insistence that I return to New Mexico with her and her husband to take care of my newly born grandson and three-year-old granddaughter separated me from the isolation of depression and began my nine years of being resident grandmother.

Flash forward twelve years to October 2015, when I once again tore two ligaments in my left leg while carrying heavy boxes down a flight of steel stairs in preparation for moving into my abode in Virginia Beach. The original injury occurred more than twenty years ago, in Bali when I twice fell into a ditch after listening to two separate gamelan concerts. A local Balinese healer exacerbated the painful injury and my knee has been vulnerable since then. My Tai Chi teacher, Patricia Hoke told me that in Chinese medicine, the function of the knee is change. The metaphor of tripping myself up did not escape me, nor did the image of being brought to my knees, because that was one way to force me to face my vulnerability.

Four years earlier I fell through a rotten wooden boat dock into the water up to my hips when I was on vacation in Maine with my family. Both legs swelled to double their size. My daughter demanded that I go to the hospital. I refused. I had no appetite for hospitals.

Healing felt easier at home. I applied castor oil packs. The next day I pushed through my pain and joined friends for a walk at Boothbay Botanical Gardens and then entertained my grandson for a week. I did have the sense to take a vacation from my Pilates class because I knew that my legs could not bear additional weight.

If I had listened to the continuous messages that my body gave me, I might have spared myself more traumas. Once again, I entered the borderlands of having no energy to support myself or to give to others. I wondered how many lifetimes it would take for me to understand that physical fitness and spiritual fitness go together?

Recycled life lessons seem more painful. Years ago, I learned the hard way that if I did not balance my spiritual work with equal attention to my body, I jeopardized my health. That's why for each hour I devoted myself to soul readings, facilitating spiritual retreats, or doing workshops, I extended equal time to bodywork and relaxation. I adopted different body centered practices—Pilates, yoga, swimming, Tai Chi, walking and massage. I smile as I remember Barbara Cookson, my massage therapist in Stetson, Maine, saying to me, "Rosie, you're growing muscles." I do feel more physically fit and present than any time in my life. I cherish the moment when Noah said with pride, "Grandmom, you are an athlete in training."

Despite my dedication to keeping my body flexible, pain was once again my teacher—this time not emotional but physical pain. I often reminded myself of the statement, "Pain pushes until future pulls." Intuitively, I recognized that my present injury felt like a repeat karmic lesson. For me, karma is soul memory. Since I believe that the main spiritual law of the earth is karma, I understand that whatever I do not learn through experience, I am destined to learn through karma. Furthermore, since I am convinced that that learning and evolution are the goals of karma, I do my best to reflect on what is being reflected to me in the situation. Looking back, I see a tendency to resist karmic lessons until I am brought to my knees—which happened for the third time!

No stranger to Carl Jung's belief that God is what we trip over, I still had more learning to integrate. This time I was determined to work through my repetitious life lesson because I did not want to endure the pain and suffering ever again.

Since I was confined to the couch for several days, the recurrent theme of learning how to be in balance between receiving and giving and work and relaxation was impossible to avoid. However, this time I met myself differently. I purposely reached out to nearby friends and invited support and I posted a request for healing prayers on my Facebook page. Being surrounded by prayers felt like belonging to community even if I had no energy to give. Friends walked into my unlocked house, and each said in her own way, "Rosie, it is a pleasure to take care of you," or "What else can I do to make you more comfortable?"

Friends showed up with flowers, food, books, jokes, hugs, music, massages, and videos. Rather than repeat my pattern of feeling like a burden because I had nothing to give back, I accepted the love, kindness, and healing. Guilt and shame did not interfere. It felt like a miracle.

During my time on the couch I asked my spiritual advisor for an emergency session because I was determined to get this life lesson right—not perfectly. Right was good enough for me. I told Meghan my injury and recovery time felt like a time of revelation because so many thoughts, connections, and aha's came to me. Then I told her how I got depressed and judged myself eleven years ago as "nothing" and "worthless" because I had nothing to give back, but this time I never felt hopeless. I got frustrated—but not hopeless. Meghan said, "It's good you have learned a few things in eleven years." Then she asked, "So no longer is your self-worth based on what you can give?"

I appreciated the succinctness of her words, especially since I'd taken about ten minutes to describe my process that she encapsulated in thirteen words.

Before I hung up, I confessed that one night the pain in my left knee was so extreme that all I wanted was for someone to hold me and comfort me by telling me everything was going to be all right. Although I knew my response was a normal reaction to extreme pain and exhaustion, I felt needy and then once again was on the edge of judging myself.

She reassured me that upwards of ninety percent of the population want to be held when they are in pain. I sighed. Some younger part of me needed to be reassured that wanting to be held by someone did not mean I was co-dependent.

Truly, I felt as if I had regressed to the first step in Maslow's hierarchy—the need to be safe. For sure, I am more comfortable with the higher-level Being places. Being aware of the fears in my heart and surrendering anyway was once again the lesson. We ended the session joking about my healing into my humanness. When will I finally understand that the spiritual journey itself is the teacher?

Returning to limited mobility after seven days on the couch felt life affirming. I reveled at my first shower, my first walk outside to get the morning paper, and my first swim. My friend Dan Urton brought over a flaming red walker and set up a table on my back porch so I could resume sculpting outside. I also made a commitment to be kinder to my bones by losing weight and exercising more. Physical therapy strengthened my knees and I learned how to walk in alignment with my bones.

Humor also accompanied my injury and couch time. My evolutionary friend Joan Chadbourne commented, "This is a hell of a way to lose weight, Rosie!" Then she channeled information about the weight of family responsibility that I carry. Since I believe that an injury or an illness also has an emotional, mental, and spiritual aspect, I listened closely. I set an intention to drop the weight of family responsibilities and, also, the additional pounds that I accumulated while friends brought me really good things to eat and I couldn't exercise.

When I am upset and in danger of sinking into my personal story that often resonates with drama, karma, and trauma, I try my best to remember to pause, take a few breaths and identify the belief that triggered my reaction. For example, I had a date for New Year's Eve and, since I usually stayed home on New Year's, I was excited to join in the revelry at the Cayce's A.R.E. Center. Before the party, we enjoyed conversation in my living room until I said something that upset him and he walked out.

I was surprised, hurt, and then angry when he did not return. His leaving triggered an old belief that I did not matter enough. I energetically tracked that belief to my tummy and I felt about five years old. When I asked my younger self, "What are you feeling?" she replied, "Angry, sad and lonely."

Appealing to her from my seventy-two year old adult, I asked, "What do you need?"

She said clearly, "A hug and a cup of hot chocolate."

I hugged myself, fixed a cup of hot chocolate and then walked over to the New Year's Eve party to join friends for the annual midnight meditation. Friends walked me home and when we wished one another a Blessed New Year, I felt grateful and cherished.

l need to remember that when I am triggered by disappointment or disillusionment, I have a choice about how to respond, as long as I remain present and aware. I know that it is my soul that offers both growth and protection, not my ego which majors in maintaining the status quo and keeping me small.

Lifetimes of conditioning dissolved slowly. Breaking rank with what I previously valued was challenging. I, who refer to myself as the Queen of Surrender based on my journey of the last ten years, was now called to a deeper surrender. In the past, I concentrated on surrendering my judgments, limited beliefs, past life vows, as well as letting go of relationships and illusions. My current assignment to surrender involves letting go of my need to know, name, understand, or control.

CHAPTER 9

Meditation

*F*or me, meditating is re-centering. I enjoy meditating alone and in community. For the last four summers, Georgia and I have meditated every morning in my meditation loft in Stetson, Maine.

I feel blessed when my grandchildren meditate with me. When Malia joined me at Friends Meeting I was uncertain about how she would respond to an hour of group silence and meditation. After the meeting she surprised me by saying, "Thanks, Grandmom. For a whole hour, I got to watch how my mind works and sometimes I was not thinking anything."

Months later at Friends Meeting, I observed myself struggling whether to speak or silence myself. I kept making deals with myself—like I would speak after I counted to ten. Still I remained silent. A couple of times, I opened my eyes to see if anyone else looked as though they might stand up and speak. Nobody did. I closed my eyes once more, sighed and then re-opened them. Barb French looked directly at me as if she were energetically asking me, "What's in your heart?" I accepted her unspoken invitation and, without thinking, rose to my feet. Then I waited for the words to come.

I began by saying that I felt I was being stalked by surrender during my daily meditations as well as my dreamtime. I said that I awoke with the words, "There are no mistakes," as if they were the conclusion of a forgotten dream. I continued by sharing that I wrote in my journal about discovering that surrendering with an open heart instead of a clenched fist was easier when I trusted that there were no mistakes. I spoke about how much I longed for my Dad's death to be easy and peaceful. It wasn't. Tearfully I admitted how I surrendered all of my knowledge of how to support him in his dying process, even though I had lots of experience of being a midwife for others who died. Letting him die in his own way and his own timing was another surrender for me and I intuit for him, too. At the end, I asked everyone to hold me in prayers.

Life has taught me that the real test of my meditation practice happens when I get up from my chair and re-enter the world in a meditative way. Driving is my biggest test. One day right after meditating, I hopped into my car to drive to the swimming pool. Another driver cut me off at the end of my street and I impatiently pounded my hand on the steering wheel. The thought that came to me was "temporarily out of service."

Since I enjoy challenging myself, I took the Edwina Gaines challenge of no negative thoughts for twenty-eight consecutive days because research suggests that it takes that amount of time to change a habit and create new neuro-pathways. Several times, I managed to get to the eighteenth day without a negative thought. Inevitably, I broke my positive record on day nineteen, always when driving. Then I had to begin at day one again. However, since I am a creative woman, I decided to walk instead of drive for the last ten days.

On day twenty-two, I walked to the Laundromat, congratulating myself all the way. When I finished loading the washing machine, I discovered that I had forgotten detergent and quarters. An expletive erupted from between my lips. Once again, I returned to day one. However, I am not a quitter and I persisted, acknowledging that discipline is a necessary part of the spiritual journey. Three months went by before I reached twenty-eight negative free days, and I treated myself to a pedicure.

I am fascinated how the stories that I attract coincide with my inner work. Once again, I return to my journal for another story:

Who knew that the power and stillness of meditation extended to inter-species communication? Today I watched a lone surfer playing in the waves. Then I spotted shiny, grey bodies surfacing and then disappearing. The dolphins were back! The surfer must have spotted them too because he began paddling fast in their direction.

They looked about fifteen feet ahead of him and as I watched the race, I realized he would never catch up to them even though he was a powerful paddler.

I wanted to yell, "Stop pursuing. Surrender. Invite the dolphins by your stillness," but I knew he could not hear my voice over the crashing waves. But when he abruptly stopped paddling and stood up on his board, I was convinced that we had connected intuitively.

Then I focused on the dolphins again and I wondered how they would respond to the upright, motionless surfer. As I watched, the dolphins changed course and swam toward him, I sank my feet deeper into the sand and questioned, "Is this really happening?" When the dolphins came within three feet of the surfer, he instinctively lay down on his surfboard. The dolphins surrounded him and swam round and round his surfboard. On the shore, I did my own version of a dolphin dance. I applauded, unable to contain my glee.

When the surfer returned to shore, I greeted him. As he reached out to shake my hand, he said, "I had this feeling that you somehow were part of that once-in-a-lifetime adventure."

I nodded and said, "I appreciated the whole thing, every moment of it."

"Awesome, huh? Who knew that if I remained still, they would circle around and visit me?"

I smiled, satisfied that the two of us appreciated what had just happened and my wide-open heart reached out to him in gratitude to the dolphins for how naturally they had responded to the surfer's non-doing. I gave thanks for this magical day and the practical lesson in applied meditation.

Enjoying the surfer's adventures, reminded me of how much I enjoy body surfing—no boards to lug and no extraneous equipment. On the way back to my house, I mused about how I instinctively know seconds before I make a decision to catch a wave, whether it will be a spectacular ride or just average. Timing is everything. My eyes are on the wave. My body is poised to dive as I hold my breath. My intention is clear. My body knows when I am "on" and when I am "off." On my longest rides, I instinctively merge with the "wave field" seconds before it washes over me.

Malia observes me and believes I have it all: a fulfilling profession, freedom to go and do anything I wish, no man to take care of, and an abundance of friends. She calls me lucky. I remind her that I have made zillions of choices to be happy. Then the teacher in me reminds her that my life is a reflection of my strongest beliefs.

"Yes, But" is often her first response and it distances her from accepting that she is responsible for her life and its transformation or misery. I am happy that I still have an influence even though being absent from her everyday life makes it hard to have an impact.

If I could wave a magic wand, my granddaughter would learn how to meditate and gain control over her emotions. Over reacting or under reacting and shutting down her feelings are two ways she has learned to cope with her sensitivity. The middle way is balance and clarity.

I am amused when Life offers me an opportunity to reinforce my meditation practice. Of course I wrote about it in my journal.

I could not have predicted that winning a four day-three night getaway at a year round timeshare resort in the Blue Ridge Mountains of Virginia offered me an opportunity to defend my daily meditation practice.

The only cost the stay involved was a mandatory ninety-minute tour that included inspecting three different condos. Initially, my friend Alice Monroney and I were relieved when our tour guide, Robert, assured us he would not pressure us. Earlier that morning I had written on the form that the only reason we came to the timeshare resort was to relax and enjoy a free weekend. He only asked that I keep my mind open. I agreed.

172

He took us on a walk around a large compound that included a swimming pool, steam rooms, two saunas, ping pong tables, noisy video games, and a basketball court. The outdoor water park was impressive but we did not linger there. Then we did a walkthrough of three different condos, each with a fireplace, a view of the mountains, a large TV, and the expected furniture and amenities. None took my breath away. We were polite but not enthusiastic.

Cookies and other potential buyers collided in the final house where Robert got out his official black book, scribbled some figures and then once again summarized the advantages of buying into the timeshare. He emphasized that my grandchildren would create memories here and reminded me that I had an option of willing my deed to them so they could remember me every time they visited. That felt creepy rather than attractive.

When we returned to the original building I thought it was the end of the tour and we would receive vouchers worth $250. Wrong! I recognized some of the people who surrounded us and I watched them listen obediently to their sales person. Then Robert extended another "last" offer with a 30% discount.

His high-power sales pitch turned me off, especially when he had promised at the beginning of our tour that he would not pressure us. I responded by saying, "Okay, if those are your terms, it is not a deal," and leaned forward in my chair to leave.

"What is your chief objection to accepting this outstanding offer?" he asked.

I firmly said, "I never make major decisions without meditating first. Besides I want to swim in the pool, check out the hot tubs and the health spa, do some art in the art studio, and walk the grounds."

Without skipping a beat, he replied, "I'll tell you what, why don't you take five seconds and meditate and then we can do the paperwork?"

Game over. As far as I was concerned, he did not honor my process.

He turned around and glanced over to the five people at the big desk who watched us. "Just a minute," he said, "my boss is over there and maybe he feels generous today and can offer you an even a better deal."

I took a deep breath and recommitted to not being bullied into signing any agreement until I had meditated.

The overweight negotiator sat down at our table and asked Robert why he had called him over. Robert said he liked us and he wondered if his boss could offer us something that would close the deal.

Before the supervisor began his high-powered sales pitch, I said, "I just want you to know that if your offer is contingent on me signing a legal document before I leave this table, I am not interested."

He smiled and said, "Yes, those are our terms and we make no exceptions because it would not be fair to all these other potential buyers."

Robert interrupted and said, "Rosalie meditates before she makes any decision and that seems like it is our only obstacle to closing the deal."

The supervisor handed us a sweeter deal, which involved taking over a mortgage from someone who had backed out of the agreement after paying for three years. In addition to a 50% discount, I would also take over his Gold Card, which entitled me to many other discounts.

"Don't you agree that this is an exceptional offer?" he asked.

I again demanded time to meditate. Request denied. Supervisor exited. I was finished. Then Robert said, "How about if I do the paperwork and you can see this offer all written up and then you can sign?"

Time was more than up. I got up from my chair and reached out my hand to thank him for the tour. He disappeared without a goodbye. I gathered up the paperwork, and Alice and I exited the building. As we walked across the lawn, Robert ran after us and shouted,

"You did not sign the sign off papers. I just left you to get the papers which you have to do as part of the completion of the tour." He motioned for me to follow him back to the big room. Then he told me that in order to get my Gift Charge card of $250, I had to see one more representative.

I felt in touch with my inner ferocity and was determined to collect the gift card and to stick to my demand to meditate before making a financial decision. In the negotiating process, I learned a valuable lesson. Meditation has more benefits than the usual health, clarity, and non-attachment. It helped me stay true to my values and thwart a predatory salesman.

I am convinced that love connects dimensions and love is who we are. When I open my heart wide to receive love, I intuitively beckon synchronicity. As I relax with awareness, synchronicity becomes my playmate. Synchronicity is like a signpost that signals that I reside in my soul story—sort of like God giggling. Surprises co-exist when I open up to my intuition and then take action. Picture me writing outside on my deck when my intuition interrupted me with the following three words: "God's time" and "beach"

Ever since I was a little girl, I have enjoyed playing in God's time. I have no idea how this game started. Nobody taught me. Perhaps I brought it in from another lifetime. I plant myself somewhere and imagine God is sitting with me. We wait together for someone to approach us or sometimes we take the initiative and join someone. No agenda. Simply shining our light.

I quickly put on my bathing suit and walked twenty feet to the beach. The tide was coming in and I watched a middle-aged woman toss bread to the hungry seagulls. I clapped as one bird caught a piece of bread crust in mid-air. The woman got up from her chair and walked over to my blanket. We greeted each other as naturally as children do when they meet each other as strangers at a park or playground.

"Are you from around here?" she asked politely.

"Right down the street," I said.

"And you?" I inquired.

"I was born here. My Dad was in the Navy. Actually, I was born in the old hospital that used to be on 21st Street. Now I live in Asheville, North Carolina."

"So, you have come home?" I responded.

"Guess you can say that. I've come back to the ocean. I hope it can bring healing and some resolution to my shattered life," she added as she closed her eyes and bowed her head.

"Water is a natural healer," I said. "It has no expectations and it will support you while you float."

We both looked away from each other and out toward the crashing waves.

"I am trying to put my life back together. It's complicated. My husband of thirty years died six months ago. We were separated when he learned that he was dying. He moved out, and we did not reconcile. I have four grown children and they are the best. The school I worked at said I was too distracted to work and at put me on a leave of absence".

Her words were labored and sounded chiseled with grief. Since I was on "God's time," which is always aligned with synchronicity, I asked,

"So, you are free to choose who you want to be and what you desire to do now?"

"Not exactly—well, maybe if I were not so exhausted from selling the house, disposing of all his precious belongings, and dealing with the myriad details of death." She sighed.

I reached out to hold her hand saying, "Grief is demanding in all ways— emotionally, mentally, socially, and spiritually. And I can imagine that your decision to separate from your husband before either of you knew he was dying makes your grief really complicated."

"Exactly. We did not do a legal separation although we both knew our marriage was done. So, I don't know if I am an ex-wife or a widow. And family, friends and even people who did not know us have stories about who I should be. And I will run smack into the middle of all their stories as well as my own memories next weekend when everyone gathers to celebrate his life at a memorial service.

She took a breath and said, "I can't believe I have just told you my whole story and we are not even on an airplane."

Then I asked, "I'm curious, if you had one wish about how you might live the next few years of your life, what would it be?"

Without thinking, she replied, "I would write. I've always wanted to be a writer and there never was enough time. But I don't know if I am being realistic or just running away from my life."

I shrugged and smiled at her.

"I have another question for you. Are you game?"

"Sure, why not? It seems like we were destined to meet and become beach buddies," she replied.

"I wonder if you dare to risk being delighted?"

She sighed and then said, "Nobody ever asked me that question before—especially recently. But I get survivor's benefits so I can support myself financially if I am frugal."

I nodded my head and then said, "I am a writer and I would have deep regrets if I had not followed my dream of being a writer."

Then she asked, "What motivated you to write?"

"The sudden death of my fourteen-year-old son, Mike. I desperately needed to reinvest in love and figure out a way to heal my broken heart and learn how to trust life, God, and the future again."

She sighed and then I sighed. Then she said, "I knew you were wise. A passion for writing and living through grief are two things that we share."

"Yes," I agreed, "and I think we have another belief in common."

"What's that?" she asked.

"We both returned to the ocean to heal. I am glad you escaped to the beach," I said quietly. "Want to go for a swim?"

"Someone warned me of the undertow earlier," she said.

"Can you swim?" I asked.

"Of course," she replied with a slight smile. "How about you?"

"I am a strong swimmer and also a cautious one. Besides how can we expect the ocean to heal us if we don't jump in?"

We scrambled to our feet and ran to the water's edge hand in hand. The last sound I remember as I dove into an oncoming wave was the sound of our laughter.

I never know how I will be asked to be of service when I am in God's time. Sometimes I wave drive by blessings or pay the toll for the driver in the car behind me. Other times I offer prayers or stop to listen to a stranger at the grocery store. When I am in Maine for the summer and fall, I invite a young person who appears to be without a home for lunch and conversation. Networking happens every time in the most surprising ways. Being in God's time is another way of being of service.

CHAPTER 10

Daughter-Mother Karma

I am not clear about where to begin writing about my mother and myself.

I believe we came into this lifetime with karma to work out. Looking back, I believe we both did the best we could do, and I gave up trying to break through the karmic knots—that is until a few months before my mother died on Valentine's Day 2016.

Edgar Cayce was convinced that nothing happened in outer reality before it was foretold in a dream. I agree. Exactly two months before she died in her sleep at home, I awoke myself from a dream of her. In the dream, we are attending a large conference and I am not sure if I am a presenter or a participant. During a break, I notice her in a group and when I pass by, I overhear her say something demeaning about me.

I surprise myself and walk over to the group and say calmly and distinctly, "Mom, let me show you who I really am." Then I fill the room with bright, white light. The brilliance of the light was so stunning that I woke myself up because I thought it was the middle of the day—not 2 AM.

I hugged myself tight and felt a huge rush of energy. From somewhere deep within me, I knew the karmic knot that we had interwoven had loosened. I had allowed myself to be seen with no cover-up, excuses or drama. Instead of returning to sleep, I walked outside and down the wooden stairway to the dark beach and did a liberation dance on the wet sand. Then I said a prayer out loud and sent gratitude to both of us for the unexpected resolution.

A few weeks after the dream, I signed up for Roger Housden's online memoir class. The synchronicity of that decision still makes me shiver and I will be forever grateful to him for teaching me the technique of writing in the third person in order to gain clarity. Although I was nervous about submitting the following assignment because I felt vulnerable writing from my own emotional experience, I sent the story off before I changed my mind.

April 15 2012

Mother and daughter sit at the long, oak dining room table playing a game of gin rummy. It is about ten o'clock. Earlier in the evening, they sipped a glass of wine as they reminisced about the missing man, the husband and father who died fifteen months ago. The mother reminds her daughter that she was married for more than sixty years.

Without any noticeable sign of being upset or angry, the eighty-eight-year-old mother looks directly at her sixty-eight-year-old daughter and says, "I have hated you from the moment you took your first breath." She speaks the truth she has held in her heart for almost seven decades as if she is announcing the weather. Then she sits motionless, never blinking, as if waiting for her daughter's reaction.

The daughter looks stunned. Then she puts her hands on her heart. A look crosses her face that telegraphs that her entire life makes sense in that moment. As the daughter watches, she intuits that she understands the enormity and the pain of the moment and she also applauds her mother for her honesty after so many years of pretending.

The daughter stares at her mother, perhaps trying to comprehend when her hatred had begun and what she had done wrong that was so unforgivable. Many minutes elapse before the daughter asks in a shaky voice, "What in the world did I do to cause you to hate me?" *as she holds back her sobs.*

"Because your Grandmother loved you unconditionally from the moment you were born. You didn't have to do anything to win her love."

The daughter smiles and replies, "Yes, we cherished each other."

"Yes, and that is why I hated you. You didn't have to do anything to earn her love and I tried unsuccessfully my entire life to win her love and it never happened," *replied the mother.*

"Soooo," *the daughter stammers, unable to make sense of the tangled history.*

"All I wanted my whole life was to have my mother look at me the way she adored you," *said the mother.*

Then the daughter pulls away from the table. The mother resumes shuffling the cards and the daughter reaches out and puts her hands on top of her mother's hands saying,

"Mom, we have to finish this conversation. The game can wait."

The mother sighs and says, "Your Grandmother loved you from the moment you were born."

The daughter is speechless and looks at her mother's face intently as if searching for more information or perhaps answers. Then she hugs herself.

Recovering her voice, she stammers, "But I wasn't even part of your original family system."

"That doesn't matter and never will," the mother screams and lays her playing cards on the table, announcing the end of the card game and the end of the conversation.

The daughter moves her chair back and stands up. Then she says with a tone of resignation in her voice, "I wish we could have talked about this a long time ago and I know there is nothing I can say now or maybe ever to make this okay. I also will not pretend. So, I am leaving now.

"Where will you go? It is late and you had a glass of wine."

The daughter looks surprised at her mother's concern and also flabbergasted. She reaches out a hand to her mother and her mother flicks the air with her right hand.

"Mom, my spirit is not safe here in this house with you and now I know it never was. I need to be somewhere I am safe."

"I will never let you go. If you leave this house, consider yourself disinherited," the mother says in a loud, threatening voice.

The daughter stifles a half whimper, turns away, and walks to the door.

Once in her car, she tries to figure out where she will stay for the night. It is thirty-four degrees outside. She watches the lights in her mother's house go out one by one. First the light in the dining room, then the light in the hall leading upstairs to her bedroom and finally the light in her bedroom. The house is dark.

Months later, the daughter tells a friend about a vivid memory of visiting her grandfather thirty years earlier when he was in the hospital two days before he died. She confides how, as she sat by his bed and held his thin, shaky hand, he asked her to make him a promise. She agreed.

'Promise me you will stop trying to win your mother's love,' he demanded in an emotional voice. 'I have lived a long life wanting love from your mother and until recently, I did not know that she does not know how to give or receive love.' He wiped fresh tears from his eyes. "I don't want you to die miserable like me because you did not feel loved by your mother. Promise me you will stop trying to get her to love you."

She would have promised him anything. She nodded. He closed his eyes and said, 'That's my girl.' Then he went to sleep.

The next morning, he was alone when she visited him. He looked up as she crossed the large, private white room to his bedside. When she leaned over to kiss his whiskery cheek and reached out for his hand, he said, "June, I didn't think you would come to say goodbye to an old man who is dying." She was startled. He mistook her for her mother. Without hesitation, she bent down once again and whispered in his ear, "I love you, Dad." He smiled and sighed and she thought she saw a flicker of joy light up his face for a moment. Then he closed his eyes and died a few hours later.

For years, I wondered if I had done the right thing. She confessed to her therapist and told a few close friends. Still the question weighed on her mind. Then she remembered the joy on her grandfather's face and knew he had died in peace."

During the four years since she walked out of her mother's home, she has grieved and healed some of the wounded places within herself where she believed that she deserved her mother's anger and hatred. She also regretted that she did not have the compassion at the time of the honest encounter with her mother to feel the anguish and isolation that her mother must have experienced for seven decades.. She also honored the paradox that her mother was a good mother to her son, Mike, and a devoted grandmother to her three grandchildren and her seven great grandchildren. The karma remained between mother and daughter.

The unloosening did not stop there. My friend Robert Powers, who practices astrology and psychotherapy, remarked that belonging, betrayal, and empowerment were huge themes in my birth chart. Months later at supper, Robert spoke passionately and regretfully about how deeply his life was impacted by his narcissistic father. I listened intently to his all too familiar story while I checked off similar experiences that I had lived through with my mother who never admitted being wrong, lacked empathy, had a deep need for validation and appreciation and could not see and appreciate me as a separate person. I was stunned by the similarity in patterns.

When he described his last visit to see his father in the hospital before his father's imminent death terminated their father-son relationship this lifetime, he sounded sad. "Nothing changed," he said and did not add any details. Those two words, "Nothing changed," zoomed directly into my heart. The tenacity of karmic patterns grabbed my attention as well as my breath. Even his father's imminent death did not interrupt or influence his father's well-learned narcissistic behavior.

As I drove the twenty miles home, my heart felt heavy and my head pounded. Looking back from a perspective of almost three quarters of a century, I appreciate that I entered an alien world where I was not allowed to be more conscious than my parents, where empathy was judged as weakness and intuition was treated as some form of black magic. My mother did not understand me and often told me that she felt overwhelmed by my Spirit. Because she seldom connected with her own soul, she could not meet mine.

I have a freeze frame memory of when she told me that she did not enjoy going places with me because she claimed that I lit up the room and everyone wanted to talk to me and she felt like a nobody. I was sixty years old and she was eighty when she confessed that secret to me. Her words astonished me, even though I was aware she had competed with me for decades. From an early age, I responded by dimming my light because being punished by her silence was too painful. Becoming less visible, less energetic, less intelligent, less intuitive, less compassionate, and less creative did not serve my soul purpose or me.

Diminishing myself was the opposite of expanding my love. What a sucky double bind. On the other hand, competing with her also felt crazy. Now I realize that my mother was describing my energy. I do carry a high frequency love vibration. Loving is authentic being for me. Side stepping my mother's narcissism did not work. People still noticed my light and wanted to be near me.

About mile ten, I committed to doing a release and forgiveness ritual. Decades ago I read about a recapitulation ceremony in one of Carlos Castaneda's books in which he recalled every incident that he remembered about a person who had been a shadow wisdom teacher for him and released and blessed and forgave each event until he had let go of every incident. I had enacted a similar recapitulation ritual a few times as a way to let go of former lovers, but this one felt different—as though it had the energetic potential to break through generations of mother-daughter karma.

Once home, I gathered a handful of long, white tapered candles, healing crystals, and sage. Very deliberately, I took a shower and decorated myself in a long, red flowered, ceremonial robe. Then I smudged myself in the traditional way before I entered my meditation room. Next I placed the candles and a photo of my mother on the altar. I said a prayer and invited all of our guides from the beginning of time to witness the ritual. Then I lit the first candle and traveled back in time to my first memory. One by one I blessed and released each memory and forgave both her and myself when appropriate. I also acknowledged that I was not the daughter that she would have wished and I also admitted that she was not the mother I would have wished. Somehow that acknowledgement freed each of us to live into our futures.

Then I paused and returned to the candle light ritual and expanded my forgiveness to extend across time to heal any and all past lifetimes when we had hurt one another. Five candles and six hours later, the letting go ritual was complete. I treated myself to another shower. Sleep came fast. I had a strong inner knowing that more karma had released and sensed the stirrings of the possibilities of peace between us. What seemed impossible to create on the human level was somehow addressed in the spiritual realm.

Four hours later my daughter called to tell me my mother had died and I realized she died less than an hour after the completion of the release ritual. She was not sick. She had no health complaints. She died in her bed and not a hospital or nursing home. I was struck with how her death coincided with the completion of the ritual and will forever be convinced that our souls communicated and there was no more to do together Earthside.

Yet I did not know how to react to her death. She had refused to speak to me for the last four years of her life. Understanding that revenge is one of the weapons of a narcissist did not ease my pain. I felt like I had already grieved her absence from my life, yet I never had a dead mother before. I was struck by the irony of her choice of Valentine's Day as her departure date. She, who had corseted her heart from me excarnated on the biggest love day of the year. I saluted her.

Looking back, I did not know where to go or what to do. Nobody in my life in Virginia Beach had ever met my mother. Few knew any of the painful details of our karmic relationship. I was going up the steps to Friends Meeting when the news came. I considered retreating to my car and then overrode that idea in favor of sitting in silence. During the meeting, I considered speaking about my mother's death but chose to be silent and present for whatever needed my attention.

I didn't expect to find myself tracking my mother in the afterworld. In the past when I tracked people's energy, I made an intention and asked permission of the Inspirited One. This was different. Even stranger—my mother recognized me by my light and energetically reminded me of the dream a couple of months before when I had shined my light. I have always believed that our personal refection of light was our soul's signature, and I was taken aback that she recognized my soul. At last. She did not seem surprised that I knew how to track and support her.

I promised to check in and help her if she needed additional support. She agreed. Ours was a relationship in evolution and we had definitely met one another. Later I called my friend Rachel Leah, author of *Safnah—Death-Birth Threshold*, who is a professional medium and asked her to check in on my mother. She called back and said, "Your mother is adjusting nicely and when I offered to assist her, she energetically thanked me and said her daughter was watching over her and that was all the help that she needed."

When I called Meghan to request an extra session to make sure I was not doing a spiritual bypass in regard to grieving my mother's death, she suggested since the historical vibrational level between us had been so far apart, it was important to look at how far each of us had come. For sure, the months leading up to her dying time contained slivers of hope, cooperation, and compassion.

I made the choice to be compassionate about how I looked at her part in the karmic knot that we had co-created because I had no idea what she had lived through. I asked countless times and she chose to be silent. I also acknowledged that she was a nurturing grandmother to my son, Mike, especially when I attended a commuter college and she cared for him full time for three years. I feared that if I button holed my compassion, I risked becoming cynical and closed hearted. In time, I hope that I will appreciate other gifts that my mother gave me. I will do my best to keep an open heart because anything less lowers my love vibration.

A few months later I learned that she had written me back into her will and my inheritance felt doubly blessed because she had let go of her long-standing grudge. That was much more important to me than being a beneficiary.

It did not occur to me until recently when I wrote in my journal that I had offered the same legacy to my mother that I had offered, on her behalf, to her father—Love—and I felt the beginning of joy arising in my heart.

I admit that mine was an ambitious and somewhat arrogant soul agreement—to introduce a higher frequency love vibration into my birth family where the generational ideals were duty, hard work and responsibility. Yet my soul was aligned with a more refined and conscious way of loving—love as reverence, love as beholding, love as Oneness.

Five months after her death I found a note written in pencil that she had written two years before she died. She wrote it during the time of silence between us. I shivered and then cried as I read, "I was proud to be your parent." How I wished she had broken through the spell of her narcissism and written, "I was proud of you."

I have sat with many families and assisted loved ones during their dying time and I am aware that transformation often happens during the transition from this world to the afterlife because everyone lets go of their egos for a limited time and soul-to-soul communication is possible. Maybe, in spite of all our emotional collisions, heartbreak and estrangement, in the end we each had a loving impact. Maybe close to the end of her life and the beginning of her afterlife, she saw me and loved me for whom I am and what I came to do. I acknowledged her for her willingness to receive me.

Remembering all the movement in the inner planes that took place weeks before my mother's death gives me hope. At the end, our souls were open to one another. I wonder how our experiences in life and with each other would have been different if we had begun our life together the way we ended it. Maybe next lifetime.

CHAPTER 11

Mother Mary and The Healing of a Past Lifetime

I wanted to be finished writing my eighth book *Soul Befriending* at about the nineteenth month marker. It took almost two years and I comforted myself when I remembered that Edgar Cayce believed that patience was an ideal, like a soul quality. Holding my energy field open to catch the call from Future Pull was not easy. My ego bullied me. Although I was impatient to complete the book, I knew I would be unhappy with myself if I ended the book prematurely. However, I knew intuitively that there was something important that I had not lived into and I overrode my ego and waited until the concluding chapters claimed me.

The first clue that caught my attention was when I was called to pray publicly three times in one week. Although I agreed, I was aware that I put brakes on myself, and I had no clue why. Ordinarily when I channel, pray by myself, or meditate, I am spontaneous and passionate. However, I was aware that I resisted connecting deeply with the emergent energy of public prayer. My heart hurt and my stomach cramped.

Although I had no specific past lifetime memories, I sensed that I was in the midst of a bleed through past lifetime. I trusted my soul memory to fill in the details. Although

I felt afraid, courage and commitment fueled my intention to remember as I overrode my ego that did its best to keep me trapped in status quo. Remembering that ego lacks a spiritual perspective comforted me.

Once I committed myself to discover why fear collided with my intention to pray in front of groups, my reality changed. Days went by and I, who considered myself a wordsmith, had no words to describe or understand what was happening inside me. Then, without warning, the traumatic details of an un-integrated past lifetime were downloaded and I questioned whether remembering was in my highest good.

For weeks, the past life trauma of being beheaded while I was engaged in rapturous prayer kept me captive to my historical personal story. Gradually, I recognized that my present day soul purpose, five hundred years later, is similar—to remind people that nobody needs an intermediary between self and God. "Go direct" is my message and practice, as it was in the long ago lifetime where I was murdered because of my passionate spiritual beliefs.

Even though I felt paralyzed when I imagined engaging in ecstatic prayer again, my commitment to reclaim rapturous prayer as a gift equaled my total commitment to raising Noah and Malia for nine years. No question that the subsequent intimate, life-changing encounter with Mary impacted me as deeply as Mike's death. I had no idea how long reclaiming ecstatic prayer would take. Yet time didn't matter. I was in.

Here's the paradox—only when I let go of my insatiable need for words, did I discover adequate words to explain my second mystical union with Mother Mary. Once again, I returned to my journals:

While meditating as I do to greet each morning, Mary, the Holy Mother, announced herself as if she had expected me. I bowed my head in reverence. She smiled and then reached out with her energy to touch my face and hands and invited me to "uplift."

Instinctively, I raised my head as if to look up and beheld her as light. She seemed miles high, as if she stretched to eternity. Her midnight blue robe created a circle of light. Somehow I effortlessly entered the light circle.

Then I heard her voice gently command, "Yes. Good. Uplift. It is your essential nature. Uplift."

Still in my body, I craned my neck in an attempt to see how far she extended.

"More, more," she intoned.

Without knowing how the rising up happened or even where I was, I ascended in my light body. When we occupied the same space—not face-to-face, more light-to-light—she directed pure light to my heart.

For an instant I felt fear since my most recent memory of my heart being pierced open with light was painful. However, Mother Mary's gesture was gentle and I opened my heart wider in order to receive more light.

The only words that I remember saying were, "Your Grace, Your Grace," and then feeling a transfusion of light enter my body. Next came tears and a total body knowing that I had waited for this sacred union forever.

Mary's voice came as if from a far-off room.

"Yes, let your tears cleanse you and appreciate the rainbows that result. You feel temporarily over-

whelmed by the spaciousness of light. Remember that you are skin, bones, organs and light.

Then she glanced off to her right and, following her eyes, I saw Jesus just as I remember Him kneeling in prayer from an old picture my Grandmother had hung over her bed. As I beheld Him, reverence and devotion flowed into me. We did not interact. Just beholding Him was more than I ever expected.

As if Mary read my thoughts, she channeled, "There will be more. This was your orientation to Indwelling."

Before I could ask more questions, she gestured that it was time to return to my physical body and my time/place self.

Gently, I re-entered my physical body. My neck remained drawn upward as if I were still in touch with Mary's light. Then I saw that the light coming in through the meditation loft's open window surrounded and illuminated my hands—only my hands. My third eye hurt as it pulsated and I felt bubble-like sensations in my crown chakra.

Out of somewhere came the words, "With your permission,"

"Of course," I said out loud without being aware of what I had agreed to because an embodied sense of rightness filled my heart and reassured me. Then I uttered, "Praise be to Thee, Praise be to Thee" as adoration rippled throughout my body and my energy field expanded and filled up with crimson red.

Then Mary said, "It is the royal red which is the vibration of Divine Love. Welcome.

Without knowing how, I understood that adoration or praise were higher octaves of gratitude. My sense of humor took over and I laughed out loud as I made the connection that "praise" and "prays" are homonyms. In the midst of sending out praise, I was seized with humility and became infused with light and peace.

My body's direct experience was the only reality that mattered. This place of instinctual awareness felt both familiar and scary. Ecstatic prayer claimed me once again. I felt deep humility and deep praise often at the same time. Then huge orgasms of adoration overwhelmed me. My inner experience was like bowing my head low in humility and then raising my head and hands in praise.

I have felt adoration when my children and grandchildren were born and in Nature but I have never felt reverence for a person. In my personal experience, Mary existed in the Bible and the Catholic Church. We didn't talk much about Mary in the Methodist Church; however, in the state of fusion, she was intensely real.

Three days later I beheld Mary in meditation again. This time she named herself, the Lady of Light and I knew her as Mary. I did not merge or fuse with her. I remained in my own body consciousness. Yet I became enthralled as I saw her outstretched hands turn to light. Then areas of her visual body dissolved into light: first chest, then face, and then lower body. Because we occupied the same expanded, energetic field, I received the light that she radiated and I sent it out to the world—receiving and giving, receiving and giving. The gesture reminds me of one of my favorite Tai Chi movements. Tears streamed from my eyes. My shoulders dropped, unassisted by me and I jumped in surprise.

Mary remained. I was aware I was tracking the process and this time I sensed it was my witness mind—not my ordinary mind which is ego driven. Now that I think about it, I believe it was my witness mind that remembered the first Mary visit.

Later in the day I decided to try to re-connect with Mother Mary through automatic writing.

Me: Thank you Mother Mary for being here.

Mother Mary: With pleasure. How may I serve you, Dear One of the Light?

Me: You just called me Dear One of the Light. I am deeply touched. So much so that I cannot remember my question. (I take a deep breath and let it go.)

Mother Mary: Your surprise mystifies me. Of course, you are of the light. That is your lineage and your heritage, just as it is for all of earth's people.

Me: (Sigh) I believe that, mostly. My connection with you feels intimate and immediate and I am at a loss for words. That makes everything deeper and fuller and vaster and I am lost for the words.

Light, joy, and rapture infused the air I breathed during my intimate, energetic infusions with Mother Mary. We played together and swapped light and healing energies. A childlike ease that morphed into magic wove its thread throughout our visits.

There were times when we interacted in pure joy. There were also times when there was no difference between her and me. I was curious about how this all worked. As if on some kind of cosmic cue, Mary began to channel through me:

Mother Mary: If the only word you had in your vocabulary was Love that would suffice.

Me: I want to relish your wisdom, without asking for explanations.

Mother Mary: Bliss does that to human ones.

Me: Yes, I have felt the edges of bliss a few times in my life. It came as a surprise and then left as suddenly. When I meditate and pray daily, I have a sense of bliss lingering even after I resume my daily life.

Mother Mary: You are making a nest for bliss in your heart. With practice you will walk through your day with bliss always within your reach.

Me: Really? I am trying to imagine how that would be.

Mother Mary: No need to try. I will tell you and then you will have a word frame to ground yourself into an expanded version of yourself. Do I have your permission?

Me: Yes, of course.

Mother Mary: "Revelatory. Your experience of yourself, others and the world will be "revelatory

Me: (Big breath.) Oh my, that sounds very serious, although when I first heard the word, I immediately thought of "revelry" which I do enjoy. Then I understood you meant revelation—like deep truth.

Mother Mary: Both are accurate. A mystical orientation need not be dull or serious. You have read too many books. Yours is the path of joy and compassion.

Me: And how do revelations fit in?

Mother Mary: Perfectly My Dear One of the Light.

And then she disappeared.

Before I stood up, I vaguely remembered a conversation I had with Mike after he excarnated when he channeled information about revelry. I found a copy of *Healing Grief—A Mother's Story* and almost fell to my knees when I read:

April 13, 1983

Embrace your essence, which is pure attraction for revelry. Sometimes revelry is quiet; other times it is energetic. Always revelry moves toward revelation. Revelry is pure, magnetized energy. Be free to offer to others what you know to be the genuine truth of living and loving.

I needed to remember to re-ground—anchor myself in my body on the earth when I returned from a Mary merging. I felt touched by magic and carried her energetic imprint throughout the day. Sometime later I happened upon the term, "vivication" which means Mother Mary surrounds you with love from her heart. Then it is up to you to live the light, allowing grace to accomplish everything.

During the vivication process with Mary, Meghan challenged me to give up what I thought I knew in favor of gaining a bigger understanding about the nature of humility. Perhaps it is my feminist perspective that caused me to equate humility with being a doormat. Since I lacked a remembered history with practicing humility, I asked Meghan to share her experience. She explained in hushed tones that for her humility was a filling up with soul. For her, humility is love in action.

Often when I desire more clarity I invite my guides in for a conversation.

Me: I feel as if my mind has been quantumized or cosmicized, or any word that extends beyond expanded.

Guide: How about seized by the Divine?

Me: How odd that I consider myself to be a student of language and yet language no longer conveys my multidimensional reality. "Spaciousness" is the word that comes the closest to describing my consciousness. And I have experienced the energy beyond spaciousness.

Guide: Essence, perhaps?

Me: Yes. Thank you.

There was something familiar about the channeling on "quantumized mind" and I found the Future Pull thread in a 2011 journal:

Me: What is mind without words?

Guides: Energy. You are capable of interacting and communicating directly with your multi-dimensional mind.

Me: What are the advantages?

Guides: There are no unconscious or shadow aspects when you engage your multi-dimensional mind. Unconscious shadow and drama become obsolete.

Me: That sounds more energy efficient than the ways I've been brought up to think and act...

Guides: Quantum knowing overrides almost all the ways you have learned how to know. Remember that all exists as energy. Thoughts are energy. Emotions are energy. Memories are energy. Energy announces itself as frequency. Mind is a frequency receiver. Humans are now at an evolutionary precipice and are capable of embracing, exploring and expanding into multidimensional knowing. Each time you embrace self as an energy being, you touch in with your quantum mind.

Me: So everyone is capable of knowing everything. I have always believed that possibility existed, but I had no idea how I knew it. Plus, I lacked the ability to sustain that way of knowing and being.

Guides. No longer.

Exposing myself as a channeler of Mary placed me firmly on the edge of my own edge. I wondered if anyone would believe that I merged with Mother Mary and not roll their eyes or question my sanity. My experience with Mary on the inner planes reminded me of how I merged with Mike after he died. I did not initiate those transformative experiences when he channeled and we connected as souls. I knew that I was hanging out in uncharted realities and one of the biggest lessons for me was to trust my own inner experience as precious and valuable. Later in the day, I wrote in my journal:

As I embrace and radiate the frequency of love somehow I intuit that for me, Mary embodies the Divine Feminine Principle. Ever since I surrendered to camping outside I have pursued the Divine Feminine. Dare I believe that the Divine Feminine was in pursuit of me simultaneously? I intuit that the next step is affirming daily that my love is the greatest gift that I have to offer to others as well as myself.

A few days later, Mary and I continued our conversation through more automatic writing:

Mary: Grace, simply grace. Within grace is perfect understanding. Grace is unity.
Once you pulsate with the frequencies of grace, understanding transforms into revelation.

Me: (an audible outbreath) I know grace consciousness. I visit with that frequency at night—sometimes when I travel out of my body and sometimes when I dream.

Mary: Yes and sometimes when you meditate or visit with the night sky.

Me: True! I am catching the irony here! Having an impact is an aspect of my soul's purpose. Yet I do not allow myself to be available for the full impact of revelation because I am afraid I will be killed even though I know I carry that traumatic soul memory from a past lifetime. Fear ruled me.

Mary: Yet you yearn for passionate revelation and for Divine connection.

Me: Yes. I sense that I must be willing to receive from the Divine and trust that I will live to have a positive impact on others because of the love frequency that gets generated when I play with the Divine.

Mary: Yes, and Presence is impact. Silence is impact. Loving is impact.

Me: I surrender. Again. I commit to clearing a space for the sacred light.

Separate from Mary's compassionate, energetic frequency, my familiar guides channeled the following message that forced me to realize that I had moved far beyond cause and effect thinking:

Dare to merge with the energy of the Divine and see what evolves.
Your assignment is to take the first step to merge with that aspect of yourself that already lives in the future.
Dare to merge with the future that flows within you.
A tangible action is required.
Just do it!
Trust that more will be revealed as you take action.
At first, one small step is all that is necessary.

Grounding and later embodying the frequency of Future Pull required purposeful action. The night sky and the stars emptied me out and filled me up, often at the same time. I rested in Nature's womb and experienced abundance as one of the organizing principles of Nature as well as evolutionary consciousness.

Deeply trusting that action leads to deeper understanding, I committed myself to silence for two or three days in a row—a promise to stay in my own cosmic jet trails. As I looked back over my life, I was touched by how my relationship with silence had changed. My mother used silence as a punishment. I too have used silence to get even. To be in a healthy relationship with silence is healing for me as my journal entries reflect:

Silence is becoming a familiar. Friends give me a second look when I tell them I am not available for social activities during my designated two days of voluntary silence each week. I wonder how they would respond if I told them I yearned to dedicate even more days to silence. Somewhere I read that silence is oxygen for the soul and I know the truth of that statement in my bones.

During my "time in" without words, I walk outside and listen to the trees, weed my vegetable garden, sculpt, meditate, and behold the beauty that surrounds me. I stay away from my phone, computer, boom box, and, of course, conversation and people. Often my guides and teachers visit, but not always and I let go of any expectations that I will be entertaining them.

For weeks, I walked in the woods in contemplation. Whether the sun was out or the rain fell, I walked and prayed silently and out loud. I imagined that each time my foot touched the ground I was loving the earth. I moved in circles and spirals and did a few trance dances. I listened to the calls of the cardinals, blue birds, robins and owls.

When friends asked me how I was different after my voluntary silence, I struggled as though I were describing a snowflake to someone who lived on the Sun! The best I could do was to say that I felt friendlier with all that surrounded me, including myself. I felt overflowing reverence for life. I often told friends that silence was like a form of spiritual hygiene. Then I continued, saying that I felt like I was part of a family of mystics who had dedicated their lives to contemplation and silence. For sure, I felt more inner-directed and I no longer grasped or clutched onto time. I was more patient and accepting of myself. I even laughed at myself when I screwed up.

Breakfast with Hiromi once again nurtured my heart. I told her about my experience with ecstatic prayer and Mary and she listened deeply. When I shared that I felt like I was living in the world as a mystic, she looked at me and said, "I have always seen you as a mystic, Rosie, and your friends have, too. You are a very powerful person, very powerful." I nodded, took a breath and allowed her words to penetrate my heart and third eye.

When I acknowledge that I am being introduced to the mystic's way of Being, which centers on prolonged prayer and dare I write, joy, I feel energized. I listen daily for how to serve God and I acknowledge that I know about devotion and discipline because of my earlier training to be strong and resilient. Fortunately, I also know how to maintain my own counsel when necessary because often I have no words. Even the word "surrender" feels like mumbo jumbo.

Later I spotted this reminder from Richard Rohr, author or *Falling Upward*

"Do not let the word "mystic" scare you. It simply means one who has moved from mere belief systems to actual inner experience. All spiritual traditions at their mature levels agree that such a movement is possible, desirable, and even available to everyone."

I would never have guessed that recommitting to ecstatic prayer was part of connecting to my wholeness. During my time of residing in my inner life, I asked my guides and myself where my own healing needed to happen. Instantly I knew that actively participating in group prayer and daring to pray out loud with passion would bring integration and peace.

That's precisely when my friend Dan Urton invited me to join Glad Helpers. Initially I was put off by the name; however, I respected Dan and agreed to attend a meeting with him and Jo Ella.

I discovered that Glad Helpers had a long history since Edgar Cayce started it in 1931 and it has served as the healing legacy of the A.R.E. Edgar Cayce organization ever since. Several of the current members have served as healing channels of blessings for more than four decades and I felt the depth and power of their devotion the first time I walked into the meditation center on the third floor of A.R.E.

In addition to offering healing prayers for those who have requested prayers, we also pray out loud for people who join us and send healing prayers to every country in the world. The two-hour service ends with the laying on of hands. The first time I attended, I sat in Glen Caldwell's chair and received hands on healing prayers. I distinctly heard two words: "Relax" and "Self Love." Then I opened my eyes and looked around to see if anyone was actually whispering in my ear.

After the hands on healing infusion, I felt tired and surrendered to deep rest. My grandmother insisted that if I were not tired, I would not be able to sleep. She was right. Later as I continued to meditate at home, I received the second part of the message, "Relax into the meaning of your name for your name is the pathway to your soul." For three days in a row, sleep continued to call me to afternoon naps and I had a sense that I was being worked with, yet I have no specific memory threads. Surrendering to rest felt right. Maybe rest is the soul's Miracle Grow!

I am now comfortable praying passionately from my heart either silently or out loud in a group. When my prayers merge with the deep prayers of others, I feel uplifted. My soul has found spiritual community—a place where I belong. Healing happened.

In my experience, healing manifests when all blocks to love's presence are removed. I believe that each time we are wounded, whether physically, emotionally, or spiritually, it is because we have lessons to learn about receiving and loving. For me, every miracle is a demonstration that love is stronger than fear.

Later I became a member of Glad Helpers and I always invited the Divine to dance through me before I participated in hands on healing completely trusting that the healing energies empowered people to remember their innate wholeness. Slowly I learned that living my truth was healing for myself and others. In 2016 I established a Glad Helpers chapter in Bangor, Maine at Maine Holistic Center.

CHAPTER 12

The Power of Beliefs

*T*he power of personal beliefs stuns me at times and I imagine that my life might be simpler if I stuck to ordinary awareness, except I do not believe my consciousness is constructed that way. I do visit other realms and dimensions and I do believe in karmic repercussions, and I do my best to avoid creating more karma this lifetime. I choose grace over karma. I returned to my journals and found this story that is grounded in the personal beliefs of four people:

Meeting Lanie at June Bro's Chat session today was a joy. I was clear upon hearing her story that moving to Virginia Beach was a destiny date. When I asked her directly if she felt moving here was a soul call, she answered, "Yes" without hesitation. I noticed that she placed her hands on her heart as part of her response. Then I asked her the obvious question, "What's stopping you?"

She replied, "I put down money on an apartment in Richmond to do the training for selling time shares before I knew that my soul did not enjoy selling and I don't have extra cash to move here."

"I have three extra bedrooms. Move in for a month and you can check the area out and maybe even land a job at A.R.E. because I live almost next door. "

"You mean it? You don't even know me," she replied flabbergasted.

"I know you have a good heart and I enjoy serving as a cosmic catalyst for someone who is answering a soul call."

Lanie moved in and we enjoyed each other's company for a month before she landed a job at A.R.E.

My granddaughter's reaction surprised me, but then I remembered I didn't even know Lanie's last name when she asked me.

"Grandmom how do you know she is not a thief or even a murderer? She could kill you and steal all your stuff. Please tell me that you did not give her a key," Malia said.

Too late. I had already handed an extra key to Lanie. Later she told me that her sister shared similar concerns and confronted her saying, "Lanie, what if she is a pervert?"

Nobody persuaded Lanie or me to give up the plan. I believe we trusted the synchronicity of our meeting and our intuitions. And we were right. Not only did we become spiritual family, but months later I met her parents and fell in love with both of them.

Malia reminds me every time we are together that she is a realist and I am an optimist and she worries about me. As I listen to how she makes sense of the adolescent world that she lives in and the adult world that surrounds her, I understand. We do see the world through different lenses. She tends not to trust people while I tend to trust others until their actions prove me wrong.

There is always more to learn and more to teach—always more invitations to expand what I imagined possible. Infinity invites and I accept. Who knew that more dimensions of soul befriending awaited me when I showed up to do a book signing for Soul Befriending at Awakened Heart Church in Wilmington, Delaware?

When I first walked into the room, I was aware of a long line of In-Spirited Ones—people who were dead and stalled between dimensions. They acted as if they had expected someone to help further them to the next dimension, except their designated volunteer never arrived. I took advantage of the opportunity and volunteered to be a "pinch hitter."

As I assisted them, one by one, to continue their journeys in the afterlife, I remembered that when I resided in the Spirit dimension, my job was welcoming the newly "Inspirited Ones." No wonder being a midwife to people who are dying feels natural to me. Once again, it is all about energy and it is energy and love that connects dimensions.

The thread of assisting people to move on after their physical death continued to weave itself into my life when a man contacted me and explained that he was not able to stop thinking that his son was stuck "somewhere" and needed help. Initially, I did not understand that his son was dead. I agreed to track his son's energy and said I could not guarantee I would be successful because his son had a vote on whether to communicate or not.

I easily connected energetically with Matthew. His Dad was right. He was stuck between dimensions and did not realize he was dead. Energetically he said to me, "I try and try to talk to my parents and my brothers and they all ignore me. Why are they all punishing me? This feels like a horrible nightmare and I can't wake myself up no matter how hard I try."

As an empath, I felt his anguish and desperation, and I didn't like knowing I was the one elected to explain to him that he was dead. A shimmer of lights caught my eye off to the side, and I intuited that the lights belonged to family members who resided in Spirit. I wondered why they had not welcomed Matthew.

"Matthew," I said energetically, "I have some bad news to tell you."

"Are you kidding? Nothing could be worse than this."

Knowing there was no good way to break the news, I said, "Matthew, you are not having a never ending nightmare. You are dead."

"Are you dead, too?" he asked immediately.

"No, I am alive. Connecting with you is part of the work that I do."

"Prove to me I am dead and you are alive."

That stumped me. Never before had anyone ordered me to prove that I was alive while connecting between dimensions.

"What's the last thing you can remember, Matthew?"

"Being in the dark alley and hearing someone running towards me and then blackness."

"Yes, your Dad told me that you were murdered in an alley in back of a bar. Your assailant shot you in the back. You never saw him. You died immediately."

"But I was too young to die. I was only thirty-six."

I nodded and tried to comfort him energetically. I knew it was not appropriate to engage in a philosophical discussion, so I resorted to skills I had learned as a psychotherapist.

"I'm curious about what you believe happened after you die."

"If you are asking me if I believe in God or an afterlife, I do not. When you die, it's over. Kaput. The end."

"I understand."

"Look, Matthew the reason your family isn't talking to you is that they can't see you because you are dead."

"You don't get it. Being dead is worse than believing I am stuck in a nightmare. If I am dead, I am nothing. Nothing. Alone and nothing."

"Look, Matthew, I am in your energy field and we are communicating, so you are not nothing."

He did not dismiss me, so I pushed on.

"Matthew, you and I have different beliefs. You see, I do believe in life after death. And I have communicated with many others who have died, including my son who died when he was a teenager; my grandfather, Bompie; my Uncle Bud; several friends; and both my father and mother, who died when they were old. I also see lights out there in the distance. Based on my experience, I believe they are family members and perhaps friends who have passed on and have gathered to help you make this transition."

"If that is true, why can't I see them?"

"I don't know. Maybe because you do not believe it is possible for life to continue after the physical body dies."

"I was a strong believer in life and where did that get me?" he said, hurling his thought form toward me.

"Look, I agreed to do my best to track you because your Dad is worried. And I am feeling a bit helpless because I intuit there are family members standing by to welcome, comfort, and help you; but, you are keeping them out of your energy field because of the power of your beliefs."

"Have you ever met someone like me before?"

"No, I have not. All of the people I have tracked so far felt overwhelmed by the love of others when they made their transitions. I am struck by the power of your belief. I also feel enormous sadness for you and the reality that you are continuing to create.

"Then convince me," he challenged.

Once upon a time, I would have accepted his challenge. Perhaps because I am older and have gained both life and cosmic experience, I appreciated what was my work and what was not.

"That's not my job, Matthew. I am here to assist you, but that does not include converting you."

"So, what now?" he demanded.

"I don't know. I am willing to hold the space while you decide if your present belief serves you."

"How many lights do you see?"

"Four," I replied.

"I still don't see anything."

"I believe you. I can't make that happen for you."

"Are you telling me that if I loosened my belief in nothingness I will see the lights that you see?"

"I can't guarantee anything, Matthew. I wish could. I wish I could comfort you, too. I can't. But I do have a suggestion. How about allowing yourself to be curious about the possibility that perhaps your relatives are waiting for you?"

"I don't know how to go about that."

"You told me you were an excellent builder of beliefs, right? What if you experiment with dismantling your current beliefs a little at a time, like taking a Tinker Toy structure apart piece by piece? Then every once in a while look for the four lights."

"How did you know I used to amuse myself with my Tinker Toy set for hours when I was a kid?"

"I can't explain to you how I know things, Matthew, I just know."

Silence. Just when I started to worry a bit, he asked, "What other choice do I have?"

"Actually, you have zillions of choices, Matthew, even now."

Then I said, "Look, I am free for the day. If you wish, I will hang out with you while you practice. Then you won't be alone."

"Okay," he said.

Then I relaxed and he did whatever he did. Every once in a while he reported, "No headlights yet. Do you still see them?"

Energetically I said, "Yes." Four hours later, he yelled, energetically "I see four lights. I see four lights."

I watched as love filled his energy body and I could not tell if it came from him or from the four lights that were coming closer and closer. I said something to him, but the lights had enveloped him, and I suspected he could not hear me. Just in case we were still somehow connected, I said, "Goodbye and God Bless," anyway and watched until the one light dissolved in the distance.

Upon re-entering my physical body, I had good feelings about Matthew's moving on. I drank a glass of water and walked around my house to ground myself a bit before I called his dad. I thought about how closely all was connected, including dimensions and how he intuited that his son was in trouble. Then I imagined his dad finding peace knowing his son was now moving on. In spite of a horrible death, I had a soul sense that all was well.

Ten days after I returned to Maine for the summer, I felt as though I were circling myself, not yet settled into a routine or the earth herself. When I visited my sacred campsite in the woods, I had a hard time doing nothing. I knew that appreciating the wispy clouds and the eternities of green in the trees nourished me, still I felt a tug to be doing something productive. My soul wanted to breathe in the beauty that surrounded me without distracting myself with an agenda, yet I was restless and on edge.

For me returning to the soft, yielding feminine instead of the rigid, driving masculine way requires patience, determination, humility, and practice. This is an inside job of re-patterning and I believe that if I slow down even more, my neurons and synapses will undergo radical renovation. When I intentionally ground myself in leisure, I notice how tiny the paws of a squirrel are compared to the bulk of its body. I bow to the first cherry buds and indulge myself in the pleasure of an outdoor massage in my backyard. I sense that leisure has the potential to bring enormous freedom, but I remain clueless about how to surrender to it. At the same time, I yearn for more spaciousness in my life. Later I wrote in my journal:

> *My ego desires control by demanding to know every detail of my immersion process. Daily I surrender my need to know, name, and understand. Lifetimes of conditioning dissolve slowly. Devotion and discipline are beginning to merge. I trust that Big Truth resides within the mystery.*

I returned to old journals for clarity and to create momentum and a sense of re-investing in my evolving self. The following entry stood out for me:

My body tells the truth. This feels like the time to rest, read, and reflect. When I surrender to not keeping myself busy, I move out of the strong Maine woman archetype. I heal a bit each time I surrender. And I have experienced that the aftertaste of surrender is equanimity. When did I introject that rest and reflection meant laziness? Time to re-imagine and experience that relaxation can lead to insight and inspiration.

As I wrote the last word, I heard, "Cherish each moment as I cherish you." A year ago, or even a few months ago, I would have insisted on knowing the source of that message. No longer.

As I continue to muse and journal about opening to pleasure and leisure, I wonder why I did not bring memories of pleasure and leisure into this present lifetime from past lifetimes? When my grandchildren visit, I always ask, "What is your pleasure for this morning, afternoon and evening?" Then we enjoy the myriad ways they instantly respond to my invitation to play. Now I ask the same question to myself throughout the day and then take action. For starters, I adore flowers. I adore beauty. I adore God. I adore creating. They bring me delicious delight.

In the purposeful pursuit of pleasure, I continue the practice asking myself, "Who do you wish to become?" in place of "What should I do?" Today the answer was clear and felt like a mini-revelation: I wish to become a woman of passionate leisure, inspirited creativity, and joy filled service

I have adopted the heart centered response, "My pleasure," when someone thanks me for a favor because giving brings me pleasure. Giving pleasure is different from being a pleaser. I give pleasure from a sense of fullness, not emptiness or expecting something in return.

I chuckle to myself whenever someone thanks me and I reply, "My pleasure." In appreciation of pleasure, my iPhone message includes the sentence, "I will be pleasured to return your call."

As if on some sort of cosmic cue, my guides add their perspective:

> Most humans have anxiety around pleasure.
> Think of pleasure as a sign of love of self.
> Allow yourself more pleasure in life, in relationship to self, and with others.
> Pleasure has an energy that connects to soul as long as your chosen pleasure does not dim your light.
> You have the capacity to fully flourish.
> Be aware of what pleasures you, inspires you, and renews you.
> Then take action.
> Allow pleasure to be part of your legacy.
> As you approach your time of dying, count the many ways you added to pleasure.

My birth family would not approve of my desire to bring more pleasure into my life. I do not know anyone who has made a commitment to apprentice to pleasure and leisure without becoming totally irresponsible. A few times, I have tripped over my inner tyrant who takes pride in being resilient and keeping a stiff upper lip. I acknowledged her long history and invited her to come along with me as I discovered more nourishing ways of being present. I am convinced, without much experience or outer validation, that as I adopt pleasure and leisure, I will be closer to embracing my inner mystic and resonating with my GPS (God Presencing System.)

Walking on the beach without a specific return time and nothing on my mind feels both decadent and delicious. Returning home with nothing to remember and no lists in my head, licking the salt from my lips and marveling at the flecks of silver sand on my toes, and laughing at myself when I feel disoriented is delightful. Is it possible that receiving and filling up with pleasure are purposeful?

My mind drifts back to when we lived in Scarborough for the first four years I raised Malia and Noah. Ferry Beach became an extension of our backyard. Each summer day I made lunch and snacks and we peeled out of the garage before nine o'clock. Most days we played on the beach, swam, and dug for clams until five o'clock. On many days, our whole neighborhood joined us. We explored the tidal pools, took long, leisurely walks and Malia and Noah were happy and made new friends easily.

Beach is in our blood. It is not a specific beach that is like breath for me. Every beach I visit spells leisure and pleasure—long days with no agendas except enjoying. Lakes and rivers are not the same for me. Even in my seventies, just thinking about the beach makes me relax and I'll bet my tranquil thoughts also lower my blood pressure.

Virginia Beach felt like an extension of Old Orchard Beach where I grew up barely a half a mile from the beach. The texture of the sand felt similar and the rolling waves felt the same. The seagulls looked like the same family although the pelicans were unfamiliar. The crabs were bigger and burrowed and scurried out of their holes unlike the smaller hermit crabs in Maine.

My most recent beach retreat was to Corolla, North Carolina on the Outer Banks where there were clusters of shells and snails everywhere. For the first time my daughter had planned this mini-vacation. I am usually the recreational director, but this time I felt like I had simply come along for the ride.

I smiled as I watched my daughter and granddaughter scurry down the beach in search of shells. I watched them lean close to the ground to pick up snails and shells that would later hang as mobiles in our homes. Then I was overwhelmed by memories of hundreds of times that Kelli Lynn and I enjoyed being beachcombers together and now Malia has joined our ranks.

My rule, which I inherited from my mother and inflicted on both of my children and now my grandchildren, was whatever anyone picked up on their walks, they were responsible for carrying. No exceptions. Malia tested by pointing out that her bag was heavy and asked if I would carry it part of the way. She smiled when I refused.

Since my mother's death, my daughter wonders if she will return to Old Orchard Beach. I wonder about that for myself, although it has been five years since I have returned to the home where I was raised.

I can easily imagine that Malia and Noah become parents the beach will be a year round attraction because beach is in their blood.I hope they will tell their children stories about the happy times we enjoyed on the beach when we were growing each other up.

Before traveling back to Virginia Beach, I participated in a four-day residential workshop at Shalom Mountain in

New York. I agreed to write a love letter to someone as a homework assignment. After considering more than a dozen potential recipients, I dedicated the love letter to myself.

Dearest Beloved Rosalie Deer Heart,

I love you with all of my heart today and all the days to infinity and back.

You are magnificent, and I delight in loving you and watching you grow more present each day in love.

Your openness to receiving pleasure touches me because I know that does not come as easily to you as giving pleasure. I pray that you continue to welcome pleasure with the same exuberance that you respond to a bouquet of flowers, or your first swim in the cold Atlantic Ocean, or your first night sleeping outside in your tent.

Your devotion to your path is awesome and serves as an example to others who may not have the overview that you have worked hard to understand and embrace.

Your work in the world changes consciousness. Even though you believed that you did not succeed in shifting consciousness in your birth family, please know there are others who respond to your love, light and laughter.

Know from the depth of your Being that you are loved and appreciated. You inspire all to be who they can be.

Your willingness to listen to your inner guidance and then take action is the primary reason that many on the invisible realms are attracted to your essence.

Your trust in your guides and now God is infinite. Continue to expand your love of Divinity and you will become even more present. No matter what you say and do, my love for you is unflinching and infinite.

Always,

Rosalie

Currently the soul call to surrender bridges my daily life with my inner life. Surrendering into vastness in order to embrace my divine potential feels profound. Although I am aware that the process calls upon me to surrender my small self so that I may re-discover my Eternal Self, I have no clue how to do it. Later I wrote in my journal:

Time feels different when I am living from my soul story. Cause and effect cease to exist. Twenty-seven nights have passed since I left my home in Stetson, Maine where I slept on the earth in my tent. Nature deepened me. The feeling of remembered radiance lives within me. I am slowly adjusting to sleeping inside in my home in Virginia Beach where the sound of ocean waves has replaced the sound of the pine branches that caressed my tent every night. Camping expanded my practice of taking silence and gratitude into the night.

During a long conversation with my spiritual director, I talked about balance again—a repeat theme from the first time we worked together two years ago. I am aware of how my life lessons sometimes come around again and offer me an opportunity to re-choose.

No excuses or pretense when I talk with Meghan. I speak candidly about how different I feel from almost everyone

I know. I used the phrase "full faith" with her for the first time. If I were younger and Catholic, I imagine I would join a convent because I do feel as though I am under some kind of private vow to serve the Divine. I feel magnetized to the unfolding mystery even when clarity eludes me. In perfect timing, I found this quote from Albert Einstein:

"I must be willing to give up what I am in order to become what I will be."

I returned to old journals to see if Future Pull left its calling card earlier in my journey. I was not surprised to find this entry while browsing through *Harvesting Your Journals: Writing Tools To Enhance Your Growth and Creativity,* which Alison Strickland and I co-authored:

March 1981 (which was thirty-six years ago)

During a visit with my guides last night, I was a teacher of spirit. My heart was hammered and chiseled open, and I agreed to teach from a "place of full heart." Was it a future lifetime that I had entered or did I meet an aspect of myself I have yet to acknowledge?

Being with an open heart was painful when I volunteered at the homeless shelter in Virginia Beach. I did not anticipate feeling the mixture of pain, hopelessness and gratitude from the people we served. I arrived two hours before supper and arranged desserts, poured milk, and eventually served a turkey supper with all the fixings to one hundred and forty-two people who were without family and money three days before Christmas. A large Christmas tree decorated the dining room and children from a local Sunday school sang Christmas carols. I did not know if that was a blessing or added to the sadness of the season for people at the shelter.

Women and men of all ages mingled. I offered them milk and love. Many came back for seconds. I often cried. One woman, who looked about my age, thanked me for my tears. We reached out across the counter and held hands. I was not prepared to feel the deep emotions that overcame me. Several times throughout the evening I was aware that I could have been on the other side of the line receiving rather than serving food. But for—I don't know how to begin to add the people, circumstances events, or maybe pure luck that made the difference.

Although my heart felt like it was breaking, I vowed to keep an open heart. Most of the time, I was aware of our Oneness and that reconnected me to empathy. Several times I did not know what to say, so I smiled and stayed in my heart. When I was not serving food, I wondered about their individual stories. Three days before Christmas and they were homeless and without family. Mostly, I felt the injustice of our system that allows anyone to be homeless and hungry.

After everyone had eaten, the kitchen manager ordered us to dispose of all the left over food. I was shocked. In my mind, I saw the food being recycled into turkey soup, casseroles, sandwiches as well as omelets, and a bread pudding. He shrugged and said,

"State law—whatever is left gets tossed."

"But…. But," I stammered and no words came as a backlog of objections and outrage collided in my heart.

A woman who appeared to be a veteran volunteer hugged me and held me while I cried. Three or four of the women to whom we had served food earlier encircled us and sighed and cried.

When I was done crying, I opened my eyes and looked at the circle of women.

"Thank you for caring," I said with a hoarse voice.

Then I added as I looked at the women I had served earlier, "I am sorry, deeply sorry." The moment I apologized I felt a fresh wave of sadness in my belly. Clearly my grief was so much deeper than the disposal of left over food. I felt vulnerable and safe with others who understood and cared which increased the pain in my belly even more.

Before I left, I decided to volunteer a couple of times a month and to keep my heart open even if I cried because I knew that compassion threatened my ego. However, I carried the experience of being deeply affected about the thrown out food and government regulations into my at home silent retreat two days later.

I wonder if I am I the only one I know who asks, "What am I loyal to and why?" That was the question that prompted me to enter into a silent, at home retreat during Christmas. Since my daughter and grandchildren had gone north to celebrate Christmas with family in Maine, I decided to dedicate Christmas Eve and the following four days to silence. The Advent season always felt like a call to reverence to me and family traditions did not include time out for reverence. Plus, the moon was full on Christmas Day and that lunar event would not coincide with Christmas again for nineteen years. In preparation for my Christmas Retreat, I went food shopping, told close friends of my plans to retreat, even posted a message on Facebook. Christmas Eve I joined other people at Friends Meeting for a carol sing and later sat in group silence. I appreciated the importance of preparation rituals.

When I returned home about nine o'clock, I intuited there was one more ritual before I entered ninety-six hours of silence. As I admired the full moon as well as the dark charcoal clouds that sometimes obscured it, I walked to the nearby beach.

The temperature hovered in the mid-fifties and Virginia Beach was deserted. I sat by the water with a full view of the moon. Then I chuckled. Of course, how could it have been more obvious, especially when I described my four-day retreat to friends as a "deep dive?" Then I stood up, removed my dress and underwear, and nimbly stepped into the water. By Southern standards, it was cold, but by Maine standards it was tolerable. Once I dove under the oncoming wave, I no longer felt at risk of hypothermia, and I swam, floated, and hummed for several minutes, until I heard a man holler from shore, "Are you a mermaid?"

I didn't know what to make of his question, so I was silent. Then he repeated it.

"No," I responded, "just a swimmer."

"Do you mind if I move your clothes further up the beach? They are about to get wet."

"Thanks," I replied and continued swimming.

The next time I looked toward the land, he was still standing there. For the first time, I wondered if I were in danger. The innocent part of me believed that since I was involved in a sacred ritual no harm could come, yet I also acknowledged that our present world is not the safe place of my childhood.

I shivered. Then I reasoned that I had two choices: to remain in the water or walk towards shore naked. Before I made a choice, the man on the beach cupped his hands to his mouth and asked, "Mind if I join you?"

Without thinking, I yelled, "Only if you take your clothes off. Fair is fair."

I turned my back and floated in the waves. Next thing I knew, he was beside me.

"Do you ever body surf?" he asked as if we were already friends.

"Yes, I did it earlier when I first jumped into the ocean."

"I'm game if you are," he said, and motioned me with his arm. Other than talking about the magnificent full moon, we concentrated on body surfing and joked about which one of us got the farthest ride. I forgot about being cold. Only sensations counted—being in the moment with all my senses alert and responsive and merging with the ongoing waves.

After about twenty minutes, I began to shiver. "Time to call it quits for this Christmas Eve," I announced.

"Me, too," he said and we walked to shore, gathered our clothes, and dressed.

Then he surprised me when he asked, "Do you not have a home?"

Maybe my brain was water logged, but I did not understand his question.

"Yes, of course I have a home. It is close by."

He bowed slightly and leaned toward me and asked, "Would you give me the honor of walking you home?"

"No thanks, I am moments away from beginning a four-day silent retreat."

Then I held out my right hand and thanked him for being part of my deep dive ritual as if meeting on the deserted beach at night was the most natural thing in the world.

He smiled. I turned away and walked up the beach to my house and he continued down the deserted beach. On the way home I reflected about the meaning of our chance encounter because I am convinced that everyone we meet on our journey is a teacher. The only explanation that made any sense to me was that I was supported by a balanced and playful male or maybe he was an angel. I gave thanks as I warmed myself in the hot shower.

It is impossible to be silent for four days and return to the talkative world the same. During the silent retreat, I kept returning to the question: What am I loyal to? The words "devotion, "surrender," and "peace" popped up many times. The final day I inquired, "What is important now?"

I have valued being a peacemaker for most of my life. When I was a college student, I drove conscientious objectors across the Canadian border in protest of the Vietnam War even though my family supported the war. I also did my best to be a peacemaker in my family. Even before I became a court appointed mediator, I did my best to find ways where everyone won. In retrospect, I realized I chose peace over honesty too many times.

Daily I remind myself that growth happens at the edges—not from what I already know. Being my authentic self is a daily challenge. I am at a choice point—whether to speak about what I know as Truth, which honors my inner experience, or to note my inner transformation in my journals and maintain my sense of privacy.

Since my visitations with Mary, angels, and God, I have grown beyond crab walking around my soul purpose. I knew from experience that each time I chose to be authentic, I was also vulnerable.

A trip to Quick Care in Bangor to ensure that the swelling in my left leg was not a blood clot gave me an opportunity to speak from my authentic self as well as receive medical attention and reassurance.

Something I said caused the doctor to ask, "Do you think past lives are real?"

I replied, "I know mine are real because I stumbled over them when I was in England, Scotland, Indonesia, Cyprus, and closer to home in New Mexico. Before those life changing encounters, I did not think much about past lives."

As I answered the physician's questions, I realized that I no longer had a need to convince anyone else of what was real or unreal about my experience. My story is my own. My own experience is all the validation that I need.

"Is it like a déjà vu experience?" he asked as he took my blood pressure.

"Yes, only they last longer, are more vivid, and the past feels real and compelling."

"That sounds very intense," he replied.

"My personal experience is my only reference point. My body knows and remembers even though my logical mind is amuck, wondering how this can possibly be real."

Then I took a risk and shared a past lifetime memory about the time I was vacationing in Cyprus. My partner enjoyed snorkeling and was eager to introduce me to a watery adventure. I stood knee deep in the water when I put on the facemask. I panicked. I thought if I put my head in the water, I would drown. My irrational fear surprised me and no matter what I did, I could not talk myself out of my reaction. Fortunately, both of us were well acquainted with past lifetime bleed-throughs and we went ashore where I re-entered the lifetime where the trauma originated. I discovered that I had been drowned as a witch. To insure that I would not survive, a wooden mask, which resembled the present day snorkeling mask, was placed over my nose and mouth. Two weeks later when we visited a museum and I saw a replica of the mask, I almost threw up!

The doctor smiled at me and I continued, "Looking back, I believe the drowning incident impacted my earlier life. I have a vivid freeze frame memory of being forced to take swimming lessons at the Royal Ambassador Pool in Ocean Park when I was eight years old. I was humiliated because I was the only kid who refused to jump into water that was over my head. The swimming instructor sat with me and patiently tried to convince me that I would re-surface if I jumped in. Still I adamantly refused to jump into the deep water. Nevertheless, disregarding the persistent demands from my mother to throw me in because that is what her older brothers did to her, he continued to talk to me. It took nearly an hour before I agreed to jump in with him with our hands joined. Nobody was more surprised than I when I re-surfaced. "

The doctor shrugged his shoulders and almost whispered, "This remains between us. I know that past lifetimes are real. I too know from experience that they have the ability to heal us; but I would never say that out loud."

I reached out and touched his hand, and said, "I am sorry that you do not feel comfortable honoring what you know, especially about healing since you are a doctor." Empathy flooded me and overflowed to include everyone else who straitjacketed their knowing. I wanted to remind him that healing demanded that we speak our truth out loud, yet I sensed he was not ready to break rank with his role as a physician.

As I left his office, I wondered how our lives and the world would be transformed if more people said what they knew and what they really felt regardless of their roles. Yet I realized from my own experience that there is always a part of us that wants nothing to do with revelation because it orphans us from our old, familiar personal story.

Driving home I realized that one of the reasons that I value past life recall is because it provides a wider lens to view a present life event. In both my personal as well as my professional experience, I have observed that sometimes trigger points can be tracked and traced to distant past memories that continue to exert a powerful force since they linger in our subconscious mind. Soul memory is real.

At times, I questioned whether my consciousness was imbued with Divine madness or Divine clarity. I did not consciously call these extraordinary events to me. Merging and eventually fusing happened in their own time. Fusion, which felt like another word for union, occurred when I totally surrendered my will to the Divine. As I reflected back in wonder at my journey, I always knew that I was light in formation. Being blessed by angels, guides, and the Holy Ones added to my light. Then I agreed to shine my light.

I welcomed the perspective of my guides when I was in the midst of an energetic shift because I knew from experience that I could count on them to broaden my understanding. I appreciated how they reinforced and refined what I half knew in my intuitive heart but lacked the words to explain. Each time I expressed gratitude, my energy field expanded.

> *You are aligning with the big picture.*
> *Note that all exists inside time.*
> *Nothing exists outside of time.*
> *The future is already here. Now.*
> *You are here. Now.*
> *All is here. Now.*
> *In order to beckon the future, you must let go of all that you are not.*

In my experience as a daughter, mother, and grandmother, I appreciate how children are born with no veils between dimensions and they are often more conscious than their parents and grandparents. They move easily through realms and seldom question their ability to access information or where the guidance comes from. For example when I told Malia and Noah that I was writing another book, Noah asked, "Are you going to dedicate your next book to Malia and me, Grandmom?"

"Nope," I said. "I already dedicated *Awaken* to you and you only get one book dedicated to you by me in a lifetime." Then I chuckled to myself as I remembered Noah's response when I showed him a copy of *Awaken* and pointed out to him that I had dedicated it to him and Malia.

His response startled me.

"Thank you, Grandmom. I just checked and found out that this is the first time in all my lifetimes that anyone has dedicated a book to me."

In present time, Noah flashed me the faraway look that I have learned from experience meant that he had tuned into the frequency of the future. After a few minutes, he said,

"Don't worry. Malia, I just went into the future and Grandmom dedicated a book to our children."

Now he had my attention! "What was the name of the book, Noah?" I asked with enthusiasm.

"I didn't look at the title. I just wanted to know if you dedicated it to us," he said matter of factly.

Malia ordered, "Well, Noah, go back to wherever you go and tell us what the title is."

Malia and I waited respectfully. A few moments later, he said, *"Cosmic Emotions."*

231

Then he looked at me intently and asked, "Do you know stuff about cosmic emotions, Grandmom?"

"Not really, Noah." But would you do me one big favor? Would you go back and see if there is another author's name on the cover?"

He nodded. I had a strong intuition that we had written the book together.

Sure enough! He returned with a huge smile and said, "It's our book, Grandmom. We wrote it together."

Then we hugged and did a celebration dance to the future.

So who knows, maybe someday in the future you may read a book co-authored with my grandson—but not until I have lived more fully into my Future Self.

Like Noah, when I am engaged with Future Pull, I too experience the world as both reciprocal and synergetic. I marvel how everything exists in relationship and that which is joined actively works to maintain the integrity of its wholeness. Maybe we were both physicists in past lifetimes.

My heart responded the first time I read this Rilke poem:

You must give birth to your images.
They are the future waiting to be born,
Fear not the strangeness.
The future must enter into you long before it happens.
Just wait for the birth
For the hour of clarity.

Like Rilke, I believe from my own experience that Future Pull is encoded in our DNA. The moment I said an honest and heart-centered yes to align with my future self, my frequency expanded and my priorities changed. I felt as though I was being quickened by an energetic infusion or transfusion and my light brightened.

As I ponder Future Pull events, I remember the first time I met Alison Strickland, my evolutionary buddy and editor of my last three books. We were sitting in the cafeteria at the Creative Problem Solving Institute in Buffalo, New York. The year was 1977. I introduced myself and ordered her to attend my afternoon journal keeping session. Except in a restaurant, ordering is not my style. Four decades of friendship, creativity, and growing up together proved that I acted as an agent of Future Pull for us both.

I marvel when I take the time to reflect on my experiences over time. Sometimes continuity happens in the blink of an eye, and other times a decade will go by until an organizing thread re-appears. My ongoing relationship with my guides is one continuity thread I know I can count on, and I do my best never to let go of the thread.

Channeling from my guides arrived in perfect timing:

You are invited to live in the frequency of your magnificence, which is the frequency of the future.

What you gift with your attention determines the frequency of your energy.

Your frequency determines what you experience and you are the guardian of your frequency.

Your frequency includes: vitality, voice, and vision.

Remember that your readiness is a frequency.

If you believe you are ready, you are.

The universe responds each time that you announce your readiness.

233

*Act as if you are already magnificent because
your subconscious mind does not respond in a time
dimension.*

*Continue to welcome the frequencies of the future
and resonate with the energy of the Divine evolutionary, creative principle.*

Later that day, I smiled as I read this quotation by Alfred North Whitehead in my wisdom journal:

"Evolution is the gentle movement toward God by the gentle persuasion of love."

I grounded the guidance by writing the following affirmation in my journal because I know that whenever I make the time to write, I deepen.

*I desire and deserve the opportunity to align with
my Future Self even though I am not perfect!*

My passion for stone sculpting is another example of Future Pull that wove through three decades of my life and Michael Lightweaver acted as a perfect evolutionary buddy when he challenged me to create a stone sculpture of Bridget, the Celtic guardian of the well and protector of women and children. He had already built her a well and all that was missing was a stone replica of her.

When I agreed to sculpt an eighteen-inch model of Bridget, I certainly did not expect to be turned inside out and upside down by the Future Pull of creative self-expression. This soul call, disguised as my first commissioned art project, took me on a thirteen-month journey and unearthed every limited belief that kept me from embracing my light and creativity.

Always before when I sculpted, I had merged with the stone. Friends often laughed when I described how I tucked a stone underneath my pillow and invited dreams about its future. The ninety-eight pound industrial sandstone that became Bridget was too big sleep on.

Michael emailed a few photos of the ancient Bridget and I designed a three-dimensional clay model so that I could see her shape as I hammered, chiseled, and filed. From the first cut, I felt more like a laborer and less like an artist. I was aware of my impatience but was clueless about the roots of my insecurities.

During my monthly session with Meghan, I spoke about my frustration with sculpting Bridget: the hardness of the stone, my insecurity about where and how to begin and my nagging question whether a past lifetime was bleeding through into my present experience. She listened intently and said, "There may be a past life theme for you as an artist being made to conform or some pressure for you to be someone other than who you were."

My body did not respond to her suggestion and I let the notion go. Then she followed up with two simple questions:

Had I any direct experience with Bridget?

Had I ever been to Ireland?

My blind spot became obvious! How arrogant of me to expect myself to sculpt a person without a relationship to her? I was shocked that I had not connected with Bridget in meditation, prayer, or dreams. No wonder I felt impotent to connect with her soul!

I agreed to create a relationship with Bridget before I resumed sculpting her, but when Meghan advised me to consider postponing further work on Bridget until I returned from a two-week trip to Ireland in September, I resisted. I was on assignment and postponing felt irresponsible. Then I struggled to discern if the voice to carry on was motivated by my ego or my soul.

Although I am a seasoned meditator, I felt shy and nervous the first time I meditated on Bridget. I began by asking her for forgiveness and then pledged myself to daily meditation. Bridget was patient with me—much more patient than I was with myself. After the end of the first week of consistent meditation, she suggested that I return to my outdoor sculpting table and sketch in her arms and hands with a permanent marker. Then she assured me that the rest of her body would take shape naturally.

Having a plan relieved my anxiety, but then my ego took over and I worried about sculpting the rest of her torso. I doubted myself many times a day and each time my ego deepened its spell and reminded me of other times that I had overestimated myself. Fortunately, I have learned to update my limited beliefs because I know from experience how my most prominent beliefs create my reality.

Several weeks went by. I continued to meditate each day before I worked with Bridget and her emerging form became more visible each day. Initially I used a black magic marker to indicate where I needed to remove stone and then I switched to pink paint to honor her feminine nature. When I listened to my intuition and took the time to merge with her essence, I felt confident and enjoyed the strong sounds that the hammer and chisel created against the stone.

Many nights I filed away with the moon as my only light and reminisced about the time that Squidge insisted I wear a blindfold in order to connect with my instincts. Friends asked me daily when I thought she might be finished. I shrugged my shoulders and said, "Hopefully before next lifetime." Time no longer mattered. I made peace with time and trusted in cosmic time rather than clock time.

Next, Bridget invited me to sculpt during the early hours of the morning with candles and the moon and stars as my light. My soul friends Dan and Jo Ella loaned me four hurricane lamps and gave me four long white candles and I placed them in the four directions. I loved working outside between two and four in the morning.

One early morning as I concentrated on smoothing Bridget's breasts, I heard two car doors slam. I wondered if I should be scared since nobody visited me at three A.M. Then I heard the sound of feet walking down my stone path, but, because of the light from the candles, I could not see who approached. Before I panicked, two policemen came into view. I was relieved I had on pajamas because I preferred to sculpt in the nude during the day so my clothes did not get all dusty.

"We were concerned there was a fire," one officer said as he looked at me curiously.

"No, only hurricane lamps and candles for light so I can see to sculpt," I replied.

"Ma'am, don't you have a home?" the other officer asked.

What a bizarre question for him to ask, I thought to myself. If I were without a home, why would I set up shop in someone's backyard?

"Of course. I live right here," I said pointing to the back door.

"Are you out here every night?"

"Nope, only when I can't sleep."

Then I assured them that I never used my hammer and chisel this early—only my files because they are much quieter. They studied me and then glanced at one another.

I felt like I was being evaluated for mental competency and decided to introduce them to the emerging Bridget.

They were polite and continued to stare at me—not Bridget.

"We have to be moving on, Ma'am. Make sure you blow out all the candles before you go inside, okay?"

"Yes, of course," I replied and thanked them for being conscientious.

I'd been working on Bridget for about four months when I became aware of another energy in the room during my morning meditation. The frequency felt high and light—not Bridget's vibration. Then I heard a low humming sound and my heart rate increased. Next came a sudden rush of energy and I began to sweat. I sensed that I was in the midst of something big and sacred. Before my mind could interfere, I witnessed myself standing before God. The suddenness and the presence of God felt huge and I felt small and unprepared; yet, I understood intuitively that He wanted something from me or for me.

God looked peaceful and intense at the same time. He radiated light and understanding. My heart exploded open and I listened to Him as though my heart had ears to receive His message: "Loan me your hands."

I looked down at my hands and turned them over. Then I looked at God. He had not moved and waited patiently as I stared at my hands. No more words were spoken. I stared at Him again. Then I returned my gaze to my hands. Neither He nor I moved. When I looked back at God, His countenance was filled with pure love. I surrendered.

He remained motionless, yet vibrated with energy. My hands felt hot and shiny and I felt intense energy moving from my arms to my hands and into my heart. We did not hold hands. He did not even touch my hands. Our energies blended. I felt lighter. My heart felt spacious. As I continued to stare at Him, He began to dissolve slowly, and then I returned to my physical body.

After drinking a couple of glasses of water and writing in my journal, I returned to Bridget. I was no longer hesitant to carve deep on her emerging body. No longer did I question whether I had the skills to birth Bridget out of stone. I felt free—like no matter where or how deeply I filed or hammered and chiseled, I could make no mistakes. The energy that surrounded us felt imbued with serene mastery and when I was my most honest and most vulnerable I recognized the energy as grace.

After the immersion of light, my talents and competencies manifested almost faster than the speed of light. I grounded myself in the over belief that everything in the universe was aligned to empower me to complete Bridget. Destiny waited as I grounded myself in the energy of serene mastery.

A week later I bumped into how I had compartmentalized God's visit by imagining that the energy infusion from the Divine was focused only on sculpting Bridget. The following week I discovered that the healing energy I transmitted when I did hands on healing with Glad Helpers at Edgar Cayce's A.R.E. Center was the same serene mastery energy. Also the energies that surrounded me when I did soul readings or wrote in my journal were imbued with the same energies. Then I laughed and imagined God laughing with me.

The same week, after an intense argument with a former husband, I was surprised when he sat in my chair at Glad Helpers for hands on healing. Although my eyes were closed, I recognized his body when I placed my hands on his shoulders. He was a perfect test of my commitment to be of healing service, especially since our previous argument had not been resolved. Nobody pushed my buttons more than he did.

I was filled with conflicting feelings. Then I remembered that when I taught my Intuition Activation class, I introduced people to the totem pole technique as a way of raising their energy if they felt stuck by using breath and focused intention. It is possible to raise your energy from the bottom or middle of the totem pole to the top. After taking a few deep breaths and consciously reminding myself of my commitment to be a Resource for the Source, I remembered the energy of serene mastery that I felt when I sculpted Bridget. Then I breathed in the energies of serene mastery as well as the focused healing energies from the Divine. As I placed my hands on my former partner's heart, I smiled in gratitude as the healing energies flowed through my hands. I was relieved and grateful to him and to myself for no longer being caught in the personal drama that we had co-created.

Thank you Future Pull.

Michael and I agreed that the replicas of the ancient Earth Mother sculptures all had small heads in proportion to their bodies and we both agreed that Bridget's head needed to be larger to signify her expanded consciousness. That part seemed easy.

When Bridget told me that she desired "a whisper of a face" so that she resembled every woman, I was temporarily stymied. I acknowledged that I was a sculptor, but an artist? Then I looked at my hands and remembered that God blessed them even though in that moment that felt long ago. I decided to call in artistic expertise and phoned my friend, Arla Patch, who also designed the cover of this book.

I have a freeze frame memory of Arla as she walked around Bridget examining her from all angles. Then she said gently, "Rosie, always look from the top of the stone downward. That will give you the perspective that you need."

I quipped, "Is that what they teach in art school?"

She nodded her head and we both giggled. Then she used chalk to mark out spots where I need to remove stone in order to give the impression of eyes, nose and mouth. As long as I looked from the top of Bridget's head down, I held a perspective of her contours.

The Blessing Bridget ritual coincided with my going away party in Virginia Beach, prior to my returning to Maine for the summer and fall. I invited family and friends to gather and they surrounded both of us with hugs, smiles, prayers and blessings for the journey. This was the first time that my daughter and grandchildren joined my spiritual family of friends. I was excited and a bit nervous to merge two important strands of my life. More than thirty people gathered in my backyard for a cookout and a farewell ritual. All I knew of the ritual in advance was I wanted it to be simple and heart-centered and I was wide open for inspiration. As I walked down the back steps to bring out platters of fresh vegetables, I had a vision of people sprinkling handfuls of water on Bridget's gray body and bringing her to her ebony blackness, which would happen naturally when Michael Lightweaver polished her.

I lit a candle before I told Bridget's story while my soul buddy Leigh Clements showed photos I had snapped throughout our journey. I told people how I had finally fulfilled my dream of being a photojournalist since I had snapped photos of Bridget from the very beginning to the end. Then I asked my circle of family and friends to sprinkle water on her and offer a prayer if they wished. Malia stood on the porch and videoed the ceremony. My friend Robert Demers, a professional opera singer, dedicated an aria to her and I imagined her dancing in response to his deep and perfectly pitched voice. My daughter, Kelli Lynne, waited until last to sprinkle water and surprised me and everyone else by pouring the remaining water all over Bridget's shimmering body. I was touched because moments before I had thought about doing the exact thing.

My thirteen-month apprenticeship to Bridget was over and I was ready to deliver her to her new home outside of Asheville, North Carolina. I had wondered over the months how I would feel when I handed her over to Michael and he placed her in her moss- covered grotto. Being with her had opened me to the energies of serene mastery. We had become companions.

When we arrived at Mountain Light Sanctuary, I remembered the welcoming energy of the land and my heart knew instantly that Bridget was home. Before I arrived, I had suggested to Michael that he sand and polish Bridget to bring his energy into the stone. We lit a candle, and I watched as Michael sanded. After working on her for an hour or so, he said he could not comprehend the thousands of hours that I had worked to bring Bridget into her final form. I breathed and received his compliment in my heart. Polishing was the final step and as I watched him polish, I thought he could create a brilliant contrast if he left her hair gray and polished the rest of her body.

"What do you think, Michael?" I asked.

He was silent for a few moments and then said, "It is not my decision. It is her decision," and I knew she was in exactly the right hands and the right place. And I knew that missing her was impossible because she was home.

A group of Gospel singers from Tennessee was staying at Michael's retreat center and we asked them if they would be part of the Welcoming Bridget ritual. They agreed to bless the ritual with music.

The morning of her Giveaway arrived. Privately, I bowed to her and thanked her for being my teacher. With her I learned more about humility, surrender, trust, persistence, and serene mastery than I could have ever learned anywhere else.

Michael invited me to lead the ritual and I agreed as long as he joined me. Then he officially welcomed her as a representative of the Earth Mother. That surprised me because I thought of her only as the guardian of the well, although I also knew her in my heart as a bridger. To Michael, she moved beyond the old patriarchy and even the older matriarchy to represent unity. For sure, she resembled the ancient sculptures of Venus of Willendorf who became known as Earth Mother.

Michael told the evolving story of how he had dedicated the land to Bridget in the spring of 2009 and built her well, which is a replica of an Irish holy well. He added that she specifically honors the source of water that springs from the earth and is a life stream, especially since her well provides the house with water. Michael ended the ritual with drumming and chanting:

Ancient Mother, I hear you calling,
Ancient Mother, I hear your song.
Ancient Mother, I hear your laughter,
Ancient Mother, I taste your tears.

Finally, he removed the white cloth from Bridget's body and gently carried her to her moss-covered stone altar at the top of her well. The sun lit up my face and I imagined that my tears transformed into rainbows somewhere. I bowed and said "Welcome" and "Goodbye."

As I walked off to be by myself for a few moments, my guides arrived and channeled:

> Your attitude of "spacious expectancy" is irresistible to the energies of the future, which are, as you are aware, part of your present. Continue to feel fulfilled and express gratitude because the energy of gratitude invites similar frequencies. Continue to be of an open heart and open mind and the frequencies of the future will become you.

Throughout my thirteen-month tenure with Bridget, I was aware of a few general principles that grounded my sculpting and now my life.

- Go deeper.
- Concentrate on what you know how to do and trust the rest will fall into place.
- Substitute curves wherever you spot edges

Note: To see Bridget's photographic evolution, visit my website: www.heart-soul-healing.com and click on the Living Future Pull tab.

I acknowledge that I am an artist. I also enjoy speaking out and expressing myself. Both require courage. However, I was not aware that creativity and courage coexisted within my heart until Lynda Marvin, a friend in Maine, thanked me for my "creative courage" in response to a photo I posted of Bridget. Upon reflection, I realized my soul is comfortable with the phrase, yet my "little self" shied away.

Later I searched my memory for an example of a woman who embodied both courage and creativity. Sadly, I found none in my ancestral lineage. Then from nine centuries ago, Hildegard of Bingen beckoned me. She has always felt like part of my spiritual family. When I taught with Matthew Fox in his Creation Spirituality program in Philadelphia, I meditated with her mandalas, listened to her liturgical hymns, feasted on her visionary theology, marveled at her poetry, and prayed to her. I also used many of her herbal remedies. Long ago I memorized one of her quotations:

"Love abounds in all things,
Excels from the depths to beyond the stars,
Is lovingly disposed to all things."

I was surprised to read Hildegard's philosophy and discover how closely our ways of being in the world fit together.

- Balance
- Focus
- Ongoing conversation with the Divine until one's life becomes a sacred poem

I giggled and imagined Hildegard, Bridget, and me celebrating the dance of courageous creativity. During a recent Friends Meeting I felt inspired to write more about courageous creativity:

Courageous creativity meant I approached the eighty-nine pounds of soapstone that emerged as Bridget with an attitude of collaboration.

Courageous creativity meant that I was more comfortable with being curious than thinking that I already knew how the future wishes to evolve through me.

Courageous creativity meant that I aligned with my eternal soul and reassured my temporal ego that there was room for all.

Courageous creativity meant that I trusted and surrendered again and again to the evolutionary, creative forces that surrounded me.

Decades ago, I heard Starhawk, author of *The Spiral Dance,* say, "Magic is the art of changing consciousness at will." What fun to notice that each time I aligned with the frequency of future self, I touched magic and the magic felt both childlike and ancient. When I see from the lens of Future Pull, life seems to be lighter. I giggled out loud when the UPS deliveryman said to me, "I will future you," referring to writing an order to himself to return the next week. I hugged myself and whispered, "If only you could."

One morning when Noah was eight years old he asked me, "What came first Grandmom, me remembering how the top of my head felt when you kiss it, or you deciding to kiss the top of my head?"

Before I figured out how to respond to his question, he continued, "Never mind, it's all the same field so it all happens in the same second."

I wonder if Rumi, the Persian poet, was a devotee of Future Pull when he wrote,

"Don't be satisfied with stories,
    how things have gone wrong,
        unfold your myth."

Last spring before I presented to the staff and volunteers at Edgar Cayce's Association for Research and Enlightenment, my guides told me to forget about planning the program and to create space in my consciousness for them to channel. I felt eager and ready to consciously collaborate! As I reached to pick up the hand held microphone, I realized I had no words—even the memory of words had disappeared. In computer vernacular, it seemed as though my hard drive had been erased and not reset.

As I looked out at the large group of people, I reminded myself to breathe into my belly and remembered that I had agreed to allow the frequency of Future Pull to lead. My next breath came more naturally. Then I smiled at the group and began to energetically connect with the heart of each person. Nobody moved, coughed, or looked away. I merged with one person and then another until I had completed my energetic introduction.

It took nearly ten minutes for a few words to return, and I trusted that the future would evolve in its own timing. Then I explained that energy was my first language and I had honored that truth by introducing myself energetically and that I believed we meet each other on an energetic level first, no matter what words we use. Some people nodded their heads in agreement. Nobody left the room.

Fortunately, words returned slowly and I told the story of how I had channeled the Angel of Findhorn because earlier John Van Auken, author of *Angels, Fairies, Dark Forces and the Elementals,* had spoken about angels. As I recounted how the Angel of Findhorn over-lighted my energy, I again felt the frequency of the angel's energy fill my body and expand out into the room, touching everyone. I became silent and filled with curiosity and wonder. How was it possible that talking about a time of remembered radiance reignited the original energy? In retrospect, this energetic phenomenon felt deeply related to Future Pull. I noticed that a few people elbowed their neighbors and I was aware that I was not the only one in the room who was aware of the angelic frequencies that had filled the auditorium.

Next I told the group how Saint Germaine, considered by many to be an Ascended Master who wielded the Violet Flame of Dissolution and amplified the energy of compassion, had appeared recently at Glad Helpers. I was surprised by his visitation until later at lunch my soul buddy Leigh Clements shared that he had invited Saint Germaine to assist with healing that day.

On my short walk home, I flashed back fifty years ago to when I was a college student and Ram Dass came to Portland. I had read *Be Here Now* and he was already my hero, but I had no idea what to expect. When he walked on stage, he looked around at the thousands of people in the packed auditorium and I imagined he looked directly into my eyes which I knew at the time was impossible since I sat in one of the back rows. He stood on stage, smiled and silently gazed into people's eyes for a long time. I'd never seen anyone connect energetically and my heart applauded. I knew I would never learn how to do that in college. Furthermore, I never dreamed that I would some day be channeling loving energy the way Ram Dass had! To both Ram Dass and my guides I say thank you and offer a deep bow and a vow to continue to be of service to Future Pull.

Almost five decades later, I realized that each time I made an evolutionary soul choice, I partnered with the frequencies of Future Pull. For example, I challenged myself in tough situations to imagine the most evolutionary choice I could make and then I followed through. Gradually I became comfortable asking, "Who do I wish to become?" in place of "What should I do?" and I blended with Future Self. Other times I stepped out of my comfort zone by inquiring what my Future Self might say or do in the situation.

On a visit to Santa Fe, New Mexico, one of my soul homes, synchronistic Future Pull events happened beyond the speed of light. Ellen Kleiner, another evolutionary buddy and the editor of my first three books, challenged me to identify the primary thread of this book.

I said that there were at least seven interweaving threads. She insisted that I give her the main thread. I took a walk and returned to Ellen's casita with my answer.

"Love and light," I said as I walked in the door.

"Rosie, that is two threads.

"Nope, light is love from the spiritual dimension, so the two are really one.

She laughed and said, "Yes, Rosie, knowing you for more than twenty years, I appreciate that your spiritual memoir is grounded in love and light."

We high-fived each other and then my cell phone rang. Lanie, an adopted member of my soul family, said, "I know you are busy working on your book, Rosie, and I don't want to interrupt you, but I had a dream early this morning that I know is important to share with you, and I don't exactly know why."

Although Lanie is in her early twenties, she has been a dream catcher for years and her intuition often shows up in her dreams. I invited her to go on.

"Well, in the dream you, June Bro, and I were standing in the kitchen in my new home. The large room was painted white and filled with light. We were talking, laughing and preparing to cook a meal. Without warning, you looked at me intensely and said, "Lanie, this is really important. I want you to pay attention while I show you my light."

Then you surrounded me with light—no words, just light. Next you turned to June and asked her to beam her love to me. She did and the dream ended. All I knew when I woke up this morning that it was important for me to tell you my dream."

"Indeed," I said, "your timing and your message are perfect. Thank you."

CHAPTER 13

The Frequencies of Future Pull

*F*lash forward to October 2106. The night before I facilitated a two-day workshop called Claiming Your Magnificence, Future Pull happened spontaneously from midnight until 4 AM and left an indelible imprint on my consciousness. I felt like my inner GPS had illuminated my consciousness. "Downloaded" was the only word I had that came close to describing my experience and it failed to carry the intensity. Six hours after receiving the downloaded information about Future Pull, I facilitated the workshop that I had designed in April. Looking back, I had intentionally left the process open-ended because I had no idea who I would be in August.

I believe that I attracted the frequencies of Future Pull because of my prolonged passion to become the woman I yearned to be. Looking back, I realized that whenever I attended to what was arising in my heart, I became a magnet for Future Pull. For example, during the weeks that preceded my encounter with the Angel of Findhorn I wrote, *"Trust, faith, and integrity are braiding themselves in me."* Then my ego freaked out and attempted to pretzel me into my familiar ways of being and understanding because it feared annihilation. Looking back, I can connect the dots between opening to the magnetic energy of Future Pull when I opened my energy field and entertained Mother Mary. My agreement to be receptive to an encounter with the Divine eventually lead to channeling the Angel of Findhorn and later beckoned Big Angel and then Mother Mary's return. If I had obeyed my ego and remained loyal only to what I could see and understand with my five senses, I would have missed the invitations of Future Pull.

Once again, I returned to my journal to record my ongoing journey:

I feel like a female version of Johnny Appleseed planting seeds for the future, which is now. During the night, I was tutored about how to consciously collaborate with the future. I almost wrote, "create" but it is like all possible futures co-existed in a horizontal and vertical pancake arrangement. It was my thoughts that added potential to each probable future. I was amazed when I discovered that I influenced future events with my thoughts, intentions, and emotions just as future events influenced me! That means that after the massive oil spill, if enough people meditated and visualized the Gulf Coast as clear and clean that would influence the probability of that as a reality.

Five hours later I shared my excitement about the downloaded Future Pull concepts and asked participants for their permission to redesign the experiential two-day workshop around Future Pull and its relationship to Future Self. Then I admitted that I felt vulnerable as well as a bit sleep deprived and I was not in the habit of teaching material that I had not embodied. The group applauded my offer.

During our next two days of creating conscious community, we identified events, people, places, and even dreams in our lives that opened us up to the frequency of Future Pull by answering the question, "If not for (list the event), I would not have become_____." I filled in the sentence with, "If not for Mike's death, I would not have realized that communication continues to take place after death." Later I added, "If not for my agreement to sculpt Bridget, I would not have become acquainted with God in such a hands on way."

Next, we explored how Future Pull magnetized each of us to become more authentic, creative, and whole by identifying themes of Future Pull that operated in our individual lives. We agreed that it often pulled us out of the gravity of our limited personal stories and invited us to embody our radiance, spaciousness, and joy. When we partnered with our Future Self, we discovered more resources and energies to blend Future Self with Present Self and heal old wounds sustained by Younger Self. When I sourced my sense of Self from the future, my Younger Self could no longer continue to interpret my life from the old lens of my personal story—that old script that read, "You are not enough," "You are too much," "Your safety rests in being invisible," "Always put the needs of others before your own," and "Work hard."

My Younger Self balked when I read excerpts from the manuscript of this book to the group. That surprised me until I figured out that my Younger Self had hardwired showing off with showing up. Since I supported others to break rank with their learned limitations, I risked being vulnerable and read from the scribbled first draft "downloaded" during the previous night. In the midst of the process, I acknowledged out loud that I had embraced my promise at the end of my vision quest three years earlier to step into a leadership role.

Later in the workshop, when I asked my Future Self her name, she replied, "Deer Heart of the Light." I clapped my hands in glee and somersaulted back through time to remember how determined I was to name myself after my divorce. Although I did not realize that naming myself was an invitation from Future Pull at the time, I knew that I wanted my new name to remind me of my spiritual path. Now I understand that my name itself was a magnet that connected me to Future Self.

Driving home after the first day of the workshop, my mind went back to 1981 when I took a role-stripping class with Michael Daniels at the Creative Problem Solving Institute. After identifying seven roles that we played in our lives, he asked us to rank order them in relationship to their importance without analyzing. Along with the familiar roles of wife, mother, daughter, friend, sister, psychotherapist, I added lover and healer. Then he instructed us to imagine eliminating the roles one by one. When I listened to my heart and not my head, the roles of lover and healer were the most difficult to let go of and that sparked my curiosity. Growing into my joy about serving as a healer took many years; yet in my heart I had privately recognized the potential decades before I owned the role of healer publicly as an essential aspect of my unique, authentic self.

I believe that most people in our lives are not aware of our evolutionary potential, Certainly that was true in my family. Often both friends and family relate to us in ways that are consistent with our past and outlived roles and they often conspire to keep us a hostage to our limited and often dramatic personal story. For example, Malia told Noah after I had published *Awaken* that they had to get used to sharing me with the world. Noah nodded his head and solemnly asked me to promise that I would still be his grandmother.

To support aligning with Future Pull, I consciously adopted evolutionary buddies who acted as my spiritual mirrors. Although I have several friends who are empathetic and present for me, the role of an evolutionary buddy is unique. My soul buddies hold me accountable when I act from habit and not awakened awareness. I have a freeze frame of the time that my evolutionary buddy Geneie confronted me, "Rosie, you have taken on much that was not yours this lifetime. You are a consummate over-giver. Fire yourself from that role."

The question that bound me even more deeply to my Future Self was, "How does this person or situation ask me to love or heal more fully?"

One of my favorite illustrations of a circle of people instinctively entraining to the frequency of Future Pull is the story of an older woman on her way to Findhorn, the international community in Scotland. She got my attention as she raised her hand in the middle of a book signing for *Soul Befriending* and asked, "So what comes after edge walking? I know from my own experience there is something more."

I sensed that she already knew the answer and that she struggled with being visible, so I softly challenged her by saying, "Then you tell me."

The energy in the room shifted. Everyone realized that she stood on the brink of breaking through her own silence and her small self and each person in the group supported her energetically without a word being said.

She sat silent and still for several minutes. We all waited. Then she said in a small voice, which did not match her energetic frequency, "I am afraid to be wrong."

I breathed and invited everyone in the room to breathe together. I was struck by the power of her personal story that caused her to regress into a little girl with a little girl's voice.

As a spiritual midwife, I am forever on the lookout for birthings. Gently, with my hand on my heart, I invited her to share what she knew and reminded her that I had neither a rulebook nor a red pencil.

At first, she spoke softly and hesitantly, "I have to listen— for God's voice—amidst all the other voices and distractions. I made a commitment—to allow God to move me—no matter what."

I said, "So you consecrated your life to being a vessel for God's love."

She sighed. The silence in the room deepened and widened at the same time.

I too remained silent, appreciating the sacredness of the moment as well as the evolutional call of Future Pull that brought us together as a group. In that moment each of us in the room served as her evolutionary buddy and we all knew instinctively that silence empowered. Furthermore, we all sensed that we were witnesses to a woman speaking her truth out loud in front of a group for the first time. In an instant, she had created sacred space. Without another word, she rose from her chair and bowed to each person in the group. The group returned her bow in silence and with deep reverence.

I gave deep bows to George Land, Robert Monroe, Ben Bentov, and Rendle Leatham who were each masters of Future Pull. Each of them became a competent and compelling time traveler and each became a teacher for me. I carry a freeze frame in my heart of the moment I met each man and I feel each ones presence dancing through me as I continue to explore Future Pull.

I have shadow boxed with myself forever—sometimes in awareness and often out of awareness. As I grow more conscious of myself, which is different from being self-conscious, I am also more aware of the impact I have on others. From conception, or maybe before, I committed myself to bring a loving impact to my original family system. Ultimately, I left. Who knows if my leaving had an impact? Later, acting as a cosmic catalyst, I made a commitment to have an impact on the souls of others. Holding space for the Holy Ones and my guides became even more essential. Receiving guidance was an essential part of the process of moving beyond the role of teacher and embracing the role of leader.

Daily I feel like I am doing mischief in the world, shaking up systems, challenging people when they are hiding, calling out what is obvious to me and yet sometimes hidden to others. Sometimes I think of myself as the Coyote, the trickster in Native American cosmology, who does whatever is needed to reveal or expose truth. Every time I do a soul reading, I am making mischief, as I align with the frequencies of Future Pull and I enjoy the role of provocateur!

The nature of my soul work is multidimensional and I have no idea what I will be called upon to say or do when I sit with a person or reach out by phone to do a soul reading. I remind people that taking action on their unique soul purpose is an evolutionary obligation. I believe that for its continued evolution our soul depends on us to alignment with agreements we have made prior to being born.

A soul reading is an example of Future Pull because it focuses on a person's cosmic report card. Often people instinctively sense their agreements to evolve and embrace their

Future Self but have yet to embody their specific agreements. Since each person has a unique soul history, soul purpose and life lessons, I feel like I jump off a cliff each time I channel. Being present is key. During my thirty-seven years of doing soul readings, I have learned to trust the guides who gather, ground, guide, and grace the process.

Three principles ground my work:

> Love connects dimensions and heals.
> Energy is information.
> Energy follows need.

Generally, the guides will begin the reading by identifying where the person is on the life time continuum: practice lifetime, somersault lifetime, integration lifetime, recovery lifetime, mastery lifetime, or completion lifetime. Identifying an individual's unique soul purpose comes next, followed by reminding the person of their soul qualities—where his or her power and healing are grounded. Then the soul reading progresses to identifying life lessons and the patterns and themes that require awareness and further action. I often remind people that their soul purpose is their "major" this lifetime and their life lessons are their "minor." I check for any past lifetime overlays, including vows that may interfere with a person's ability to align with present day soul agreements. There are zillions of vows—humility, invisibility, mediocrity, and stability, to name a few. There is sometimes a potent love vow—"I will love you and only you forever and ever." This vow, like all the others, was made in the passion of the moment. If the person who made the vow does not release it before dying time, the soul contract remains and he/she will experience challenges with intimacy because their heart belongs to another. Equally potent, the warrior vow states, "I will never give up the fight." Let's assume that peace is a life lesson for this long time warrior. That conflicting vow will attract pain and struggle, not peace. Other times, my job is to release a spell, curse, or entity.

I have included a few excerpts from the thousands of soul readings to offer an inside view of the multi-dimensional nature of the world in which I live.

TRUDY - Grandmother, who was a therapist, suspected her granddaughter, Trudy had entities. She told me two other healers had confirmed her suspicions but were unsuccessful at freeing her of her uninvited guests.

When we first met, Trudy was underweight, appeared quiet and meek, and her large blue eyes were amazingly bright. Initially, her guides offered specific details about a traumatic past lifetime, which continued to hold her hostage. Here is their story of her karmic bleed through lifetime.

In her most recent past lifetime she was born into a family of respected healers. From birth she knew it was her destiny to follow the lineage of her ancestors. She developed her psychic skills naturally and was adept at reading energy and making precise interpretations.

At nineteen, she decided to explore the world. She traveled extensively, and wherever she went people sought her out for her healing skills. Her life appeared to be laced with grace until a black magician arrived. In the past they had experienced a karmic lifetime, and he was jealous of the light she carried and decided to take her down. He was adept at shape shifting, and since she had never met someone who was an expert at robbing people of their power, she was clueless about his deception. She did not expect to encounter evil.

Too late she admitted to herself that he was not of the light and his intentions were not good.

She refused to believe that anyone would forgive her for trusting him and working with him. Furthermore, she was furious with her guides for not warning her about his malevolence and cursed them before she ordered them to leave. Then she wandered bereft and alone. At the end of that lifetime she had made two vows: never to be tricked again and never to trust her guides and her intuition again. She was in a recovery lifetime this trip, and her soul purpose was centered on opening her heart and reclaiming her healing gifts; however, the power of the self-imposed curse continued.

Calling in her guides was painful. Her body shook and her voice cracked, as she asked, "What if they won't come? What if they are angry with me?"

Working with her to break the vows, I encouraged her to let it be easy. After she released the vow never to be tricked again, she exclaimed, "I feel free, unburdened, lighter, as if I can see more clearly." Earlier we had established, despite her initial denials, that she read energy all the time. I pointed out to her that she was reading her own energy and she said, "I do that all the time—doesn't everyone?"

During the reclaiming part of the release process, she filled up with self-love, worthiness, clarity, dedication to her path, and beauty. Then she easily let go of her vow never to trust her guides again and reclaimed innocence, discernment, freedom, willingness to be a healer, and faith in herself and the future. Her energy field filled up and she looked iridescent.

Then she asked me how to call in her guides. She cried at the thought of being in connection once again. Then she felt afraid that they wouldn't come and they would never trust her again. Her guides channeled that she needed to forgive herself for being duped. Then they suggested that she invite them back to support and guide her. When she got in touch with the heart-breaking theme of this past lifetime, she began to feel compassion for her former self.

"Let's call them in and see," I invited.

"Do you know their names? Do you see them or hear them or what?" she asked.

"Your guide who channeled most of this reading goes by the name of "Gemcy." He carries a masculine energy and gives you strength and insight. He is practical and committed to seeing you complete your soul purpose. Earth attracts him, especially canyons. Your other guide goes by the name "Flame," and she carries light, magic, playfulness, and the ability to see through deception. She is attracted to glass chimes.

Trudy was eager to communicate with them and they suggested she keep a journal exclusively for them. She also agreed to set time aside to call them in and listen, and then take action on their guidance.

One of her major life lessons is trusting that she can complete and stay on her path to experience fulfillment and prosperity. When she walked out the door she was a different person because she was free to be in her own energy this lifetime.

I have learned over three decades that the most effective way to resolve karma is to forgive. Forgiving frees everyone affected by the karma. The cosmic and human interweaving of karma and grace helps us to align with our soul purpose. Remembering that grace is not earned by our efforts, but is bestowed as an aspect of God's divine forgiveness creates hope.

SANDRA- I have a distinct remembrance of the evening that I received an urgent call from a woman for whom I had done a soul reading for her after the death of her son. Seven years before she had come with her teen aged daughter and I enjoyed channeling for both of them. For me a soul reading is a sacred encounter. Working with a Mom or a Dad who has outlived one of their children feels like a soul agreement between all of us that somehow existed before our appointment.

Sandra was concerned because she had lost communication with her dead son and wondered if she had done something wrong, if there were something she did not understand, or if he had abandoned her.

When I checked in, her son no longer resided in Spirit. He had reincarnated. I gave the news to his mother and she burst out crying, then moaned, "So that means I am no longer his Mom. Where does that leave me? This feels like another phase of grief, and I don't think I could live through more."

I had no easy answers and slid back to my own memories of how I felt when my son Mike, reincarnated. I remembered feeling disoriented—happy that he chose to live on the earth plane again and sad because I was not his mother this time. The bond we had created that survived his physical death had dissolved and I had grieved once more while at the same time I celebrated his choice to reincarnate.

As silence grew between us, her guide drew my attention to an etheric message that her son had left for her. The best way I could explain this process was comparing it to leaving a forwarding address at the post office. I was fascinated because this was the first time that I had encountered this type of messaging service. The message said that in about twelve years that they would pass each other in a shopping mall, and they would both recognize the other. They would not exchange words, but their energies would merge in their hearts and impact each other. Love would emanate from both of them, and their souls would salute one another. Then, because love would be enough for each of them, they would smile and walk on.

As I communicated the message to her, I had tears in my eyes. She did, too.

Neither of us said anything for several minutes. Then she said, "I don't have a clue how to wrap my arms around this. Who would have expected any of this?"

I shook my head and held her hands. Finally, I said, "You have plenty of time to grow into this energetic reunion." She agreed.

Next I met with her daughter who had just entered high school the last time we had sat together. I had no idea what her reaction would be to her brother's choice to reincarnate. When I told her the news, she clapped her hands and sighed deeply. Then she said, "You mean I no longer have to be afraid that he will be born as my child? I have dreaded making love to my fiancé each time because I was petrified I might get pregnant with my brother and I don't know if I could handle the responsibility."

I asked her how long she had lived with her fear and her body shook as she said, "Almost three years and I didn't dare tell anyone because, I thought they would think I was crazy." Instinctively, I moved over beside her and cradled her as she wept in relief.

During my therapy training, I learned to wait until my client withdrew from a hug first. I have cherished that wisdom for decades. When Marcie's body stopped shaking and she had released many tears, she pulled away. We looked each other in the eyes and she thanked me for returning her passion to her. I was struck by how much younger she looked. Freedom had replaced anxiety. She had returned to herself.

Joanna - Another soul reading that stands out in my memory is one that I did with a woman who was three months pregnant. This was her first pregnancy and her doctor had indicated there were problems. She wanted to know if she should abort the baby. When I reminded her that healing was her soul's purpose, she sighed loudly. Clearly, being pregnant was a soul call.

She told me she had hoped that I would make the decision for her. I repeated that healing was her soul's purpose. I empathized with her because the stakes were huge. Yet we do not agree to a specific soul purpose without the resources to succeed. When she left, I had no idea what she would decide.

Two years later I was a guest of a friend at a big party in Taos, New Mexico. Imagine my surprise when the woman who greeted us at the door was the woman who had sat on my couch and agonized whether to have an abortion or continue her pregnancy. We recognized each other instantly. She hugged me and announced to her friends, "This is the woman who is responsible for Josh's birth." As if on cue, a pudgy little boy with blond hair ran across the room and lifted his arms for his mom to pick him up. Tears came into my eyes as she lifted him up and put him into my arms. I hugged the little boy and the mom and I smiled. Later she told me she had taken a few courses in energy medicine and based on the feedback of her instructors, she believed she was a healer.

Wendy - Working with an entity is often the most challenging part of my work. I was surprised when I answered a call from sixteen-year-old Wendy, for whom I had done a soul reading a few months earlier. She reported that she felt depressed and had gained about twelve pounds in two months. I remembered her soul purpose, helping Inspirited Ones (dead people) who were stuck in their afterlife and failed to move forward. She reported that she had seen ghosts and sensed she was supposed to do something to help them, but had no clue what to do. Her mother, who accompanied her to see me, did not believe in ghosts and worried that Wendy might be mentally ill. We made an agreement that I would mentor Wendy and her mother would continue to parent her. Before they left on their first visit, I loaned them a copy of *The Unquiet Dead* by Edith Fiore for an overview about entities because, in my experience, people who act as midwives between dimensions often attract entities.

When Wendy revisited, I explained that entities have a range of consciousness that goes between clueless and malevolent. They attach to someone alive in order to get their needs met and that means that the hostess or host also has an unmet need or wound. Then I explained that she did not need to feel ashamed for attracting one, and we would work together to identify her unmet need. She agreed.

Without going into all the details, I asked Wendy temporarily to take everything in her energy field that aligned with light and place it in a nearby chair. She seemed a bit hesitant until I reassured her that she would call all the energies aligned with light in her consciousness back after we released the entity.

Next I dialogued with what was left.

Me: Greetings. Do you have a name?

Entity: Yes, Sara.

Me: Thank you for speaking to me. I am here to help you and Wendy. This co-housing arrangement has not been good for either of you. Would you agree?

Entity: Yes.

Me: How are you feeling in Wendy's body?

Entity: Starved and like I am suffocating.

Me: I am curious. About how much of her energy do you occupy?

Entity: Sometimes as much as ninety percent.

Me: That's a lot! No wonder that she is feeling depressed and you are feeling trapped. I am curious about what at-tracted you to her?

Entity: Her aliveness. She was lonely and needed a friend and I did, too.

Me: So you promised her friendship and she let you into her energy field?

Entity: Yes and I wanted to experience life again.

Me: Why is that?

Entity: I drowned when I was the same age as Wendy and I wanted to see what life felt like beyond the age that I died.

Me (Note to self: Was the drowning purposeful or accidental?)

Me: I am sorry that your life was cut short. I am wondering what you learned about love in your previous lifetime.

Entity: Nothing. I was too stubborn.

Me: Do you have a memory of your guides and teachers in that lifetime?

Entity: None. I don't think I had any, or if I did, I pushed them away.

You know, Wendy has guides and they are her friends. She works with them to help people who get stuck after they die.

Entity: Yes, I know and I don't like them and I have pushed them out.

Me: Why?

Entity: Because she was paying more attention to them than to me.

Me: You sound angry.

Entity: You bet! I am trapped and starved.

Me: Do you have any feelings for Wendy?

Entity: I care for her. I won't lie and say I love her because I don't know how to do that. I do want her to be safe.

Me: Have you ever cared for anyone else?

Entity: No.

Me: I need to remind you occupying ninety percent of Wendy's consciousness is not okay. And interfering with her connection with her guides is not okay, either.

Entity: I know that now. I got scared when I almost convinced her to kill herself and I feel bad that I don't know how to help her erase that thought. I didn't mean to cause her to suffer, and I don't know how to get out. I just wanted to see what life was like.

Me: Look, I can help Wendy return to herself. I can also assist you to exit and be transported to where you came from and ask healing angels to accompany you so that you can heal. Eventually when you have healed, you will have the choice to return to a body of your own. Plus, once Wendy asks you to leave, under universal laws, you must leave.

Entity. : I am ready to leave.

Me: Before you leave, do you have anything to say to Wendy?

Entity: I am sorry. You would be much happier with another name. And your orange bedroom is not good for you. Try painting it buttercup yellow and you will be happier.

Before furthering Sara, I asked Wendy if she had anything to say to her.

Wendy said, "You have taught me a lot. I wished that I had known how to help you. I will make friends with kids at school. Good luck!"

After we had completed Wendy's session, I invited her mother to join us, and I supported Wendy as she summarized her experience. I wanted to find a way that her mother could voice her concerns if she sensed that Wendy was in trouble without Wendy turning oppositional. Together we worked out an agreement for mother and daughter to communicate concerns.

When I finished writing this section, I laughed out loud. For decades I have not only called in the guides from all dimensions, but also I have called in the energies of evolutionary consciousness that have made a commitment to the wellbeing of our planet and her people. Looking back, I do not remember learning how to do this from a teacher. Could it be that Future Pull was responsible?

Sometimes pain pushes until Future Pulls. Moments before I sent the manuscript of this book off to Alison for editing, I spilled water on my computer and my external backup drive. The light went out and I rushed to find a hair dryer in an attempt to revive my computer.

Then I bullied and judged myself until I realized that my demeaning behavior did not serve my emerging Future Self. Gradually, I replaced self-abuse with compassion and later, curiosity. I followed through with a daily swim with Georgia at Sebasticook Lake, understanding that nothing I could do would fix my unresponsive computer.

As we swam and delighted in the antics of the family of seven ducks that we had watched for weeks, I wondered if the computer failure might be the universe's big push to force me to re-commit to explore pleasure and leisure in addition to working on this book.

As I stretched out on the blue noodle and merged with the sky, I shifted my way of framing the computer crash from why did this happen "to me," to why did this happen "for me." I shifted my attitude from blame to receptivity and curiosity. To the wind I said, "Time off!"

The next day I consulted with three people about repairing my computer and each person told me to expect a three-week wait. Pleading for faster service would not work. No doubt I had more reflection to do while I waited for my computer to be fixed. I had planned to bring it with me on a family vacation. No more. Although the man who sent my hard drive off for repair offered to loan me a sixteen-inch laptop to "tide me over" until mine came back, I declined. Since I did not believe in coincidence, even those that happen because of my carelessness, I decided to back off the book and enjoy my vacation with my family.

Autumn came, and a few weeks before I left Maine to return to my abode in Virginia Beach, Steve Raymond, one of my evolutionary buddies, invited me to be a guest on his television program, "Spotlight on Aging." Initially, I questioned what I could contribute, until he reminded me that I could talk about Living Future Pull or Bangor Glad Helpers, the prayer-healing group that I initiated in July. Then I thought about dying as another example of Future Pull and I agreed.

Steve is a natural interviewer, and we enjoy the synergy that erupts when we are together since we deeply trust and appreciate each other, we agreed to be spontaneous as the cameras rolled. Steve announced that instead of looking at social or legislative issues, we planned to focus on the individual interiority of aging. Whenever I do not have an agenda, I am surprised at what comes out of my mouth. After Steve introduced me and handed me the microphone, instead of beginning with Future Pull and its possible connection to dying, I described my passion for community and the inherent healing power of a group of people who share an intention. I used my experience with Glad Helpers in Virginia Beach as an example and then talked about my passion for creating a chapter of Glad Helpers in Bangor, Maine. Our conversation deepened as we discussed awakening to group consciousness, the power and potency of group intention and the communion that evolves when a group leaves their ego and defenses at the door and agrees to serve as channels of blessings in order to serve the greater community.

Steve mentioned that I often bragged about being a fifth generation Mainer and added that in his experience many native Mainers ground themselves in strong independence and resilience and had a challenge allowing themselves to be vulnerable. I admitted I had prided myself on my independence and strength for decades and that summer I broke rank and apprenticed to pleasure and leisure and exposed my vulnerable self. I relished boasting that I attended five performances at Ogunquit Musical Theater with my soul buddy, Linda Harris, swam almost everyday with my soul buddy Georgia, tented out beneath the night sky, sculpted, and vacationed with my daughter and grandchildren,

We agreed that life events caused us either to open up or close down, and Steve brought Mike's death into our conversation. I spoke of the painful, heart-piecing experience and said that I eventually chose love because my two-year-old daughter deserved a mother who practiced love. After that happiness, creativity, and peace became daily choices.

I added that the feminine way of being holds the field where all possibilities can exist without rushing to a conclusion. Being receptive to what is unfolding is part of being willing to discover what is emerging. That takes trust and more trust. I advocated relationship, community building, and listening to dreams as ways to connect with feminine ways of knowing.

As the conversation drew to a close, Steve asked me what legacy I wanted to leave. Without thinking, I said, "Hope, creativity, and love"

(To listen to the tape, visit my website at www.heart-soul-healing and click on home page.)

CHAPTER 14

The Challenges of Aging

*A*ging has an agenda. At a book signing, I referred to my last book, *Soul Befriending,* as "my coming of sage book." It was. Although I never hesitate to request senior citizen discounts, I continue to think of myself as an "in between woman"—positioned somewhere between middle age and old age.

I don't know how to begin writing about my aging body. When my women friends gather, we often talk about our aches and pains and subsequent medical interventions. Many of my friends have already undergone eye, knee, and hip surgery. I am aware that I walk more slowly and carefully since my knee injury. Jogging is out of the question for me although I still delight in body surfing.

Befriending my body is one of my lessons this lifetime. I no longer take my body for granted. I am aware of my limitations and remind myself that just because I can does not mean I have to. Each day when I wake up, I send out thanks for both my breath and for the experience of having a body that continues to support me.

Like my mother who attended Curves three days a week until she was eighty years old, I have prided myself on my fitness. I swim laps at least four times a week for an hour.

I also walk the beach every day and push myself to hike at least three miles. Once a week I enjoy Tai Chi lessons. Many trainers have reiterated that I am flexible and that I also need to concentrate on strength building. For sure, hammering and chiseling industrial sandstone is a perfect way to improve my upper body strength while being creative at the same time.

I have a strong intention to bring more awareness and compassion to my body as I age. Meditation keeps me in my body and expands my awareness. My daughter cautions me to buy sandals that have more support and checks to be sure I am up to date with my prescription glasses.

I added this poem to my wisdom journal to celebrate my aging process:

> I Am Not Old
> I am not old...she said,
> I am rare.
> I am the standing ovation
> At the end of the play.
> I am the retrospective
> Of my life, as art.
> I am the hours
> Connected like dots
> into good sense.
> I am the fullness
> of existing.
> You think I am waiting to die...
> But I am waiting to be found.
> I am a treasure.
> I am a map.

And these wrinkles are
Imprints of my journey.
Ask me anything.
-Samantha Reynolds

I remember the day, October 9 2015, when I drove home from an exercise class and realized I had been driving a car for fifty-seven years. I was stunned. My mind, which has a tendency to wander, has its own labyrinth made up of memories that carry some sort of energetic resonance that lies in wait somewhere in my unconsciousness. I remember the day that I told my Grandmother that she could no longer drive because she was a danger to herself as well as others. She surrendered her car keys to me and later told me that day was one of the worst days of her life. At the time I felt compassion for her. Recently I have begun to dread what my life might be like without the freedom to hop in my car and drive to the store, or the park, or off for an adventure, and I dread that day.

Looking back, I do not remember either my grandmother, who lived to be ninety-three or my mother, who lived to be almost ninety-two, talking about either menopause or growing old. "Grin and bear it" was part of the Puritan Maine philosophy I inherited and I wished that I had asked more questions or at least listened more attentively.

I have a freeze-frame memory of how and when I adopted June Bro as my mentor for aging gracefully. She is kind and energetic, and she has dedicated herself to living a life based on Edgar Cayce's ideals of love, cooperation, service, patience, and faith.

My first morning in Virginia Beach, I visited Edgar Cayce's A.R.E. Center because I could not sign my lease until the afternoon. June, at 93, was the featured speaker. According to the brochure she was one of the few people living who had worked with Edgar Cayce, the most studied psychic of all time. When I walked through the door, I was not prepared for the instant recognition that erupted between us.

I sat down opposite her and we both smiled like Cheshire cats. Then she leaned toward me from across the table and she asked intensely, "What brought you here?"

I felt tongue-tied because I intuited one of the reasons I had been pulled to attend June's Chat was a long awaited destiny date! My impulsive self yearned to whisk her away from the group and fill each other in on our many lifetimes since we had walked the earth together, but I restrained myself.

Within a month June and I had officially adopted one another as spiritual family. Together we attended a Search For God study group for two years and our prayers opened my heart wider. This year we enjoyed being together on New Year's Eve at Cayce's A.R.E. Center and I celebrated her as I watched her dance, visit with long time friends, sip red wine, and enjoy herself.

I watch her and marvel at her generosity and innocence. She continues to be genuinely interested in everyone she meets and greets each person's stories as precious. Although each week people from all over the world come to listen to her talk about working with Edgar Cayce, she remains humble. I often remind her that people have come to listen to her stories about working for Mr. Cayce because she is more interested in hearing their stories than telling her own.

I remember how earnestly she listened to me as I read her first drafts from this book. I felt vulnerable. She listened to each word and smiled, and I was overjoyed when she urged me to read more and more. When she responded to my words with some of her stories, I felt doubly blessed. With the exception of June Bro, I have missed mentors for this transition into elderhood.

When I offered a sneak preview of this book at Maine Holistic Center in Bangor, I grabbed a pink and gray flannel blanket to ensure that I would be warm before I began reading excerpts. Susan Ortiz, who founded the center, hugged me as she said, "You look like a tribal elder." When I glanced at myself in the mirror, I agreed.

I belong to PEO, a national philanthropic organization of women that raises millions of dollars for college scholarships for women. Our local chapter includes a group of women who sing to elders in nursing and retirement homes. The last time we joined with residents for a sing-along in Virginia Beach, I realized that I was older than some of the residents.

Reminders of aging come more frequently now but still surprise me, as when my family doctor prefaced a statement with, "At your age, I recommend a pneumonia shot," or my optometrist warned me that I am growing cataracts but it is not unusual for "a woman of my age."

Lately, I have noticed that my daughter complains that the volume on my television is too high, and some friends have bragged about their designer hearing aids. I remember the day I volunteered to drive my grandmother to an appointment at the hearing aid clinic. Actually, I kidnapped her because I knew she would have refused to go had I told her in advance. Initially she protested and then enjoyed being able to participate in conversations again with her new hearing aids.

Noah reassures me that he will be my memory when I forget things like people's names and places. Malia challenges me when I buy sun dresses for her that I think she will like saying, "Grandmom, don't you know I am fifteen? This dress is too young looking for me. You wear it. It would look good on you." When I remind her that I am growing older, she laughs and tells me I will always be middle-aged to her.

During an extravagant seventy-third birthday celebration in Puerto Rico, paid for by my daughter, I felt celebrated by a culture that honors elders. Younger people helped me climb over slippery rocks that lead to a swimming hole in the rain forest, strangers sang Happy Birthday to me, and I was welcomed as an elder rather than a burden even when our hiking group waited for me to catch up. Later when we joined others on a snorkeling trip, I felt welcomed even though I could have been a great grandmother to most of the other people aboard. Perhaps my friend Darlene was right when she insisted to live out senior years in Mexico because elders were honored in that culture.

As an older woman, myself, I have learned to give thanks for all of my stories.

As an older woman myself, I appreciate that my ego and my soul co-exist and pain often pushes me until future pulls.

As an older woman myself, I respect that I lose traction with myself whenever I exert my will to initiate a creative project before time is on my team.

As an older woman myself, I marvel about the paradoxes and dualities I create in my daily life whenever surrender pops up as a teacher.

As an older woman myself, I appreciate the balance between story making and silence.

As an older woman myself, I honor that grace is a dimension of consciousness that is our birthright and I am determined to choose grace over karma this lifetime.

As an older woman myself, I am aware that my body is aging and I am determined to create healthy ways of growing into my elder years.

As an older woman, I appreciate that my soul growth and my soul story are experiential—not mental.

As an older woman myself, I realize I have the potential to become a visionary of my own life and I work hard to integrate and expand my voice and my vision.

As an older woman myself, I practice letting go daily in preparation for greeting my dying time as God's approach.

CHAPTER 15

The Powers of Place and Grace

L and welcomes and speaks to me until I have learned what I needed to know or remember and then it spits me out and I am free to travel to my next right place. Some friends describe me as a "gypsy" and wish a permanent home for me. I smile and affirm to myself that my journey is my home.

When I move from my eight-month sojourn in Virginia Beach back to Maine for four months, friends greet me with, "Welcome home." When I once again return to my home in Virginia Beach, friends greet me with, "Welcome home, Rosie." Home feels in my bones. Being home means settling into my bones even more.

I have always known that locations possess specific vibrations. I was surprised to learn that my soul can have more than one! Looking back, Crater Lake in Oregon was right place; Taos, New Mexico; was right place, Mountain Light Sanctuary in North Carolina was right place; the Gathering Place in Stetson Maine was right place, and Virginia Beach was right place

I had driven past the entrance to Camp Etna, in Etna, Maine several times and wondered what attracted me when I obeyed the impulse to drive down that dirt road into the campgrounds. Nobody was around. The office was open but empty. The chapel doors were open and nobody was there either. I drove by several small houses and nobody was home.

Feeling like a trespasser, I got out of my car and explored the woods, walked down to the pond and discovered a large healing stone in a clearing in the woods. I giggled because I felt like the land and I were becoming friends again and I felt happy that I had followed my whim. My mind wanted to know more. I stopped by two more times in the same month and walked the land before I met Rosy coming out of the office. She gave me a brochure describing the camp and its activities and invited me to the Healing Light church service the following day.

Although I had never attended a Spiritualist Church before, I felt at home since the first part of the service was dedicated to hands-on-healing. I had missed my weekly opportunity at Glad Helpers in Virginia Beach to act as a channel of healing. I resonated to the line in the creed that stated, "And I will do my part." Being responsible for our own healing felt right to me.

Although I have no specific past lifetime memories of the early churches, I imagined that hands on healing was an essential part of ministering to one another. Participating in the healing segment linked me to my life in Virginia Beach, and my heart felt at home. After a short inspirational message, mediums channeled messages from the Inspired Ones to family and friends.

Later in the month, Georgia and I decided to attend the early morning meditation at Camp Etna rather than sit together in meditation in my loft because we both sought to become part of a larger spiritual community.

A month later at Sunday worship I entered the group meditation with no expectations. The guest minister had a soothing voice and I relaxed. Immediately, I felt the Presence of God in front of me. I recognized his energy from our first encounter when he requested that I loan him my hands.

I was delighted to be in God's Presence once again and also a bit anxious about what He might ask of me next as well as what He might offer. My heart expanded to take in more love and light and I aligned my will with God's will. Once again God's eyes mesmerized me and my anxiety melted. The feeling of being "at home" or more precisely "in home" filled me. I sighed. Then He energetically beckoned me to move closer. Our energies blended.

Once again, He looked at my hands and I intuitively recognized that He was inviting me to put my hands in his outstretched hands. The last time when He asked me to loan Him my hands, I experienced an exchange of energy, but our hands did not physically touch. This time our energetic interaction felt even more intense and intimate. Somewhere deep inside I knew that if our energies merged and then fused, I would be forever changed.

Our energetic eye-lock comforted me. The human part of me realized God was calling me to break rank with all I knew to be possible with no guarantee of whom I might return as—yet none of that mattered. When I nodded my head to surrender, the merging process began.

I did nothing. The only analogy that comes anywhere close is the process of whipping heavy cream into whipped cream—like colloidal suspension happening in my energy body and physical body simultaneously until our two bodies became one energy field and then fused into pure light. How

I managed to unmerge and return to my skin and bone self, I do not know.

When the meditation ended, healers were called to do hands on healing. I volunteered because the healing energy that suffused my body needed an outlet. My hands were hot and later people told me that my cheeks were tomato red. Initially, I feared that the energy running through my hands might be too much, but I breathed and reminded myself that God was in charge.

I don't remember much of what happened during the hands on healing time, but I carried a freeze frame of God in my heart. Several people sat in my chair for healing as intense healing energy flowed through my hands. Later people commented on my open heart and the light that came through my hands, and I felt Goddess bumps all over my body.

In the days that followed, I cleared my work schedule and moved deeper into silence. The timing of my monthly consultation with Meghan was perfect. When I summarized my surprise encounter with God, Meghan reminded me that my recent merging with God was a natural progression. I agreed and let go of my ego mind that once more challenged me with, "Who do you think you are?"

She invited me to ask God what He desired from me. The thought of merging once again and having a conversation excited me. When I returned to my meditation loft to pray, God met me. Once again, we gazed at each other. I have no idea how long we held the intense gaze because eternity cannot be measured. His answer to Meghan's question, "What do you desire from me?" was simple, practical and profound. "To bless by Your Being and shine Your light to others as a Beacon of Becoming."

For a while I stumbled over my humility. Affirming that my light is a gift felt huge. Then I remembered Meghan's definition of humility—love in action. Later I imagined flashing my business card that says "cosmic catalyst" and has an added background of rays of light extending from a luscious red heart. Surrendering to my fullness, my body's complete presence and infinite possibilities feels like art.

Flash forward to September 2016, when I accepted an invitation to be the inspirational speaker at Healing Light Church at Camp Etna. Two weeks earlier I had introduced the idea of Future Pull at a weekend workshop and we applied the organizing principles of Future Pull to create a greater sense of our individual wholeness.

I challenged myself to compress the general principles of Future Pull into a twenty-minute presentation. Naturally, I invited my guides to collaborate because I enjoy our cosmic collaboration. Unlike my presentation at A.R.E. four months before, I made a few notes. Before I spoke, I opened my heart wide and invited both my guides and the energies of evolutionary consciousness, which may indeed be the same, into my energy field to have their way with me. For sure, I felt like a volunteer magnet for Future Pull.

Publicly announcing myself as a cosmic catalyst felt right. People responded positively. They understood from their own experiences how the frequency of Future Pull invited them to come home to their Full Selves—not their wounded self or their younger self—their whole self.

My guides added their perspective:

Evolutionary consciousness is the signature of the Eternal One.

Was it God who called me to Camp Etna the first, second and third times? Was it Divine energy that was in the wings waiting all the time? If I had not picked up the earlier clues, would this destiny thread have disappeared? The idea of cosmic choreography left me breathless and curious. I honored its magnetic attraction and aliveness and became convinced that embodiment is an example of awakened divinity.

The Future Pull of Camp Etna did not stop there. The thread continued to weave itself through my life. A few days after delivering my inspirational message, my guides directed me to once again to turn into the driveway to Camp Etna as I returned home after an early morning massage.

During the four years I spent in Europe, my guides educated me about memories and resources that they called energy pellets that I had left behind in past lifetimes. They channeled that I had agreed to integrate those aspects of consciousness into my present day life. I recovered past lifetime memories in Scotland, England Cyprus, Egypt and Spain. Closer to home, Taos, New Mexico and Crater Lake held powerful gifts and talents that I have written about in *Awaken* and *Soul Befriending.*

Places have power. In my experience, when I have integrated the lessons and added to my wholeness, I am free to move on and answer another Future Pull call. Sometimes it is my choice to move on and other times circumstances dictate the re-location. For instance, I thought I would return to the Gathering Center in Stetson, Maine and continue to enjoy the summers in community with Georgia and Dennis Kosciusko until I died. Both the land and the vision of offering workshop on spiritual growth and community appealed to my soul. Yet after Georgia retired, they needed year round income from my apartment and I realized my soul yearend to live on the water. Destiny and evolution collaborated and I was free to explore options.

After a leisurely swim in the lake, I bumped into Diane Jakeman as she left the newly renovated healing center she had worked on for several weeks. When she asked me what I was doing there in mid-week, I, somewhat embarrassed, said, "I don't know yet." Then I asked her if anyone at the camp might rent a cottage for the next summer. She smiled and said, "You came to the right woman. Don and I talked last night about touring the country in our RV for two months next summer if we could find someone energetically compatible to rent our cottage." She winked and said, "We would give you a good deal."

My guides cast their vote saying, "Grab it now." She invited me to take a look at their cottage. The space was cozy and the energy felt healing. Now I look forward to living beside the lake that is part of Camp Etna and kayaking or sculpting in the backyard and enjoying community during the summer of 2017. I recognized the intervention of Future Pull by the ease and the spontaneity of the event.

As I conclude this book, I am aware that I look forward to more time to breathe into the immensity of what I understand about Future Pull. I believe my guides hold my soul history as I move closer to embracing my evolving consciousness. At the same time, I am aware of the simplicity interwoven within the immensity of Future Pull and trust that all pulsates with a unity beyond my ability to grasp at the moment. I know in my heart and bones conscious evolution is alive with Future Pull. I am discovering that the more I open my heart and the clearer my intention is to live in the center of my soul story, the greater the probability that Future Pull will continue to further my conscious evolutions.

No longer is my identity confined to my human self. At this point in my evolution, I do not know for sure if Future Pull is connected to my Eternal Self, and it truly doesn't matter because I'm convinced Future Pull resonates with quantum mind that exists everywhere and every time simultaneously. No longer is cause and effect thinking my reality. In my everyday world, which is alive with Future Pull, simultaneous events occur like fireworks set off at the same time at the end of the Fourth of July.

I am curious and excited wondering what other threads of Future Pull exist. Perhaps you are wondering the same thing as you finish reading this book. I learned that wonder opens the dimensional doorways and often creates feed forward momentum. In the process of weaving this book from the myriad threads of my life—my body, relationships, creativity, Nature, breaking rank, inter-dimensional visits with the Holy Ones, as well as edge walking and eventually inhabiting my soul story—I appreciate how I am the ending of some stories, the carrying on of others, and the beginning of many that I may not finish. That simple and profound understanding fills me with humility and gratitude.

I am a library and repository of ancient stories of first loves and betrayals. Later stories of births, achievements, and affairs became my familiars. Still later stories revolved around menopause, disease, travel, triumphs, and dark nights of the soul claimed my attention and my heart. Recent stories include those about grandchildren, faith, loss of faith, longing and belonging, and more frequent deaths of friends and family.

I often begin workshops and retreats with a poem. I end this book with a poem and an invitation for you to breathe into the many stories that live within you. Then I encourage you to share your stories with your evolutionary buddies and open your hearts to the possibilities and the blessings of Future Pull that ground and center your soul stories.

Tell Me, She Said

Tell me, she said:
What is the story you are telling?
What wild song is singing itself through you?
Listen:
In the silence between there is music;
In the spaces between there is story.
It is the song you are living now,
It is the story of the place where you are.
It contains the shapes of these old mountains,
The green of the rhododendron leaves.
It is happening right now in your breath,
In your heart beat still
Drumming the deeper rhythm
Beneath your cracking words.
It matters what you did this morning
And last Saturday night
And last year,
Not because you are important
But because you are in it
And it is still moving.
We are all in this story together.
Listen:
In the silence between there is music;
In the spaces between there is story.
Pay attention:
We are listening each other into being.
-Sally Atkins

As a writer, artist, and woman, I struggle with endings. I often frustrate myself when on one hand I drive myself to finish a project and at the same time I yearn for a perfect ending. Although I had written a first draft of the conclusion to this book, I was not satisfied. My intuition nagged me that something more was needed but provided no guidance. Once again, patience and trust were the calling cards of Future Pull.

Two days before I flew to Florida to join Alison Strickland and edit this book, my friend Nancy Carlson died. Her death was not unexpected, yet her dying shook me. We held each other's histories. Before she became a trusted friend, she was my therapist, and she was both brilliant and empathic. She welcomed all of me and listened intently as I struggled through depression and worked out my responsibility for the karmic relationships that defined my life. A few years after I had "graduated" from therapy, we decided to work at becoming friends.

During the last year of her life, she moved from Virginia Beach to live with her brother, Bob, because she was too weak to care for herself. We spoke on the phone at least three times a week. Often, I read her excerpts of this book and she gave me honest feedback. She was excited when I stumbled on the concept of Future Pull and together we reviewed my life for further evidence of it.

When her brother called to tell me that Nancy had died in the night, I was surprised. I thought I would know when she made her final transition. We were that close. Then I laughed out loud as I remembered how I had been jolted awake at 2 AM by a message, "Close the front door." I knew it was not a dream fragment. Sure enough, the front door was wide open. I did not make the connection until Bob told me that Nancy had died around midnight.

When I asked him what I could do for him, he replied, "I know you know how to talk to dead people about how they are doing and I would appreciate it if you could track Nancy's progress."

I didn't expect that request. I happily agreed. After preparing myself by meditating and praying, I lit a tapered silver candle. Without effort, I merged into Nancy's energy and felt her amplified frequency. "Giddy" was the first word that came to mind. Then she communicated energetically, "I am soaring like a lark."

I applauded her for her swift exit and remembered how we had joked many times that the ability to die swiftly was a mark of a master. Then she channeled that she was more familiar and comfortable in her new "home" than she had been during her life on earth. That surprised me since she had dedicated her life to understanding the human experience.

The day after Nancy's death I sent her Light for the Journey prayers, although I laughed at myself because I knew she was evolving beautifully. When I finished my forwarding prayers, I felt a nudge to go outside to look at the emerging sunset. A twenty foot pink "angelic bird" cloud rested directly over my house. I applauded and did a bird dance in honor of Nancy's life and Spirit. Later I posted the photograph and the following words on Facebook:

"I am left with the knowing that we are all so much vaster than we allow ourselves to imagine. Thank You, Nancy for reminding me once again of both our human potential and our Divine potential."

Note: To view the lark soaring photo, visit my website at www.heart-soul-healing .com and click on the Living Future Pull tab.

Right now, I feel a deep reverence for life and the afterlife. I also appreciate how love is the glue that connects dimensions. I end this book by returning to the original question that I challenged myself with as well as you, the reader: "What if our journey on earth is as simple as believing and trusting that each of us is the meeting point between earth and heaven? What if my life were as simple as believing that God is having a Rosalie experience here on earth through me?"

I now believe that my two original questions were prompts from Future Pull, calling me to embrace my wholeness and step more confidently into my Future Self. My present sense of place feels grounded in everywhere-ness and my sense of time feels grounded in everywhen-ness. My heart is filled with love and overflows with possibilities for the emerging future. I am confident that I am the meeting point between earth and heaven. For this entire journey, I am grateful.

If you are interested in exploring your own unique story, please visit my website at heart-soul-healing .com and click on the Living Future Pull tab for quotations, reflective questions, activities, and field notes that I designed to support and inspire you as you write your way home to yourself.

Other Books by Rosalie Deer Heart

Soul Befriending

Awaken

Celebrating The Soul of CPSI
with Dorie Shallcross

Harvesting Your Journals,
with Alison Strickland

Healing Grief—A Mother's Story

Affective Education Guidebook
with Bob Eberle

Affective Direction
with Bob Eberle

Books are available at
www.heart-soul-healing.com

CPSIA information can be obtained
at www.ICGtesting.com
Printed in the USA
LVHW082150260219
608763LV00004BA/292/P